Managing natural catastrophies

T0345922

Anja Reissberg is Director at Malik Management, Hawaiʻi, and Consultant/ System Expert at Malik Management, St. Gallen.

Anja Christina Reissberg

Managing natural catastrophies

Viable Systems to prevent human tragedy –
the Hawai'ian example

Campus Verlag
Frankfurt/New York

ISBN 978-3-593-39621-7

Copyright © 2012 Campus Verlag GmbH, Frankfurt am Main
Umschlaggestaltung: Guido Klütsch, Köln
Satz: Fotosatz L. Huhn, Linsengericht
Gesetzt aus: Adobe Garamond Pro
Druck und Bindung: Beltz Druckpartner, Hemsbach
Printed in Germany

Dieses Buch ist auch als E-Book erschienen.
www.campus.de

Contents

German preface for editionMALIK

Die alte Welt vergeht,
weil eine neue Welt entsteht.

Wirtschaft und Gesellschaft gehen durch eine der tiefgreifendsten Umwandlungen, die es geschichtlich je gab. Als Begriff wählte ich 1997 dafür »Die Große Transformation«, denn bereits damals war das Ausmaß des heraufziehenden epochalen Wandels deutlich zu sehen. Was heute lediglich als eine finanzielle und ökonomische Krise zu eng gesehen wird, kann weit besser als die Geburtswehen der neuen Welt des 21. Jahrhunderts verstanden werden.

In dieser neuen Welt werden Organisationen eine höhere Ebene des Funktionierens erreichen. Sie werden doppelt so gut wie bisher funktionieren, aber nur die Hälfte des Geldes dafür benötigen. Die universelle Herausforderung wird für sie das Meistern von bisher noch nie erfahrener Komplexität durch neues Management sein.

Geld ist dafür aber weit weniger wichtig als Intelligenz, Vorstellungskraft, Information, Kommunikation und Gestaltungswille. Das neue Wissen hierfür und darauf gestützte neue, biokybernetische Lösungen sind bereits da. Deren Kern sind die ®Evolutionären Naturgesetze aus Kybernetik und Bionik für das Selbstorganisieren und Selbstregulieren. Diese Gesetze zu verstehen und sie zu nutzen, ist das neue Kapital der neuen Welt und die Grundlage für Leadership von Personen und Organisationen.

Die editionMALIK ist die Plattform für das zuverlässige Funktionieren von Organisationen in der hochkomplexen Umwelt des 21. Jahrhunderts. Sie ist die systemische Orientierungs- und Navigationshilfe für Leader, die den Wandel vorausdenken und -lenken.

Fredmund Malik
St. Gallen, Januar 2010

Über Malik sagt der Doyen des Managements, Peter F. Drucker:

>Fredmund Malik has become the leading analyst of, and expert on, management in Europe as it has emerged in the last thirty years – and a powerful force in shaping it … . He is a commanding figure – in theory as well as in the practice of management.«

Introduction: Natural disasters in the light of management cybernetics

Natural disasters seem to be on the rise worldwide and their increasing frequency and dimension [Munich Re Group, 2004] make them more and more the focus of society's concern [Annan, 1999]. But do natural disasters really occur more often than before? Are they more disastrous because of their physical manner or because they are socially constructed, with society increasingly 'getting in nature's way'? The latter appears to be the case. For example, globalization has led to more direct linkages of distant places than existed in the past. The rising interconnectedness and dependency of elements within human systems increase this complexity while the nature of those connections gets more complicated and the number of system elements increases. Factors such as population growth, agglomeration of population and capital value in metropolitan areas, rising living standards, settlement and industrialization of very exposed areas, vulnerability of certain elements and groups in modern society, and the increasing number of high-risk technologies, all play a role [Munich Re Group, 2004]. Further, an increasing complexity of infrastructure, especially communication systems, makes human society more vulnerable to natural hazards. Trust and dependency on information technology, in particular, enhances vulnerability even more. Environmental degradation, such as surface sealing, global warming and climate change, are other dynamic pressures on the stability of human systems. Consequently, the effects of events like natural disasters are felt more quickly. A more effective response is needed in order to address these many negative impacts.

In the Pacific, small island states are especially vulnerable to hurricanes ('typhoons', 'cyclones') due to their small size, isolation, fragile ecological systems, poorly developed infrastructure, limited fresh-water and other natural resources, fragile economies, limited financial and human resources and low elevation above sea level. Among these islands, the Hawai'ian Islands have the highest population density of them all [Pacific Regional Environment Program, 2003]. Urbanization has increased the concentration of people and capital in Hawai'i's coastal areas, especially on O'ahu. A direct hit on O'ahu by a hurricane would put in jeopardy a significant portion of its population and economic wealth. Further, Hawai'i's isolation makes outside assistance very difficult to provide – the neighbor islands, the west coast of the United States, and Guam are the nearest responders. Transportation of resources by air or sea takes on average five hours or several days, respectively, coming from the west coast of the United States or Guam. Infrastructure damage to the islands will limit the functionality of those life-sustaining transportation corridors.

In response to these vulnerabilities, an effective disaster-management system must be based on the fact that the nearest responders are the State's least damaged islands. Except for the limited assistance that the least damaged islands might provide, Hawai'i State Civil Defense estimates that the population of the Hawai'ian Islands will be without outside assistance for at least one week after a major hurricane event [Teixeira, 2007b]. Focusing on O'ahu, Ed Teixeira, Deputy Director of Hawai'i State Civil Defense, has observed that planning for a high-impact-low-probability event like Hurricane Katrina on O'ahu has not much evolved: 'because it was unthinkable and too hard to think about' [Teixeira, 2007b].

Society's concerns are often underrepresented in disaster management decisions since long-term mitigation measures often cannot compete with short-term politically motivated measures and funding sources are polarized, which results in a continuation of the present situation regarding the disaster vulnerability in Hawai'i. Often, disasters are exacerbated by policy problems and thereby caused vulnerabilities due to failure to address root causes, for example by certain land use or settlement policies, population distribution or degrading habitats [Comfort, 1999]. These are initiated under the legal framework of development policy. The complex problem of disasters consists of four factors: first, the rate of social and environmental change exceeds organizational capacity to manage it effectively. Secondly, the understanding of the components and consequences of that change is inadequate. Third, interactions among individuals, organizations and governments are uninformed and fourth, change in public policy and practice is needed. 'If the complexity of interacting scientific, social, political, and economic conditions exceeds the existing capacity for organizational control, decisions taken by local actors govern the direction of the evolving process' [Comfort, 1999, p. 42]. Yet, an integrated process of hazard reduction requires coordinated action across jurisdictional and disciplinary boundaries. Building resilient communities as a policy is at the core of the participatory approach and is one of the main solutions academia offers. Management Cybernetics offers such participatory and non-hierarchical approaches that are capable to reduce vulnerabilities on all scales.

The assumptions of the Federal Emergency Management Agency (FEMA), expressed in the Concept of Operations (CONOP) for a catastrophic hurricane impacting the State of Hawai'i, offer little consolation [Federal Emergency Management Agency, 2007]. A massive federal effort will be needed, it states, because O'ahu's support infrastructure faces potentially catastrophic inundation and damage: the main power production facilities (both electric generation and liquid fuels), Honolulu International airport, and the cargo-handling facilities at Honolulu harbor and Pearl Harbor. The *problematique* is further exacerbated because 80 % of Hawai'i's population lives on O'ahu and is especially vulnerable due to lack of resources. Making the situation worse, the other islands are dependent on O'ahu for energy, food and other commodities, which will greatly limit their ability to assist O'ahu. No transportation for evacuation will be available or feasible; the evacuation of tourist population faces similar issues of capability and feasibility [Rosenberg, 2007b]. Air evacuation of visitors leaving the State of Hawai'i would require 400–500 aircrafts, Boeing 747 equivalent [FEMA, 2007]. Even if it would be considered, prioritizing evacuees would become a problem. The most pressing problem will arise in the aftermath when in a competitive situation mass control becomes a major issue. In case of a false warning, the governor would possibly face 180,000 angry tourists, an upset airline and hotel industry and a low chance of getting elected again. Overall, the governor can make only recommendations to the Tourist Board, which is an independent commercial board. The Board could start canceling people coming in and making people leave [Rosenberg, 2007a]. Reality, as seen the night before Hurricane Katrina hit New Orleans 2005, looks very different: hurricane parties are abound.

Overall, hurricanes are by far the most costly disasters in Hawai'i (see Table 1).

From 1860 to 1962, floods from tsunamis, hurricanes and rainstorm caused more than 350 deaths and over $82 million in property damage in Hawai'i. Damage from floods from 1963 to 1982 total about $395 million [Department of Land and Natural Resources, 1996]. Hence, within 20 years the damage developed fivefold compared to the 100 year period. For a period of 20 years in comparison, it would be a 25 fold increase. Numbers cannot be directly related in this way, but the trend for the tremendous increase in damage potential is obvious. It results mostly from increase in population density and increase in value and agglomeration of value in the Hawai'ian Islands. Therefore, a massive federal effort is assumed for a major hurricane impacting the whole State of Hawai'i.

Since the risks and damage potential of natural events cannot be changed or managed, it is crucial that human-caused vulnerabilities be kept to a minimum. One way to achieve this is through an effective and efficient disaster management system, which this dissertation aims to explicate by critiquing and offering suggestions to improve the effectiveness of disaster management on O'ahu. The VSM aims at enhancing effectiveness of the elements already in place, rather than proposing new disaster management elements. Lessons learned from this case could be applicable to the management of disasters of any type and size in Hawai'i.

Vulnerability leads to destabilized social systems – what does management cybernetics have to offer? Vulnerability can be defined in a variety of ways. For the purpose of disaster management, it is 'the characteristics of an individual or social group or a situation to anticipate, cope with, resist and recover from the adverse effects of a natural hazard' [Blaikie, et al., 2004]. In cybernetic terms, vulnerability is the potential for a system to become unstable. When unstable for a certain time and not returning to a stable system, the system becomes non-viable. The timeframe for a system to become then viable again is called 'Relaxation Time'. Vulnerability can be caused by a variety of sources internal and external to the system. For example, disasters can be socially produced displaying internal disturbances: instabilities persist in the daily routine of people's lives such as a incorrect flood-plain mapping system leaving a family ignorant to the fact that evacuation is necessary at certain times or simply a non-working fire-extinguisher. Those facts by itself are not a threat but in connection to other events, such as a flood or fire, they become key to a circumstance developing into a disaster or not. Ultimately, the term lends itself to many aspects of interest – e.g., physical, natural, environmental, social, economic or cultural vulnerability – and therefore underlines the need for a holistic approach. This also means that the vulnerability of the whole system depends on the vulnerability of its units. This gives rise to the argument that the government should be responsible for or give leadership in making society a safe and secure place in form of integrating anticipatory disaster mitigation into development strategies. This systemic viewpoint underlines the statement that the whole is more than the sum of its parts, which argues against reductionism and advocates a holistic approach, such as the VSM. It is also helpful to elucidate the challenge of complex systems through relating viability and stability. A system is viable if it remains stable in the face of an unexpected event [Beer, 1994a]. In terms of the disaster management system, viable means capable of responding effectively, or remaining invulnerable. Even though small instabilities can endanger the viability of the system as a whole a certain minimal degree of instability within the system does not yet risk its viability because those systems are capable to survive by absorbing certain perturbations [Holling, 1977]. Setting those limits on a small scale will help to alarm the system at large to avert a viability-threatening concatenation of events, even if every single circumstance seems only as a small disregardable risk. But, risk and vulnerability are two sides of one coin. Increasing vulnerability leads to increased disaster risk. Hence, reducing vulnerability by building disaster-resilient communities is key to disaster risk reduction. In a systems thinking view, vulnerability and the risk of incurring instabilities within the system at large has great potential to be stabilized through revealing the driving mechanisms and deep structures. In another stance, the social sciences emphasize that risk cannot only be defined in terms of physical damage, but have to include risk perception or acceptance. Behavior is greatly affected by whether or not risk is taken voluntarily, since people's risk posture (i.e., if they are risk averse, risk neutral, or risk-seeking) has been shown to vary along this dimension.

Overall, a disaster is the destabilization and disruption of the social system, its units – communities, social groups, individuals – and its connectivity. The environmental, economic and social reverberations caused by this destabilization lead to positive feedback loops until countermeasures balance the system as a whole and it returns to a stable state again. This systems approach is valuable, since it is multi-dimensional, includes all temporal and spatial scales, and emphasizes the disturbance of the collective routine. The Environment of the system affects the system with natural and human-induced disturbances – for example, a natural hazard such as a hurricane. My work incorporates all natural disturbances, also termed hazards, that are the trigger of 'natural' disasters as well as the human-induced aspects. Since a disaster can be caused by a Variety of hazards, e.g. by hurricanes, earthquakes or tsunamis this systemic approach is applicable to all hazard types.

Management cybernetics was chosen because much of hazard management research only describes what goes wrong during hazards and why things do not work. Some approaches offer explanations for damages, such as people's poor perception of the phenomena and poor choices of response, the nature of the geophysical phenomena themselves or the nature of insti-

HAWAI'I'S COSTLIEST NATURAL DISASTERS

A preliminary damage estimate of $80 million from the Oct. 30 Flooding in Mānoa Valley would make it the fourth-costliest natural Disaster in Hawai'i history. Here's a list of the state's worst:

1. Hurricane 'Iniki	Sept. 11, 1992	$2.6B, 4 dead
2. Hurricane 'Iwa	Nov. 23, 1982	$307M, 3 dead
3. Big Island flood	Nov. 1, 2000	$88.2M
4. Floods	Jan. 6-14, 1980	$42.5M
5. New Year's flood	Dec. 31, 1987	$35M
6. Tsunami	May 22, 1960	$26.5M, 61 dead
7. Tsunami	April 1, 1946	$26M, 159 dead
8. Kīlauea Lava Flow	1990	$21M
9. Floods	Mar. 19-23, 1991	$10M- $15M
10. O'ahu flood	Nov. 7, 1996	$11M

Source: Hawai'i Civil Defense

Table 1: The most costly disasters in Hawai'i

tutions that create or exacerbate risk and vulnerability for society or particular groups within it. Ways to improve hazard management in general and in a proactive stance are rarely addressed. As a fresh breeze, management cybernetics offers solutions. This work is original and unique because the VSM was never applied to disaster management systems, a loosely coupled network of systems that are hibernating and not always in place.

The VSM lends itself perfectly for this analysis because it deals with messes – not defined problems – and can illuminate why things go wrong. Its theory says that the sum of the elements is greater than the sum of its parts. Instead of examining the cause and effect in a linear manner, the VSM specifically looks at the links that hold the system together in a holistic fashion and therefore takes a system's full complexity into account. Since the VSM can integrate quantitative and qualitative measures, it can provide a common language and framework to discuss the management support and coordination needed by the groups working in the very complex field of disaster management – private and governmental agencies, non-governmental and volunteer organizations. Improvements to communication channels within and between disaster management organization can save valuable time and can promote high levels of effectiveness and efficiency. The VSM can support research incorporating different disciplines without having its basic structure and dynamics obfuscated. Highly valuable is its ability to diagnose hibernating and temporary systems that jump in and out of existence.

Viability is most commonly understood in terms of longevity and persistence, where success is measured in terms of survival, but the VSM does not neglect organizations that are less long-lived and based on goal-oriented action. Beer's main message in *The Heart of Enterprise* [Beer, 1994a] specifically states that the aim is not single-goal oriented, e.g. maximizing profits, but viability and survival, which is ensured through effective organization. The reader needs to understand that in essence the means for survival, the 'how', are most important. Hence, effectiveness of the Hawai'ian disaster management system is the measure of viability per se, independent of how long this organization exists. Moreover, two aspects should be highlighted to show the VSM's applicability to disaster management: time – a disaster needs a quick response – and smooth coordination – not confusion. One advantage of using Beer's VSM in a disaster management context is its convenient framework for experiencing and examining interactions among several groups responding to a disaster. This also includes the democratic management style within volunteer organizations and the command and control approach used by the military. The VSM enables one to distinguish among the different operations and management units along with their communication channels and this secures its flexibility in terms of different management styles. Specifically temporary disaster management systems, which jump in and out of existence depending on when a disaster strikes, do not necessarily have a base of commonly understood conventions and relationships on which to build. The methodology is explicitly linked to this purpose and involves 'qualitative measures of cohesion, identity and ethos as well as the more usual quantitative measures' [Leonard, 1993, p. 79].

From a practical standpoint, the federal disaster management system is constituted by the Federal Emergency Management Agency's (FEMA) Incident Command System (ICS), which is a systems approach. So it is both inviting and highly useful to diagnose this system with a similar approach coming from the same field of thinking. Overall, the VSM seemed to have great potential to improve the effectiveness of hurricane hazard management.

1. The Hawai'ian hurricane tale

The Hawai'ian Islands lie at about 157 degree Western Longitude and 20 degree Northern Latitude (see Figure 1) and are the most remote islands worldwide. Extending from the Big Island of Hawai'i to Kure Island, the State of Hawai'i extends 1200 miles, and is composed of 26 islands, reefs and sea-mounts. The Islands of Hawai'i are shown in Figure 2 [FEMA, 2007]. The major islands of O'ahu, Maui, Kauai and Hawai'i are also designated as counties.

The City and County of Honolulu covers the entire island of O'ahu (see Figure 3), approximately 600 square miles in size. Its resident population was 910,000 in 2006 [Department of Business, Economic Development and Tourism, 2006]. It rises from sea level to a high point of 4,020 feet

Figure 1: Hawai'i's location in the Pacific Ocean

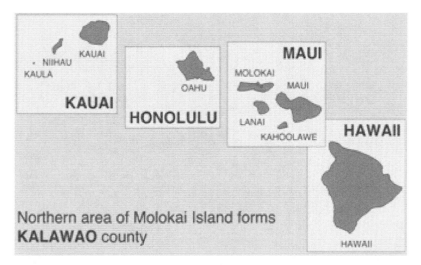

Figure 2: The Hawaiʻian Islands

Figure 3: The island of Oʻahu

on Mt. Kaala in the Waianae Range. The island is situated approximately 2000 miles, or 5 shipping days, from the continental United States. Housing 80 % of the State's population, Oʻahu measured from its farthest points

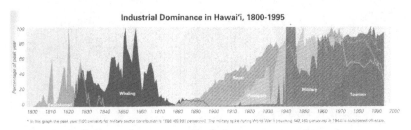

Figure 4: Predominant industries in Hawai'i 1800–1995

is 44 miles long by 30 miles wide. The 112 mile coastline holds the two largest harbors in the state, Honolulu and Pearl [FEMA, 2007, p.17].

The other designated counties and main islands consist of Maui, Kauai and the Big Island. Hawai'i's economy is centered around tourism, the dominant source of export earnings (see Figure 4) [Department of Geography, 1998, p.239]. The neighbor islands have more prominent agricultural and tourism sectors than O'ahu because O'ahu attracts other businesses such as financial and health services, as well as defense. The former importance of plantation agriculture and defense diminished over the last decades due to stagnation in agricultural output and prices and the end of the Cold War, while a growth of tourism in general persisted [Department of Geography, 1998].

The State is heavily dependent on resource imports: 89% of Hawai'i's primary energy depends on imported petroleum [FEMA, 2007]. Hawai'i's small market size inhibits the exploitation of manufacturing economies of scale, resulting in an overdependence on imported merchandise [Department of Geography, 1998].

1.1 Background on State of Hawai'i and O'ahu

The term hurricane has its origin in the indigenous religions of past civilizations. The Mayan storm god was named *Hunraken*. A god considered evil by the Taino people of the Caribbean was called *Huracan*. Hurricanes are products of a tropical ocean of 28 degree Celsius or more and a warm, moist atmosphere [U.S. Department of Commerce, National Oceanic and Atmospheric Administration, National Weather Service, 2006]. Hurricanes develop from tropical depressions with sustained winds up to 38 mph to tropical storms with sustained winds of 39 to 73 mph before becoming hurricanes with winds of 74 mph or more. The Saffir-Simpson Scale categorizes hurricanes depend-

Hurricane Category	Central Pressure (Mm of mercury at 32 degrees F)	Sustained winds mph	Peak Gust (over land) mph	Approximate Storm Surge Height (ft)	Damage Potential Indications
Tropical Storm	979-1007	40-73 mph		2-3 ft	**Some.** Minor damage to buildings of light material. Moderate damage to banana trees, papaya trees, and most fleshy crops. Large dead limbs, ripe coconuts, many dead palm fronds, some green leaves, and small branches blown from trees.
1	980-992	74-95 mph	82-108 mph	4-5 ft	**Significant.** Corrugated metal and plywood stripped from poorly constructed or termite-infested structures, may become airborne. Some damage to wood roofs. Major damage to banana trees, papaya trees and flesh crops. Some palm fronds tron from the crowns of most types of palm trees, many ripe coconuts blown from coconut palms. Some damage to poorly constructed signs. Wooden power poles tilt, some rotten power poles break, termite-weakened poles begin to snap. Low-lying coastal roads inundated, minor pier damage, some small craft in exposed anchorage tron from moorings.
2	965-979	96-110 mph	108-130 mph	6-8 ft	**Moderate.** Considerable damage to structures made of light materials. Moderate damage to houses. Exposed banana trees and papaya trees totally destroyed, 10%-20% defoliation of trees and shrubbery. Many palm fronds crimped and bent through the crown of coconut palms and several green fronds ripped from palm trees; some trees blown down. Weakened power poles snap. Considerable damage to piers; marinas flooded. Small craft in unprotected anchorages torn from moorings. Ecavuation from some shoreline residences and low-lying areas required.
3	945-964	111-131 mph	130-156 mph	9-12 ft	**Extensive.** Extensive damage to houses and small buildings; weakly constructed and termite-weakened houses heavily damaged or destroyed; buildings made of light materials destroyed; extensive damage to wooden structures. Major damage to shrubbery and trees; up to 50% of palm fronds bent or blown off; numerous ripe and many green coconuts blown off coconut palms; crowns blown off of palm trees; up to 10% of coconut palms blown down; 30-50% defoliation of many trees and shrubs. Large trees blown down. Many wooden power poles broken or blown down; many secondary power lines downed. Air is full of light projectiles and debris; poorly constructed signs blown down. Serious coastal flooding; larger structures near coast damaged by battering waves and floating debris.
4	920-944	131-155 mph	156-191 mph	13-18 ft	**Extreme.** Extreme structural damage; even well-built structures heavily damaged or destroyed; extensive damage to non-concrete cailure of many roof structures, window frames and doors, especially unprotected, non-reinforced ones; well-built wooden and metal structures severely damaged or destroyed. Shrubs and trees 50%-90% defoliated; up to 75% of palm fronds bent, twisted or blown off. Many crowns stipped from palm trees; numerous green and virtually all ripe coconuts blown from trees; severe damage to sugar cane; large trees blown down; bark stipped from trees; most standing trees are void of all but the largest branches (severely pruned), with remaining branches stubby in appearance; trunks and branches are sandblasted. Most wood poles downed/snapped; secondary and primary power lines downed. Air is full of large projectiles and debris. All signs blown down. Major damage to lower floors of structures due to flooding and battering by waves and floating debris. Major erosion of beaches.
5	< 920	>155 mph	> 191	> 18 ft	**Catastrophic.** Building failures; extensive or total destruction to non-concrete residences and industrial buildings; devastating damage to roofs of buildings; total failure of non-concrete reinforced roofs. Severe damage to virutally all wooden poles; all secondary power lines and most primary power lines downed. Small buildings overturned or blown away.

Table 2: Saffir-Simpson Hurricane Scale Ranges with additional Hawai'i damage indications

ing on their maximum sustained wind speeds (intensity), but other characteristics must be considered as well to estimate damage potential and extent as outlined by the State Civil Defense (see Table 2) [State Civil Defense, 2005]).

Overall, hurricanes pose a Variety of threats. The damange potential of a hurricane depends on strength (size of storm), storm life, moving speed and path [The World Meteorological Organization, 1997]. Additionally, it is influenced by the rainfall intensity during the storm. A 'dry' hurricane

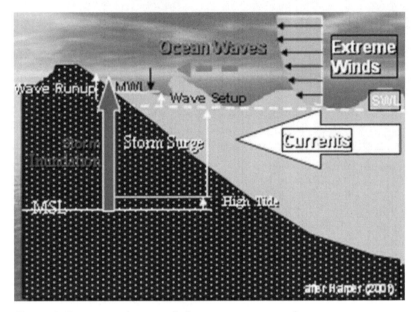

Figure 5: Storm inundation including wave run-up and setup

event does not cause rainfall-related damage such as landslides or flooding. Further threat factors are storm inundation and related surge, astronomical tide, wave setup and wave run-up; high winds and possible magnification by terrain and possible tornados; and heavy rains and associated flash flooding, which can also be terrain enhanced [Browning, 2007b]. Wind gusts within a hurricane may exceed the sustained winds by as much as 50 % [FEMA, n.d.]. Due to underwater topography around Hawai'i, such as depth and slope steepness, and the large wave setup and wave run up effect (see Figure 5), surf and storm inundation can vary widely. Wind waves associated with a major hurricane may reach 30 feet or more as seen during Hurricane 'Iniki in Kauai 1992 with high water marks from storm inundation up to 27 foot on the south shore, Poipe, but the storm surge only measured 6 to 9 foot. On O'ahu, it caused 15 to 20 foot surf with a three to four foot storm inundation. During hurricane Katrina, the cause of the storm inundation was mainly the storm surge due to the size of the hurricane. [Browning, 2007a]. Hurricane Katrina's maximum storm inundation was 27.8 ft but the National Hurricane Center at Miami speculated that this level was likely exacerbated by extremely large waves offshore. One buoy measured the largest wave ever documented by the National Data Buoy Center at 55 ft. Those

uncertainties pose a vulnerability to decision makers in disaster management due to the wide range of damage potential.

1.2 Background on hurricanes

Figure 6 shows the tracks of all Central Pacific hurricanes from 1949 to 1997
[Businger, 1998]. The shading from red to blue is important because 80°F
is the minimum Sea Surface Temperature (SST) for hurricane formation.
The climatology of hurricane tracks over the central Pacific shows a mean
track passing to the south of the Hawai'ian Islands and a maximum hurricane occurrence during the late summer when the ocean surface is warmest
(Figure 7) [Businger, 1998]. Hawai'i's hurricane season prevails from June
1st to November 30th, with the highest probability of occurrence in August
[Browning, 2007b].

   Those are important considerations because the climatic phenomenons
of El Niño, La Niña and La Madre that seem to become more and more
influencial in the region due to global warming [IPCC, 2007] will influence
the hurricane paths, their strength and life time. A warmer climate correlates with an increased frequency and intensity of ENSO events [Mack-

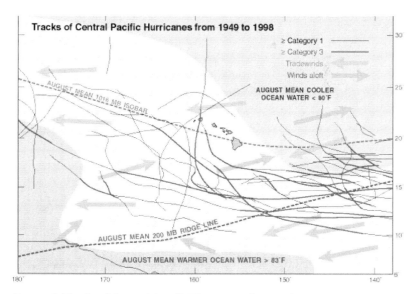

Figure 6: Tracks of Central Pacific Hurricanes from 1949 to 1997

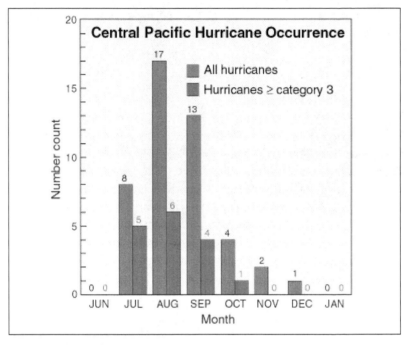

Figure 7: Central Pacific Hurricane Occurrence

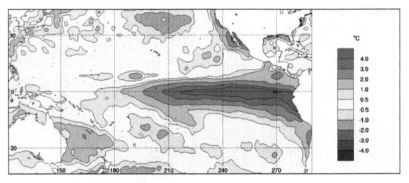

Figure 8: Departures from average ocean surface temperatures in December 1997 at the height of the 1997/98 El Niño

enzie, 2003]. Figure 8 shows the warm SSTs, which developed during the El Niño 1997/98 [Bureau of Meteorology, 2008] and Table 3 suggests that in ENSO years the probability of hurricane development is enhanced in the Pacific (see Table 3) [University of Hawai'i at Mānoa , 1993, p. 53]. Meteorological observations conclude more specifically that during El Nino conditions with warmer waters on the West coast of Mexico more intense and more numbers of hurricanes develop that could potentially threaten Hawai'i [Browning, 2007a].

Year 19..	70	71	72	73	74	75	76	77	78	79	80	81
Storms	5	5	7*	2	3	1	4*	0	7	0	2	2
Year 19..	82	83	84	85	86	87	88	89	90	91	92	
Storms	10*	6	5	8	7*	4	5	4	4	3	11*	

Table 3: Frequency of hurricane events and correlation with ENSO years
* denotes ENSO year

Further, a warming atmosphere contributes to sea level rise through expansion of seawater and melting ice on land. These factors further increase the

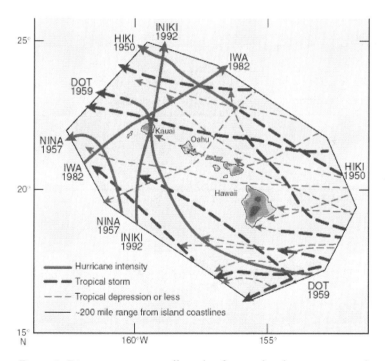

Figure 9: Diagram capturing all tracks of tropical cyclones passing within 3 degree Latitude of the islands between 1950 and 1992. Major hurricanes are named.

vulnerability of Hawai'i's coastlines and enhance the damage potential of hurricanes in Hawai'i. The effects in the Hawai'ian Islands result in worsening of coastal erosion, beach will narrow or be lost, coastal properties and roads will be overtopped more frequently, some lands will become completely submerged and coastal lands will become more vulnerable to coastal hazards including tsunamis, storm surge and high waves.

All major islands in the Hawai'ian Island chain were struck by strong wind storms since the beginning of history. Until 1950 no official data was collected about tropical cyclones approaching Hawai'i. It is only since 1969 that there is geostationary satellites available monitoring storm development in the Pacific. Documents identified storms before that time period, but no exact data on storm intensity and other relevant data are available. From 1832 to 1949, 19 tropical cyclones were identified from scattered written records and ship reports [Shaw, 1981]. Data on hurricane history for the Hawai'ian Islands do not allow the calculation of a statistically significant frequency of tropical storms and hurricanes, but nonetheless show that the islands are at risk. 'Hurricane threats will be frequent and actual strikes will be rare' (see Figure 9) [Businger, 1998][University of Hawai'i, 1993,

Name	Year	Peak winds	Winds at land-fall	Remarks
Nina	1957		No landfall	Close approach, record Honolulu wind
'Iwa	1982	92 mph	No landfall	Eye Northwest of Kauai
Fefa	1991	105 mph	< 30 mph	Rain producer
Fico	1978	115 mph	No landfall	South of South point
Uleki	1988	120 mph	No landfall	Threatened recurvature
Fabio	1988	125 mph	No landfall	Heavy rains from remote range
Estelle	1986	130 mph	No landfall	Surf damage Hawaii, Maui, rains on Oahu
Susan	1978	138 mph	No landfall	Greatest threat for Hilo
'Iniki	1992	145 mph	130 mph	Direct hit on Kauai
Dot	1959	165 mph	81 mph	Eye over Kauai

Table 4: History of hurricanes in Hawai'i

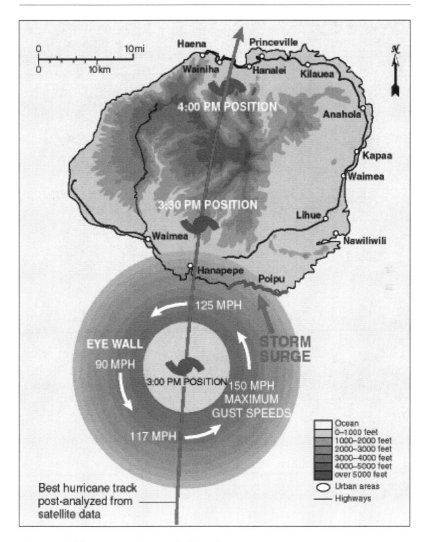

Figure 10: Track of Hurricane 'Iniki 1992

pp. 2]). The hurricane risk for a strong hit or near miss on O'ahu lies at about 1–3%. This probability seems low, but risk is mathematically constituted by the probability of an event times the magnitude of the consequences of the event. Consequently, the severity of the impacts needs to be considered. As various vulnerability analyses show [Federal Emergency Management Agency, 2007; Reissberg, 2010], those impacts would be catastrophic. Only considering the minimal probability is mis-leading for responsible disaster

Figure 11: High resolution infrared image of Hurricane 'Iniki

managers as well as politicians. But of course, emphasizing the low probability of High-Impact-Low-Probability (HILP) events comes in handy if long-term expensive measures are not favourable to politicians who want to be reelected, for example.

Kauai received the brunt of Hurricane 'Iwa, which struck on 23 November 1982 and produced an estimated $234 million in damage. Hurricane 'Iniki in 1992 was the most costly disaster in Hawai'i, ever [Businger, 1998]. Table 4 shows that hurricane Dot was the strongest hurricane in terms of peak winds, but 'Iniki made landfall with the highest wind speed (130mph) [University of Hawai'i at Mānoa , 1993, p. 3]. It is important to note that a hurricane does not have to be a direct hit to cause great damage [FEMA, n.d., p. 1].

By any measure except loss of life, Hurricane 'Iniki, which hit Kauai on Sept. 11, 1992, was by far the worst natural disaster in recorded Hawai'i history [Starbulletin, 2002c]. Figure 10 shows the hurricane track crossing over the island of Kauai [Businger, 1998]. It caused over $1.6 billion in losses to residential property, visitor accommodations, public utilities, public buildings, and agriculture on Kauai. Six months after the storm the unemployment rate was still over 16 %. Kauai County lost an estimated $14 million in property tax revenue during 1993 and 1994. Property losses from 'Iniki also precipitated a statewide property insurance crisis, the bankruptcy of one insurance company, and the cancellation of over 40,000 property insurance policies [University of Hawai'i at Mānoa , 1996]. Figure 11 shows the hurricane making landfall on Kauai at 3:15 PM HST on 11 September 1992. The image was taken by a NOAA polar orbiting satellite about 500 miles above the Earth [Businger, 1998].

O'ahu is much more vulnerable than Kauai and costs will be enormous. It cannot expect resource support from the other Hawai'ian Islands due to their dependency on O'ahu's resources and the fact that they will be impacted to some degree as well. Because of the technical condition of their harbors, containerships are offloaded on O'ahu and resources are barged to the other islands [FEMA, 2007]. During hurricane 'Iwa (1982) and 'Iniki

Figure 12: Aerial photograph of debris line on Kauai after Hurricane 'Iniki 1992

Figure 13: Category 4 destruction on Kauai

Figure 14: Flying debris during Hurricane 'Iniki 1992

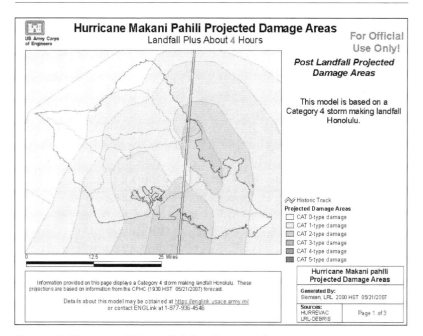

Figure 15: Hurricane Makani Pahili – Projected damage areas

(1992), Kauai received resource support from O'ahu and consequently, Kauai recovered faster. Further, Kauai was less reliant on infrastructure than O'ahu. O'ahu's infrastructure is more vulnerable, specifically the harbor's supply infrastructure, the electricity system and the water system [Richards and Tengan, 2007]. People on Kauai were more self-sufficient and less dependent on modern infrastructure. Kauai's electrical system was less complicated and could withstand more pounding. Additionally, according to 1990 population data, 837,000 people lived on O'ahu, but in Kauai County had only a population of about 52,000, a fraction of O'ahu's population [U.S. Census Bureau, 1990]. Consequently, food and resource requirements were less. Not only would the numbers be higher on O'ahu in general, but due to multiplying effects and the interdependency of critical infrastructure systems, damage would rise exponentially.

The following three images demonstrate the extent of possible damage. Figure 12 shows an aerial photograph of the debris line on Kauai after Hurricane 'Iniki 1992 [Browning, 2007a]. Figure 13 exemplifies hurricane Category 4 destruction on Kauai and Figure 14 shows flying debris caused by Hurricane 'Iniki in 1992 [Browning, 2007a].

The United States Army Corps of Engineers (USACE) developed a model showing projected damage areas after a Category 4-hurricane landfall on Oʻahu plus four hours, (see Figure 15). Category specific damages are estimates of the USACE relating to the NWS standards [Siemsen, 2008] and are outlined in Table 2.

Extrapolation from damage on Kauai in 1982 and 1992 resulted in the total estimate costs for an ʻIniki strength storm on Oʻahu is *between US$19.4 and US$32.4 billion* (updated 2005) [FEMA, 2007] but do not include a Variety of costs to Federal, State and County governments, private businesses, and individuals, for example expenditures for disaster assistance, damage to Federal facilities, losses in business income, losses of State and County tax revenue and others. This estimate falls within several other calculations of insurance companies and private contractors: potential insured losses were estimated at about US$35.7 billion [University of Hawaiʻi at Mānoa , 1993]. It is important to note that the damage in dollar amount only covers the quantifiable physical asset and economic impacts, but do

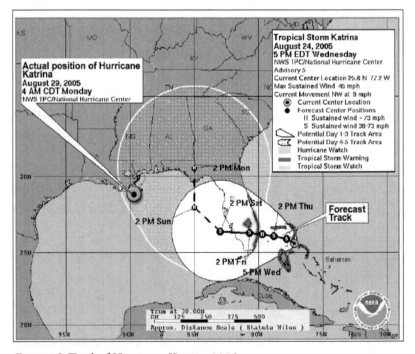

Figure 16: Track of Hurricane Katrina 2005

not measure intangible costs such as the effects on plant and wild life, the human suffering and other social costs.

High-impact-low-probability events rarely get predicted, but cynically, science pretends to be able to calculate their probability *after* the event. Taleb [2007] argues that, if looking at history, no high impact event has been predicted and that history jumps, and does not crawl [Taleb, 2007]. Consequently, science gives us a false sense of security, where we can control nature to a certain extent. It seems inacceptable and unmanageable to admit that those uncertainties cannot possibly be calculated or be controlled. This should motivate us to prepare for the worst case. Ultimately, if prepared for the worst case minor events will have less impact. As mentioned before, it has been shown that the reduction of risk and damage potential does save four dollars for every dollar spent [Rabenold, 2006]. If this win-win situation would be considered with more seriousness, much risk could be reduced. The problem with HILP events are their opportunity costs, such as financial costs for mitigation measures or loss of political popularity.

Hurricanes are the most predictable short-term natural triggers of disasters with a forecast time span of several days. Geological hazards such as earthquakes and volcanic eruptions, floods and the effects of El Niño Southern Oscillation (ENSO) are much harder to forecast. Figure 16 shows the forcast for hurricane Katrina and the final storm location over New Orleans [U.S. Department of Commerce, National Oceanic and Atmospheric Administration, National Weather Service, 2006].

Forecasting weather patterns was and will always be challenging. Consequently, decision making in hurricane hazard management, e.g. regarding the timing of evacuation, is problematic because minimal changes in hurricane location have major impacts regarding damage potential [Richards, 2007b].

Besides those natural factors, the progression of vulnerability cannot be addressed outside of the context of social and economic facts that play significant roles in determining 'Who is vulnerable and why', which will be discussed in the next chapters.

1.3 Hurricanes in Hawai'i and the risk of a future hit

The catastrophic nature of this event will require a massive Federal response to support State efforts to save and sustain lives, protect property and promote economic and social recovery. Critical infrastructure including energy, transportation, communications, food, sanitation and water distribution and emergency services will be severely impacted. The results of loss of infrastructure and key resources and the disruption of emergency services will be greatly exacerbated by the distance of the Hawai'i Island Chain from other areas of the United States and the world.

1.4 Damage scenarios and vulnerability analysis for O'ahu

1.4.1 Storm track and inundation scenarios

The Federal Emergency Management Agency developed in 2007 a Concept of Operation for a catastrophic hurricane (Saffir-Simpson Category 4 to 5) hitting the island of O'ahu (CONOP) with wind speeds of 131 mph or greater. The State Civil Defense led annual hurricane exercise Makani Pahili is based on a storm track shown in Figure 17 and Figure 18. On picture 1 of Figure 17, it is assumed that the hurricane will pass Hawai'i but then it turns north for a direct hit (Figure 18).

A significant portion of the highly populated areas of the City and County of Honolulu will be inundated based upon a likely twenty-foot (20ft) storm surge and wind swells and waves, associated with a category 4–5 hurricane.

1.4.2 O'ahu's vulnerability to hurricanes

So far, the natural vulnerabilities for the Hawai'ian Islands were elaborated, which cannot be managed or changed. In the following, the focus will be the man-made vulnerabilities that are imposed on society by human activity through economic circumstances, environmental or cultural conditions and therefore can be managed or changed in order to reduce vulnerabilities on all scales.

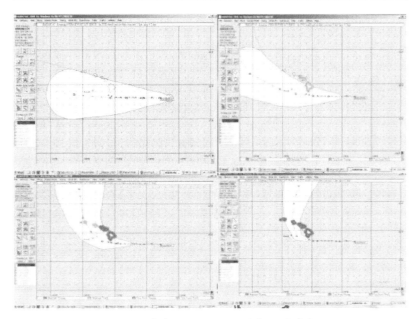

Figure 17: NWS storm track during Exercise Makani Pahili 2007

Figure 18: Storm track of Makani Pahili 2007

Compared to the damage extent of Hurricane Katrina still vivid in the memories of many O'ahu faces a much more vulnerable situation due to its isolation, high population density and fragile infrastructure. In human terms, the biggest difference appears to be the infeasibility of evacuation of the island's population. As the past has shown, under a hurricane threat the population will not even consider evacuation, both the local population and tourists. The fact that 80 % of Hawai'i's population lives on O'ahu makes the population especially vulnerable due to limited fresh-water and other resources. It is highly dependent on imports and other islands cannot assist O'ahu because they themselves are dependent on O'ahu for energy, food and other commodities. Its support infrastructure faces catastrophic inundation and damage, especially the harbor and airport facilities and also the main power production facilities (both electric generation and liquid fuels). 80 % of the island's infrastructure will fail [Rosenberg, 2007b], Honolulu International Airport will be unavailable for an extended time and the extensive damage to harbor facilities of Pearl Harbor and Honolulu and smaller inland

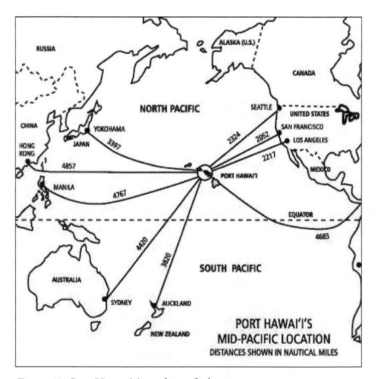

Figure 19: Port Hawai'i's mid-pacific location

airports will limit the island's resource access to a great extent [Rosenberg, 2007b]. Food and water shortage will become a major problem after about 10 days [Rosenberg, 2007b]. Power outages for large parts of O'ahu will last for weeks if not months due to the highly vulnerable power distribution system: Only 44% of HECO's power lines are underground and temporary power outages occur due to local high wind events. The power system is the most critical and life-sustaining element on O'ahu. Most of the power plants are located in surge inundation areas, resulting in the potential loss of power generation post landfall [FEMA, 2007]. Hawai'i is specifically vulnerable due to its long coast-lines and its isolation. The State of Hawai'i cannot be sustained by air due to the massive amount of resources needed and consequently the harbors are the most important element [Richards, 2007h]. O'ahu is critical because it has the only fuel terminal and its infrastructure supports distribution of fuel, food, and essential commodities to the neighbor islands [FEMA, 2007] [Rosenberg, 2007b]. Figure 19 shows Hawai'i's distance to support locations [FEMA, 2007, p. 11].

A chaotic situation with almost one million people in Honolulu would emerge and the daily life for O'ahu's population will be greatly disrupted for a long time after landfall of a catastrophic hurricane. An estimated 75% to 80% of O'ahu's residences may be damaged or destroyed due to the inundation of a significant portion of the highly populated areas of the City and County of Honolulu, and most that are habitable will need to have temporary roof repair to allow residents to remain with their homes [FEMA, 2007]. Roofs will be blown away resulting in water damage. Homes will collapse or have major damages to roofs from high winds and have no power. Downtown, the majority of the buildings' windows will be broken due to flying debris. This will result in a large percentage of the population requiring emergency shelter and other services. Officially, the shortfall of shelter space on O'ahu amounts to 153,000 units [Tengan, 2007b], but this number seems grossly underestimated for a catastrophic hurricane. Transportation is hindered due to blocked roads and staffing problems for emergency workers. Streets are clogged with debris and downed utility poles. Roads are jammed with abandoned vehicles. Banks are closed due to the power outage. Many bank buildings in town have sustained major damages due to the high winds and broken windows. Telephone service is down throughout most of O'ahu. Cellular telephones are operational in a few sporadic locations. Water pressure in many high-rise buildings is low or non-existent' [Hawai'i State Civil Defense, 2007d]. Sand and debris have clogged many storm drains, and standing flood waters, large sinkholes, landslides and mudslides disrupt life all over the island. Hazardous materials such as oil spills and broken glass hinder the progress of the disaster response. Debris clearing is dangerous due to downed power lines, and resource distribution is severely disrupted. Due to Hawai'i's subtropical climate health concerns will become rapidly imminent. Widespread flooding would cause widespread sewer system failure [FEMA, 2007]. Lacking refrigeration and suffering a broken sewerage system, health hazards and disease outbreaks will become a problem and will affect the availability of disaster workers [Breakout Session Infrastructure, 2007]. County and State emergency workers are overwhelmed and some areas will not be restored for months.

Cases of acute vulnerabilities and risks to O'ahu's population

The following should give a deeper insight on how mismanagement can lead to highly vulnerable situations that threaten the life of the population on all islands before, during and after a catastrophic hurricane. Since all other islands are on all scales dependent on the air and ocean harbor systems of the island of O'ahu, all islands will be massively affected.

Debris management – the entry into restoration of O'ahu

The three most critical infrastructure components to make life sustainable on O'ahu after a Category 4 to 5 hurricane are the power, transportation and communication system. All other systems are highly dependent on those systems, e.g. resource distribution and storage capabilities [Suizo, 2007]. But, restoration of the islands critical infrastructure and subsequently the reestablishment of sustainable life conditions are first of all dependent on debris management.

To mention the most urging factors first: the time for debris removal was estimated at at least one year [ICCMA, 2006]. The sheer amount of debris poses a serious problem for the functioning of the island's life (Figure 20). A volume of 25,120,000 cubic yards of debris will be accumulated [Hawai'i State Civil Defense, 2007a]. Besides the problem of hazardous material, e.g. asbestos, and its disposal, the Army Corps of Engineers' estimate for the amount of debris equals 240 football fields being 50ft high [Teixeira, 2007b].

Only two landfills exist on O'ahu. Consequently, the debris will have to be shipped off. H-POWER at Campbell Industrial Park that burns 90% of the waste will be destroyed, which emphasizes the urgency for a debris

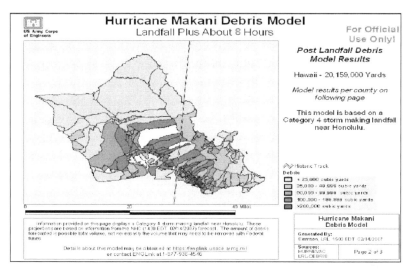

Figure 20: Hurricane Makani Debris Model

management strategy [FEMA, 2007]. Without infrastructure to support the power distribution lines, transportation and communication capabilities a hurricane's impacts will not be overcome. On the other hand, without power, no debris removal or pumping system will be operational, which makes these factors a key to vulnerability reduction.

As of now, no salvage and dredging capabilities exist on the islands, so it has to be brought in from the mainland via ships, assuming that the airports with landing capability allowing large equipment will not be accessible [Rosenberg, 2007b]. The time to stage equipment and ship it to Hawai'i must be estimated at about one week: five days are needed for shipping time in addition to the staging time. Obviously, pre-staging is of major importance. The time span to clear areas of high priority is estimated at two to three weeks of dredging operation and adds to the time until the major corridors to sustain life on O'ahu will be available [Rosenberg, 2007a].

Intensifying the situation after the storm are lacking communication capabilities. Currently, the State of Hawai'i has no coastal surveillance systems nor *any* port or port approach surveillance capability, visual or radar. The State's critical infrastructure (e.g., Hawai'ian Electric Company, water and sewage systems, ports, hospitals and shopping malls) has continued to improve their individual surveillance and protection systems, but no means exists to provide any coordinated or centralized monitoring at a County or State level [Hawai'i State Civil Defense, 2007ab].

Infrastructure vulnerability

In the event of a direct impact from a Category 4 to 5 hurricane on Oʻahu, the loss of critical infrastructure and the challenges associated with providing emergency logistics support from across the Pacific Ocean will require early and massive efforts from the Federal government to sustain the local and transient population [Rosenberg, 2007c]. Concerning the most significant factors, State Civil Defense officials assume that Oʻahu would lose 80 % of its infrastructure in the case of a catastrophic hurricane making landfall near Honolulu, the scenario given for the Makani Pahili Exercise and that Honolulu International airport will be unavailable for a long time [Rosenberg, 2007b][Richards and Tengan, 2007]. The support infrastructure of Oʻahu including the power production facilities – most importantly the two oil refineries Chevron and Tesoro –, Honolulu International Airport, Honolulu Harbor and Pearl Harbor face potential catastrophic inundation or damage to cargo handling facilities. The largest critical infrastructure at Campbell Industrial Park, adjacent to Barbers Point Kalaeloa Harbor, lies between five to 10 foot above Mean Sea Level (MSL) [Nolan, 2008] on the West Side of Oʻahu within the inundation zone (Figure 21) on around 1,400 acres with both power production facilities (Chevron, Tesoro) and major manufacturing, recycling, import/export, power generation, construction, warehouse and distribution industries [Enterprise Honolulu, 2008].

The interrelatedness and interdependence between power and fuel availability, the transportation capability and communications makes those systems highly vulnerable. The progress of efforts depends on power availability. Without fuel, no power or gasoline can be produced. Transportation and distribution of goods, medical services, refrigeration and other life-sustaining activities would become impossible. Also, the communication system would fail. For the transportation network, as much as for the power distribution network, debris removal is essential, for which again fuel is needed. The dependent Emergency Medical System need all of the above to function, and is only one example for the importance of the critical infrastructure to establish 'normal' life conditions on Oʻahu after a catastrophic hurricane landfall.

The power system and consequential risks

Campbell Industrial Park with the main critical infrastructure support on site – specifically the off-shore pipelines that transport that imported bulk fuel on land – is the bottle neck for power production and will be inundated (see Figure 21). From there, power is carried over the Koolau Mountains to the Windward side and to downtown and eastern Honolulu. If the facilities at Campbell Industrial Park fail, the whole island of O'ahu will be without power, except for some small generation units and self-sustaining units of the private and public sector. Adding to O'ahu's and Hawai'i's vulnerability is the dependency on one single energy source: imported petroleum accounts for 89 % of Hawai'i's primary energy, which is the highest dependency in the United States. Hawai'i itself has no oil resources and of all the oil imported, 32 % is used for electrical production, 34 % for air transportation and 27 % for ground and water travel [FEMA, 2007].

Main problems to be considered are the potential destruction of the off-shore pipeline system, the fuel terminals, the oil refineries and the distribution system, a potential contamination and the shortage of fuel supply in general since the supply of jet fuel and gasoline on the island is about 1 month [Hawai'i State Civil Defense, 2007d]. Bulk fuel might be available and stored in tanks around the island, but if it cannot be made available through the distribution network, it is without use. Further, for many first responders' activities, gasoline is needed because bunk fuel is not usable for all needs. Consequently, the oil refineries are of major importance. Power is needed to pump gasoline at the stations in most cases, even though some small trucks have self-pumping systems [Rosenberg, 2007a].

Oil is offloaded to mobile buoys at open sea – because of safety and efficiency concerns – and runs via pipeline to Campbell Industrial Park. This means that the only access of oil supply runs from ships to land. In case of a major disaster, oil could be offloaded by docking ships, which would be less efficient and time-consuming, but feasible. Oil supply underground and in pipelines will sustain limited damage. Most of the power distribution network runs under or along H1, which is only 13 ft above sea level [Rosenberg, 2007a]. Consequently, those underground fuel tanks and the distribution pipelines are at risk [Breakout Session Infrastructure, 2007].

Further pipelines support the harbors with ship fuel and Honolulu International airport [FEMA, 2007]. Salt water inundation to cargo terminals and cranes at the harbors, in addition to the blockage of the channel from debris would pose major problems.

The CONOP states even that 'much of O'ahu's power distribution infrastructure, including poles, wire and transformers, will fail due to pre-landfall winds' [FEMA, 2007, p. 58]. Power outages can begin at 40 mph sustained and widespread power outages can occur with gusts to 60 mph

[FEMA, 2007]. Only 44 % of HECO's power lines are underground and almost all the 138 kV lines, the largest on their system, are above ground including all major lines running out of the power plants. Oʻahu, analogously to Kauai after past hurricane, would be entirely dependent on generators for some time.

Since HECO's power network is a circular system it is highly vulnerable when any part of the system fails because transmission and distribution can only be served from two sides. Once the electricity system fails, there is no centralized backup generation in place. Plus, electricity generation does not have much redundancy: even the day-to-day generation does not enough backup for disconnected island system elements and the reserve margins are narrow. Clearly, if one major HECO plant is lost, a very dire situation will develop. Another factor contributing to the system's vulnerability is HECO's dependency of 95 % electricity produced from oil, the rest from coal and renewable trash. As stated before, 89 % of Hawaiʻi's primary energy is produced from imported petroleum [Rosegg, 2007a].

The heavy concentration of power generation in one single location – Campbell Industrial Park – and a location that is most vulnerable to even the edges of large storms and to inundation makes the power system of Oʻahu highly vulnerable. It stands on its own without any backup for the entire island [Rosegg, 2007a]. The island's isolation makes the situation even more difficult. After a complete shutdown, if there is no damage to the power system, it takes 24 to 36 hours to restore it in the urban area due to a protection system. The risk of damaging the system by bringing it up too fast or too early is very sensitive due to transportation or availability difficulties: the equipment needs to come from the mainland United States [Zingman, 2007]. HECO's generator systems are small and not capable of supporting hospitals, critical facilities or even hotels who will depend on own emergency generation or potential military support.

Problems that are not a direct result of the hurricane but are a consequence of power system failure are a major threat. Without power, the Emergency Medical System and the hospitals' capabilities are limited. Loosing refrigeration would mean a threat to the food supply as well as a loss in medical capabilities with potential health threats in densely populated areas.

This results in environmental vulnerability: the loss of electricity can cause sewage spillages, e.g. into Lake Wilson when the ultraviolet disinfecting unit at the Wahiawa Wastewater Treatment Plant lost power, according to the city's Department of Environmental Services. Before emergency generators could kick in at the Sand Island Wastewater Treatment Plant, "clarifiers" could overflow and spill wastewater within the plant, as seen in 2006 [Honolulu Advertiser, 2006a].

An USACE assessment of temporary power generation requirements for critical facilities on the Island of O'ahu showed that 510 facilities potentially requiring temporary power are only covered by 89 FEMA generators ranging in capacity from 10 kW to 640 kW on island at FEMA's Logistics Center in O'ahu [FEMA, 2007].

The above-ground utility poles are not built to withstand any hurricane winds of 74 mph or more, most above-ground poles on O'ahu will fall. It is not known or tested, if only the underground cables would be working or if this would shut down the total system [Rosegg, 2007b]. For comparison, the island of Kauai lost all electricity and telephone service following Hurricane 'Iniki, a category 4 storm, which passed over the island on September 11, 1992, and only 20 % of the power was restored on Kauai as late as four weeks after the storm. A catastrophic hurricane impacting O'ahu could destroy over 40 % of the power transmission and distribution poles, transformers, and wire, requiring months for the system to be restored [Rosenberg, 2007a].

Resource availability and distribution on O'ahu

The most imminent problem impedes due to the blockage of resource imports. It would be impossible to bring goods on land without power, and before debris management is in gear. Open transportation corridors are – besides power on land – the bottle neck in the progress chain in order to start debris removal [Rosenberg, 2007a]. Priority is given to the Emergency Medical Services, evacuations regarding the transportation to and from shelters and commodities supply.

It might be possible to use the transportation units that bring resources to O'ahu as evacuation space for the population, which stands in competition to issues regarding debris management and removal and depends on the conditions of the means of transportation. Those prioritization issues are not worked out by neither FEMA nor the State or City and County of Honolulu departments.

90 % of the critical commodities come in via ocean transport to Honolulu by ship and only 10 % via airlift [Rosenberg, 2007b]. As a consequence, the air corridor cannot sustain Hawai'i and its resource requirements due to the large population [Richards, 2007e]. Without functioning harbor facili-

ties the population is unsustainable in the State of Hawai'i. The total time to plan logistics of loading ships and plane additionally to the difficulties offloading ships and planes in Hawai'i after a catastrophic hurricane poses serious impediments to efficient disaster management efforts. Commercial shipping from the mainland on calm seas requires an average of 10 days (typical vessel total execution time) including on- and off-loading.

The ability to restore critical infrastructure will be hampered by significant damage to the harbor facilities of Pearl Harbor and Honolulu and the possibility of debilitating damage to major airports on O'ahu [FEMA, 2007]. There will be near total destruction to commercial port cargo handling equipment due to storm surge and catastrophic wind conditions. Their docks would be extensively damaged and their channels would be blocked due to lose containers, broken free ships, loose gantry cranes and washed up sand, Barbers Point Harbor is assumed to be closed [Hawai'i State Civil Defense, 2007d]. Salt water inundation to motors of cranes and other equipment will render them unusable. Ships with cranes and on-load/off-load facilities are essential for the operation in those conditions [Rosenberg, 2007a] and have to be brought in from the mainland. Pre-staging of equipment is also here of major importance.

Honolulu International Airport with eight to twelve ft elevation above sea level, will be unavailable for some time as well as Hickam Air Force Base and Kaneohe Marine Corps Base [Hawai'i State Civil Defense, 2007a]. One O'ahu inland airport will be available earlier but does not have the capacity of Honolulu International, where e.g. the Russian cargo plane Antonow is able to land (Kauai, 1992).

Since self-sustainability is of high importance, first responders might not be at their job immediately and a high influx of workers is necessary. But if airports, specifically Honolulu International Airport, are destroyed, the needed personnel influx is hard to manage and would be at current times a 'mission impossible' [Breakout Session Infrastructure, 2007].

Abandoned vehicles, downed utility poles, land-, rock- and mudslides, debris, sinkholes, flooded streets and hazardous material spills would bring the road system on O'ahu to a closure [Hawai'i State Civil Defense, 2007a]. Figure 22 exemplifies one scenario of roads blocked post landfall [Hawai'i State Civil Defense, 2007a, p. 35].

The City and County of Honolulu Emergency Operations Plan of January 2007 states that 'federal resources originating from out-of-state should not be expected to be available for a period of time' in case of a major disaster [City and County of Honolulu, 2007, p. 4]. No plan to pre-stage resources before a hurricane strikes is in place, which would be majorly important specifically regarding the logistics priorities. A time-phased delivery data list is needed and a plan about in which order to load resources, for example [Rosenberg, 2007a]. All public warehouses will be destroyed with a Category 4 hurricane on O'ahu. Safe warehouses are needed to even start a response post-storm. Key facilities need to be identified where supplies can get to [Breakout Session Infrastructure, 2007].

Drinking water supply will be a very critical issue. Potable water is anticipated to be non-operational due to the degraded power distribution post hurricane [FEMA, 2007]. The water pressure in many high-rise buildings would be low or non-existent [Hawai'i State Civil Defense, 2007d] and contamination of water sources will worsen the situation. USACE contracts will be used to support the substantial requirement for water. The limited quantities that may be sourced will be for critical facilities. The distribution of water will be to Task Force staging areas and/or Points of Distribution as identified by the State of Hawai'i [FEMA, 2007]. Most storage facilities and warehouses lie in floodplain areas (FEMA warehouse in Halawa, JTF-HD warehouse in Kunia, State warehouse on Sand Island) [Richards, 2007h] and refrigeration will be lost. The population is informed to have two weeks to one month of food self-supply because the shelters might be destroyed [Richards, 2007h]. First responders coming to Hawai'i are to carry a minimum of one to two weeks of self-supply because propositioned food on site will not be enough to cover emergency response workers [Breakout Session Infrastructure, 2007]. The question of how much food supply exists on O'ahu for the entirety of the population could not be answered, due to unclear inventories of the private sector, among other factors. The only solution to secure the food supply for the Hawai'ian Islands is to ship food from California and other places. Therefore, organizations of all kind have to be contacted to summarize inventories and to start planning logistics. Plans for such a coordinated effort are not in place.

Communication system

In Hawai'i, the physical IT communication system is fragile and highly vulnerable. It depends on other systems' capabilities such as power and its distribution system. In New Orleans, initial response efforts were hampered because police, fire and other rescue personnel had difficulty talking to each other, with their networks crippled by lack of power and flooding or due to incompatible communication systems. The situation in Hawai'i would be similar [Rosenberg, 2007a]. Power outages start at 40 mph sustained winds and will be widespread at over 60 mph gusts, and cell phone outages occur with over 60 mph sustained winds. Consequently, only satellite and amateur radio will be left for communication. Satellite communication is difficult in Hawai'i due to its location in a strange satellite position. Hawai'i is not able to use a lot of mainland satellites and there are limitations on usage [Weyman, 2007a]. Battery-supported communication will be limited and will break down when battery capabilities are exhausted. The Federal Emergency Management Agency (FEMA) deployable disaster communication capability to restore local infrastructure capabilities including communications is the Mobile Emergency Response Capability (MERS). In 2005, during hurricane Katrina, communication failed even though today, technical capabilities including its interoperability are no limitations.

During the earthquake on O'ahu in October 2006, which causes minor damage compared to the here discussed scenario, it became obvious that the cell phone system is very fragile: it failed due to heavy usage. Actions to harden that communication system through landlines, dedicated cell lines, out-of-the-public lines for emergency responders, and numbers that are not widely published, were obviously needed. The Hawai'ian Electric Company (HECO) has an internal microwave system around the island that enables machinery and computers to coordinate with each other, which sustained itself well in the earthquake and is designed to withhold disasters. Communications with other the HHMS departments and agencies rely on landlines or cell phones, which are very fragile. Cell phone providers were down due to outage, their emergency generators went out, ultimately due to fuel shortage or other problems. In the longer term, cell phone usage would be impossible. The use of landline is preferable because it is easier to use and there is greater control over getting emergency access between critical facilities than with cell phones. 45 % of landlines are underground, but those are susceptible to other problems, e.g. flooding. There is no escaping from a plethora of problems for a direct hurricane hit. Helpful is the advance notice so parts of the system would be shut off before hurricane to protect the system [Rosegg, 2007a].

The distribution of public information as well as information exchange of first responders for damage assessments is of high urgency. But, as mentioned above, the communication system is dependent on power and fuel. The Makani Pahili exercise assumptions expect telephone service to be down throughout most of O'ahu and cellular telephones to be operational in a few sporadic locations. All radio and TV stations would be heavily damaged due to high winds and able to transmit intermittently [Hawai'i State Civil Defense, 2007d]. The recovery of telecommunications depends on mainland resources [Department of Emergency Management, 2007].

Urgent upgrading and repairs of Hawai'i's communication system would reduce O'ahu's vulnerability immensely. An upgrade of the 60-year-old siren system would take over seven years and about $19 million as per State Civil Defense [Starbulletin, 2006b]. Roughly 10 % of the sirens typically don't work when the system is tested each month. In 2006, 100 older sirens were flagged for replacement and about 148 more emergency sirens are needed on the four main Hawai'ian Islands to cover gap areas. Half of O'ahu's 24 vital communications towers, like the one on Koko Head shown in Figure 23 and Figure 24, need repairs and are vulnerable to catastrophic storms.

An 'Iniki-type storm hitting O'ahu would knock out a significant portion of its communications infrastructure due to, among other factors, a lack of system maintenance, so Gordon Bruce, director of the city Department of Information Technology [Honolulu Advertiser, 2005b]. The back-up systems are powered by generators or with batteries. Without power for a long period, fuel supply shortage, battery draining along with transportation difficulties will contribute to a system breakdown.

Local governments understand the need to anticipate and prepare for loss of communication. Similarly, information technology plans are essential for continuity of government, and those plans should include storage of backup data outside the immediate area. GIS map expertise with printer capability is especially helpful in emergency operations centers so that crews from out of town can assist in rescue and recovery efforts. The county EOC has direct lines to dispatch centers of the Honolulu Police Department, the Honolulu Fire Department (HFD), the Emergency Medical Services (EMS) and others. Those hard-wire lines will work as well as the satellite phones. The power requirements are supported by three generators, but unfortunately without redundancy. Those are used for the Department Communication Center, the Department of Information Technology (DIT) and the county EOC and if one generator fails, the system will fail. The Department of Facilities and Maintenance responsibility is to replace the generators every five years, which is only suggested, but not implemented [Gilbert, 2007b]. This underlines the system's vulnerability and demonstrates the difficulties of keeping real-time, which is essential though for a system to function effectively. We cannot manage the past, only the present and possibly the future by indirect control as cybernetics aims to explicate.

Figure 21: Areal image of Campbell Industrial Park

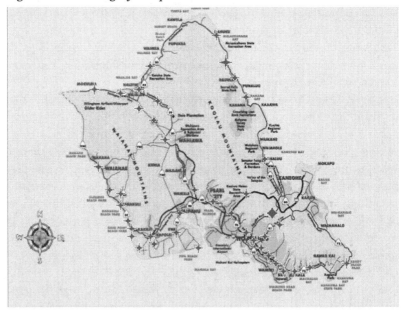

Figure 22: Areas with roads blocked post landfall

In case of a catastrophic hurricane, the data submission via internet, landlines and cell phones will fail and there will be no way of collecting damage assessment data. The data collection has to go via satellite [Observations, Oʻahu Civil Defense Agency Emergency Operation Center, 2007]. Rosenberg stated that that kind of communication is not set up yet and that a partnership with private industry that holds 80 % of the critical infrastructure is necessary. Currently the telephone landlines and cell phones are not capable of operating that system and the physical infrastructure system is very fragile. The communication plan in the Concept of Operations (CONOP) for a catastrophic hurricane impacting the state of Hawaiʻi is much undeveloped. The system in place has no sophistication and operates with a Variety of phone lists [Rosenberg, 2007b]. Further, a team solution is needed for the State Civil Defense (SCD) joint communication operations. Those fail due to data network issues (firewalls) and the entities cannot get on each other's network [Rosenberg, 2007a].

Several real-time devices exist on Oʻahu and in the State of Hawaiʻi to enable efficient communication and decision making processes: radio and TV stations, amateur radio operators RACES (Radio Amateur Civil Emergency Services), the Traffic Management Center run by the Department of Transportation with cameras, radios and broadcasters and the Emergency Alert System (EAS) network that enables the President of the United States to address the American people during periods of national emergency. The Conference Bridge is a virtual connection of all Emergency Operation Centers (EOC) of all islands. It connects to the National Weather Service that reports the real-time development of the hurricane. Hawaiʻi Electric Company and others also communicate through bus drivers while they are still operating. Those devices are highly vulnerable though as well. Internet-based information systems are dependent on power distribution and communication system availability. A Variety of software applications (Web EOC, E-Team, Hurrevac, Islands Mass Management Tool, National Disaster Medical System etc.) exist to accommodate real-time information exchange within entities during a disaster, but their incompatibilities and user interfaces are not in sync.

Health care and sanitation infrastructure

The chaotic situation after Hurricane Katrina with 50.000 people left in New Orleans makes a scenario with almost one million people in Honolulu vivid. Without refrigeration and a broken sewage system, sanitation, drinking water availability, health hazards and disease outbreaks will become a problem and will affect the availability of disaster workers [Breakout Session Infrastructure, 2007]. Widespread flooding would cause widespread sewer system failure over a long time [FEMA, 2007]. How easily that system is overwhelmed showed the local disaster involving major sweage spills along all coasts of Oʻahu caused by 46 days of rain in Spring 2006. Many sewer lines were still in repairs and above ground in August 2007 [Breakout Session Infrastructure, 2007].

The major sanitation plant for Honolulu with almost 400.000 people is located on Sand Island, an area on the coast which would be heavily damaged due to inundation. It is a branched network, not a loop, which is very inefficient because of its single-point-failure setup: if a part of a branch is lost, everything behind it is lost as well. In case of system failure the sewage backup will contaminate the water and people in high-risers buildings will be without flushing water, among other issues. As a result all drinking sources in that area will be contaminated. Within days health threats such as cholera and typhus will spread [Rosenberg, 2007a]. This situation with devastating consequences is not accounted for in the CONOP [FEMA, 2007].

Regarding the medical facilities' capabilities, the Makani Pahili exercise assumptions suppose that Queen's Hospital on Beretania Street is at high risk of inundation and will not be available immediately after the storm. Trippler Army Medical Center laying mountainside, Straub Clinic and Hospital and Kapiolani Medical Center, would suffer major damages to its facility and would be 50 percent operational. The Blood Bank would run low on their blood supplies and would need about 750 donors to donate blood [Hawaiʻi State Civil Defense, 2007d]. Besides the vulnerability due to inundation and winds, certain agreements should be in place to make an efficient workflow at and between hospitals possible. For example, Trippler Hospital is owned by the military and therefore agreements would be needed to be able to treat civilians here in case of a disaster [Rosenberg, 2007a].

The shelter system – Oʻahu's population at risk

The shelter system depends on all of the above mentioned systems.

There will be minimal pre-landfall evacuation of both the resident and tourist population on Oʻahu off the island. The tourist population on Oʻahu on any given day is approximately 131,000. Active and Guard military facilities on the island of Oʻahu will sustain extensive damage and initially be able to provide only minimal material support through inherent assistance authorities. Specific plans to designate shelters and provide emergency services including medical treatment and food and water distribution, and to develop a systematic process for restoring critical transportation, communications and energy infrastructure are urgently required [FEMA, 2007]. The significant loss of dwellings will result in a large percentage of the population requiring emergency shelter and other services [FEMA, 2007]. Some hub-shelters are fully equipped with sufficient generators and communication systems, capabilities for the special needs population and pet-friendly sheltering and other shelters will depend on them due to lack of funding [Tengan, 2007b]. The Makani Pahili exercise assumptions deduce that all American Red Cross shelters would be at maximum capacity and would be in need of water and food; approximately 60,000 residents would be displaced throughout Oʻahu and that public schools would be closed and used as shelters [Hawaiʻi State Civil Defense, 2007d] (see Table 5) [FEMA, 2007, p. 50].

Those numbers are grossly underestimated because they are calculated for a Category 1 hurricane only, but the CONOP scenario handles a Category 4 to 5 hurricane [Rosenberg, 2007a].

The combination of major low-lying area inundation and flooding from storm runoff, coupled with extensive wind damage, creates exceptional potential for catastrophic loss [FEMA, 2007]. Major emergency sheltering will excessively be needed because the numerous lightly constructed buildings and dwellings are highly susceptible to severe damage or being destroyed in hur-

Figure 23: Koko Head communication tower 1

Resident and Visitor Space Needs / Usable Shelter Space for Oahu						
Oahu CD District	Council District	Est. Pop.	Shelter Spaces *	Hurricane Scenario Needs (Winds 74 mph or higher)		
		Residents		Resident	Visitor	Shortfall
I	4,5,6,7 (Honolulu)	408,111	131,830	128,555	37,133	(33,858)
II	2,9 (Waialua)	100,952	23,305	31,800		(8,495)
III	1,9 (Maile)	51,687	18,199	16,281		
IV	2,3 (Kailua)	120,176	25,982	37,855		(11,872)
V	2 Kahuku)	18,774	12,213	5,914		
VI	1,8,9 (Pearl City)	192,384	55,795	60,601		(4,806)
Totals		892,084	267,324	281,006	37,133	(59,031)
				318,139		
*Includes estimated total shelter spaces Category 1, 2,2A and Visitor Shelter space.						
Multi-Hazard Pre-Disaster Mitigation Plan for City and County of Honolulu, 2003, Section 6.						

Table 5: Shelter spaces and needs

ricane force winds [FEMA, 2007]. Flying debris from these structures and airborne vegetation increase the potential for serious damage to neighboring properties and utility lines. It must be assumed that 80 % to 90 % of roofs will be lost on O'ahu [Breakout Session Infrastructure, 2007]. An estimated 75 % to 80 % of residences may be damaged or destroyed, and most that are habitable will need to have temporary roof repair to allow residents to remain with their homes. The USACE performs this work under its Blue Roof mission [FEMA, 2007].Through an agreement between the State Civil Defense, the City & County of Honolulu, the Hawai'i Hotel and Lodging Association (HHLA) and the Hawai'i Hotel Visitor Security Association (HHVSA), major hotels have plans to shelter hotel guest in place. The agreement provides liability clause and planning for 72 hours of provisions [FEMA, 2007]. If residents and visitor seek safety at locations structurally not designed to withstand the wind load, there could be a need for search and rescue and mass medical treatment at numerous locations across the island. Due to a lack of anticipatory and proactive policy measures, both the regulation of building standards and insurance options are limited.

A vulnerability of major importance is the fact that shelters in Hawai'i in general are designed for the response phase: that means, for people to get out of the storm and then return back home after the storm passed. People going to shelters need to bring their own bedding and food. Shelters do not have mass feeding capabilities. In pamphlets given out by the American

Red Cross Hawai'i Chapter it is outlined to have a three-day food supply at home and to bring a three-day food supply to the shelter [American Red Cross, n.d.]. If people should have to stay long-term – which is to be expected considering the excessive damage of a catastrophic hurricane, additional shortfalls regarding shelter equipment exist: generators, communications equipment, secure storage for equipment, refrigerators for medication and kitchen facilities, among others [Tengan, 2007b].

Inundation zoning interferes in some cases with the need for shelters. For example, McKinley High school at the corner of Kapiolani Boulevard and Pensacola Street is a designated shelter but lies within the inundation zone (see Figure 25) [McKinley Community School for Adults, n.d.][Rosenberg, 2007a] and will be under water [Breakout Session Infrastructure, 2007]. Alarmingly, the shelters of the best category are only designed for a maximum wind speed of 85 mph, an average Category 1 hurricane, and stronger wind forces are not accounted for. Under conditions of higher winds, the roofs will come off the shelters [Richards and Tengan, 2007]. These facts uncover a high vulnerability of O'ahu's population to a hurricane disaster.

Information management and risk perception

It is not known by the public in general, that Active and Guard military facilities on the island of O'ahu will initially not be able to provide material support through inherent assistance authorities due to sustained extensive damage [FEMA, 2007]. But in fact, O'ahu depends on the Department of Defense resources for its infrastructure repairs.

Within O'ahu's five Divisions the locations for staging areas and base camps are identified [FEMA, 2007] showing its height above sea level and the storms impact (see Table 6)(own interpretation).

Awareness of the general public about this situation would change attitudes, because people trust in the heavy presence of military on the islands and consequently rely on a false sense of security [Rosenberg, 2007a]. 80 % to 90 % of the population now living in hurricane-prone areas have never experienced the core of a major hurricane [U.S. Department of Commerce, National Oceanic and Atmospheric Administration, National Weather Service, 2006], only weaker storms or outer rain bands of intense hurricanes and cannot imagine a major hurricane's damage potential. Complacency and delayed actions can result in more injuries and loss of lives.

In general, information management is a great source of social vulnerability. Disaster information is a highly sensitive issue and could cause public commotion or panic if not used wisely. Also, false alarms could cause the public not to react in a potentially fatal situation. Because the situation on Oʻahu for a catastrophic hurricane is so dire, it is not in the state's interest that the general public is informed about Hawaiʻi's short-comings, which would cause unnecessary public discomfort or maybe panic when the state does not have the means to fix the situation. In the state's viewpoint, people are supposed to be prepared [Richards and Tengan, 2007]. On the other hand, social vulnerability is enhanced if people cannot foresee the seriousness of the situation. This gap of information status is a great source of vulnerability since it influences the general public's risk perception. It is a political issue though to reveal shortcomings. For example, it is not known or communicated how much food will be available after refrigeration is lost; or, the National Weather Service will inform HECO if an approaching hurricane is dangerous long before this would be communicated to the public [Rosegg, 2007a]. At a presentation contracted by HECO in the summer of 2006, it was said that hurricanes are a low risk, and consequently upgrades to HECO's poles would not be urgently needed. This economically motivated interpretation of information ultimately results in social vulnerability due to the public's dependency on HECO's electricity distribution network and on information available to them.

Those support installations and facilities, including Staging Areas, and Base Camps, are planned to be used to support response and recovery operations. Considering the damage potential this list gives a false impression of available resources for the assumed hurricane scenario and consequently, in addition to the surprise and reduced capability to respond, vulnerability is increased by this kind of misleading information management. Fact is that Wheeler Army Airfield is in Central Oʻahu and the only one secure from storm inundation and its location is well positioned to support air operations if other airports are damaged due to storm inundation. Load limitation places constrains using the site for an air bridge supporting a Federal Operational Staging Area [FEMA, 2007]. The Diamond Head Base Camp is the only base camp secure from storm inundation. All other locations listed are at high risk to be damaged. Analogously, the CONOP identifies that Honolulu International Airport will likely be unavailable post landfall for a period of time depending on the overall impact to the runways, debris accumulation, and infrastructure damage [FEMA, 2007]. In the Makani Pahili exercise, the availability of Honolulu International Airport is assumed, which has large-scale implications.

Division A (South)			height SL	Impact
Staging Area	Honolulu International Airport / Hickam Air Force Base		10ft	Flooded
Base Camp	Honolulu International Airport / Hickam Air Force Base		10ft	Flooded
Base Camp – Alternate	Hawaii National Guard Fort Ruger (Diamond Head)			OK
Division B (East)				
Staging Area	Marine Corp Base Hawaii		13ft	Flooded
Base Camp	Marine Corp Base Hawaii		13ft	Flooded
Division C (Central)				
Staging Area	Wheeler Army Airfield		837ft	OK
Staging Area – Secondary	Dillingham Airfield		20ft	partially flooded
Base Camp	Wheeler Army Airfield		837ft	OK
Division D (Maritime)				
Staging Area	Naval Station Pearl Harbor		SL	heavily damaged
Base Camp	Naval Station Pearl Harbor		SL	heavily damaged
Division E (West)				
Staging Area	Kalaeloa Airport (Barbers Point)		33ft	potentially flooded
Base Camp	Kalaeloa Airport (Barbers Point)		33ft	potentially flooded
Supporting Installations				
Initial Staging		Wheeler Army Airfield		OK
Federal Operational Staging Area		Hickam Air Force Base		Flooded
Federal Operational Staging Area		Honolulu Harbor		heavily damaged
Alternate		Kalaeloa Harbor (Barbers Point)		heavily damaged

Table 6: Flooding at designated staging areas and base camps

Potential loss of life

Most of the loss of life happens in the first week [Breakout Session Infrastructure, 2007]. Hurricane Katrina provided the opportunity for evacuation that a Category 4 to 5 storm in the State of Hawai'i does not. For comparison, 92 % of the affected population, about 1.2 million people, evacuated and only 8 % of the population sheltered in place to face the storm, about 105,000 people [The White House, 2006]. Still, Hurricane Katrina caused about 1500 deaths [Munich Re Group, 2006]. Assuming that a substantial portion of the population being left to face the storm in Honolulu, a death rate of 1,4 % would mean about 15,000 deaths. This rough estimate lacks accounting for the different features of the island of O'ahu and the City of New Orleans, besides the different issues of mass control, among others. To control and provide resources for over one million people in an isolated area of the world poses different challenges than a situation where 105,000 people face a storm in an area on the mainland where resources can be obtained from neighboring counties on roads. Overall, a storm comparable to Katrina impacting the island of O'ahu could yield substantial fatalities.

Economic and environmental vulnerability – a Catch 22 for Hawai'i

In general, O'ahu's economy is very fragile because it is highly dependent on tourism, its geographical isolation and high power and resource requirements. Tourism that would suffer substantially from a catastrophic hurricane event since its natural beauty that attracts tourists would be diminished and most importantly, the infrastructure would be destroyed to the point that tourism will not be possible nor attractive for an extended period of time. An inundation to King Street points out the vulnerability of life sustaining infrastructure in Honolulu: underground conduits, fibers and cables would sustain massive impacts and consequently a failure of the power distribution system and the communication system is to be expected [Breakout Session Infrastructure, 2007]. Figure 26 shows the approximate area of Honolulu below 10 feet elevation with an inundation to King Street [Browning, 2007b] with all of downtown and the Waikiki area under water – the most economically vulnerable area in Hawai'i.

Restoring the tourism industry in a reasonable amount of time is of high priority because otherwise the economic impact will be overwhelming due to sinking employment rates. Job availability is essential to support the population [Rosenberg, 2007a]. On Kauai, after hurricane 'Iniki in 1992, it took two years to restore the tourism industry. Losses in tax revenue, unemployment, job losses and negative publicity for the tourism sector also have negative impacts resulting from a hurricane hit and an economic recovery strategy needs to run long-term [Teixeira, 2007b]. It was estimated in 1993 that tourism would recover to 75 % of its pre-storm conditions in the fourth quarter after an 'Iniki-type storm hits O'ahu [University of Hawai'i at Mānoa , 1993]. This estimate seems optimistic looking at the recovery process of Hurricane Katrina. Mayor Kusaka stated that Kauai's economy returned to normalcy 1999, seven years later. In 1996, hotels had only 30 % to 40 % occupancy [Starbulletin, 2002e]. A boost in advertising for Kauai improved that situation. Perception and information management are a major factor ultimately influencing the re-

Figure 24: Koko Head communication tower 2

covery of Hawaiʻi's tourism industry, specifically consumer confidence, particularly among travel agents booking Hawaiʻi vacations on the mainland. Interruption of life would also be caused by banks being closed due to the power outages [Hawaiʻi State Civil Defense, 2007d]. The insurance capability after a storm is highly problematic because insurance companies might drop their coverage, charge huge premiums or impose very large deductibles. Insurability might be at risk and more stringent building codes can make rebuilding expensive.

The extensive damage to Hawaiʻi's economy from the landfall of a catastrophic hurricane on Oʻahu will be extremely costly. If ʻIniki had hit Oʻahu, asset damage alone would have been over $18 billion. The visitor industry would have lost an estimated $3.6 billion in revenues within the first twelve months following the storm and somewhere between 71,200 and 111,3000 would have been unemployed between October and December 1992. A year later, 44,500 would have still been unemployed [University of Hawaiʻi at Mānoa , 1993, p. 86]. It must be noted that hurricane ʻIniki was a Category 3 storm only, not a catastrophic hurricane of Category 5.

As a side effect, a disaster will also result in gains to economic activity, e.g. for construction businesses and government supported recovery employment, but it will take an immense amount of time to reach the breakeven point in economic terms [Hawaiʻi State Civil Defense, 2007d]. Wide-

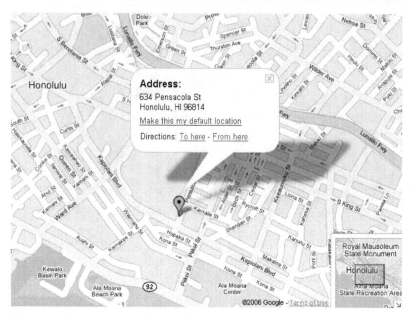

Figure 25: Location map of McKinley High school

spread flooding would have major impacts on crops, but the agricultural sector only makes a partial contribution to the whole economy.

Long-term environmental impacts, such as oils spills on beaches also concern tourism and lead to long-term economic losses, besides the cost for nature's reinstatement. Additionally, the consequences of the amounts of debris as discussed earlier would have serious environmental impacts, but also the quality of the debris and the security and safety regarding debris removal pose immense tasks. Hazardous materials, e.g. asbestos, and trash, e.g. white trash and electronics, and its removal are major obstacles. The analysis of potential threats are currently under works and an educational program is needed [Breakout Session Infrastructure, 2007].

International considerations

The State of Hawai'i has close working relationships with foreign governments, non-governmental organizations, federal agencies and national organizations. Hawai'i is a vital Port of Call for international commerce as well as a destination for recreation and immigration. In case of a catastrophic hurricane on O'ahu, the international community would participate in the response due to concerns for nationals on island before and after storm events, and in the recovery phase for restoration of foreign owned infrastructure and property [Rosenberg, 2007b].

Cybernetic support – don't panic after you panic

"Just don't panic after you panic" said Andrew Marr, pro-surfer for the XXL Billabong Contest in 2007, when I asked him how he can possibly survive a 25m high ocean wave of ice-cold water washing him when he doesn't make that wave. To me, that would be a very hopeless situation. Planning by no plans while being in a state of 'Wu-wei' – effortless doing – can be the only solution; and, inserting a negative feedback loop – you just don't panic after you panic. But what it needs is a system that is fully cybernetically sound to function that way. Andrew Marr certainly managed to be exactly that.

Considering the potential consequences resulting from the current conditions and the high vulnerability of O'ahu's population Federal and State officials realized the hopelessness of this complex disaster situation. If the after-impact scenario for the Makani Pahili exercise would have been realistic, it is clear that this situation is beyond solution, simply looking at the evacuation feasibility, debris management and power situation. All subsequent problems are only exponentially exacerbated by those facts. Realistically, the population will have to live self-sufficiently for a longer period of time or leave the island eventually or when possible. New Orleans, hit by hurricane Katrina in 2005, is today still not close to the lively city it was back then. Cybernetics says that seemingly insolvable problems are first to be considered by self-confrontation (Beer, 1986). Information arrives, and information is what changes us (Beer, 1994, p. 282 ff.). To confront oneself with the fact that those vulnerabilities are as bad as they are instead of dealing with damage and exercise scenarios that are not even close to reality further giving a false sense of security, can only worsen the situation. The (self-)confrontation of what is (=realisation), changes it. This principle is also known in quantum physics where the observer changes the observed due to the light waves or energy.

Must such a chaotic situation ensue just because a hurricane has hit O'ahu? After all, hurricanes are not sudden, unforeseen events. Residents of the tropical Pacific are well-acquainted with hurricanes and their genesis and paths are monitored, charted, and announced meticulously. Is there something deficient about the way government, the private sector, and other organizations on Oʻahu are currently structured and interact that all but guarantees such chaos and pandemonium? If so, is there some way to ascertain what it is, to diagnose its ills, and are there any tools available to guide the redesign and repair of such structures and interactions? Fortunately, there is. The science of cybernetics and the methodological tools it offers provide just such diagnosis and guidance. This dissertation will use a particular cybernetic approach, the Viable System Model by Stafford Beer, to illuminate major deficiencies in the hurricane hazard management approach currently in place in the State of Hawaiʻi.

Given the picture of great potential problems, there is a need for a way to maintain a society's internal stability and reduce the vulnerability in face of such an external threat. Cybernetics in general and the VSM in particular, seemed to offer potential solutions.

2. Keys to solutions of a complex disaster management world – the Viable System Model

Cybernetics as the science of communication and control in the animal and the machine was applied to management by Beer, who named it then science of effective organization [Beer, 1985, p. ix]. It aims at managing complexity in a holistic way. Jackson argues that it integrates 50 years of research in the academic discipline of organization theory and provides 'an applicable management tool that can be used to recommend very specific improvements in the design and functioning of organizations' [Jackson, 2003, p. 106]. Beer used the VSM in consultancies for four decades and demonstrated increases in efficiency of between 30 % and 60 % [Walker, 2001]. The VSM is thus a proven management assessment tool based on successful business practices. It does not render a prescription *per se*, and a normative model cannot be elaborated on a general basis. Rather, the Viable System Model is used as a diagnostic tool in this dissertation to point out 'alarms', or red flags, across the system to be investigated and induce action to proactively prevent the failure of the disaster management system as a whole. One 'alarm' or red flag would not matter to the system, but many small ones can. Blaikie [Blaikie, et al., 2004] stressed that it is not one single event that leads to system failure, but the concatenation of events.

In sum, the VSM does not re-invent the wheel through prescribing a certain structure, but improves a system's efficiency through fine-tuning. Overall, a Viable System is one that is able to maintain a separate existence and that is capable of maintaining its identity independently of other systems within a shared Environment [Beer, 1989a]. When Hurricane Katrina hit the Gulf coast in 2005, an example of a non-viable system in the United States was revealed. During the storm, resources were available to deal with this catastrophic incident, but the management was ineffective and urgently needed resources were not in the right place at the right time. And, indeed, numerous reports have identified the lack of interagency cooperation and communication as a leading factor for the overall failure of the governments' ability to prevent or respond to catastrophic incidents such as Hurricane Katrina [U.S. House of Representatives, 2006]. The VMS would have set red flags well in advance before the disaster situation emerged, advising the managers of the disaster management system where and why the system will not be able to respond in time. In other words, the VSM suggests ways to overcome proactively a potentially overwhelmed system by setting red flags, or alarms, on unstable situations that would lead to overall system non-viability. Practically, if there are not enough funds and resources to be plugged into the system, the system does not exist and a disaster response cannot be accomplished effectively. But the VSM can set up a system ahead of time to enhance a system's effectiveness with given those resources.

The origins of System Sciences and Cybernetics

The Viable System Model belongs to the cybernetics part of system science. The origins and broader contexts shall be elaborated here so that the reader may understand the reasoning behind cybernetics in general and the placement of cybernetics within system science [Umpleby and Dent, 1999].

In the mid-20th century, several different research traditions in system science developed independently of each other. The main streams of system science besides *cybernetics* are the *systems approach*, *operations research*, *general systems theory*, *system dynamics*, *learning organizations* and *total quality management*; other lesser streams might be added. Due to these different research traditions, quite different understandings of the field of system science developed. Ultimately, it is hoped that an awareness of the various research traditions will promote the integration of the field of systems science.

System thinking in general is an approach in social sciences using systems theories to solve problems in a holistic manner. Systems theory is concerned with the complexity of systems in nature and society and is widely applicable due to its interdisciplinarity. System science is the research surrounding these systems theories. In this dissertation, *cybernetics* as a systems theory is combined with disaster management and shall employ system thinking to solve an interdisciplinary problem. The fields of research this entails belong to social and natural science as they include management science, climatology, behavioral studies, political aspects and a broad spectrum of geographical interests and environmental issues. Further, legal aspects need to be accounted for as they influence heavily the efficiency of disaster management measurement. Overall, systems thinking is said to focus on the structure of systems whereas cybernetics concentrates on how systems function and hence the two are inseparable because the structure and function of a system can only be studied cohesively [Heylighen, 1999].

Cybernetics – deriving from the Greek word *kybernetes* (meaning 'steersman') – was founded by the mathematician Norbert Wiener in 1948 as 'the science of communication and control in the animal and the machine" [Wiener, 1948] and stands in close connection with Ludwig van Bertalanffy's General System Theory, which will be explained below.

Cybernetics itself can be differentiated into several traditions named after their principal advocates: Norbert Wiener, Alan Turing and Warren McCulloch. All these traditions emerged in the 1940s. Wiener's work on control systems [1950] led to the establishment of the Systems, Man, and Cybernetics interest group of the Institute of Electrical and Electronics Engineers. Turing's work on computation and machine intelligence was the base for the field of computer science and artificial intelligence, and McCulloch's efforts to understand human cognition and epistemology by studying the nervous system are continued by the American Society for Cybernetics [Umpleby, 1997]. Essential to all three traditions of cybernetics was the series of conferences funded by the Macy Foundation between 1944 and 1954 and chaired by McCulloch.

Wiener's Cybernetics emerged from the collaboration with the biologist Arturo Rosenblueth [Bigelow, et al., 1943]and started with the design of a machine that would sense its Environment and act in a fashion suited to a changing Environment. Wiener, an applied mathematician, also worked with W. Ross Ashby, whose key research conclusion was that a regulator required a model of the system being regulated [Conant and Ashby, 1970][Ashby, 1956]. Wiener's book 'Cybernetics' [1948] suggested a second industrial revolution where machines replace the human capacity to process information and make decisions.

Turing developed the universal Turing machine and the Turing test. He also worked on the decoding of messages of the German

Wehrmacht during World War II. That successful experience led to support for the National Security Agency during the Cold War. During the Vietnam War, this computer science tradition contributed to the idea of an 'electronic battlefield' [Umpleby and Dent, 1999, p. 94].

McCulloch was a philosopher and neuroanatomist and his cybernetics was concerned with experimental epistemology – understanding knowledge by understanding the brain. His neuro-philosophical research was deepened by Humberto Maturana and Heinz von Foerster and influenced the fields of management [Zeleny, 1981] and family therapy [Watzlawick, 1984]. From the mid-1970s on, 'second-order cybernetics" developed. This idea emphasizes the inclusion of the observer in the domain of science, since observers interpret the results of experiments. Constructivism as contrasted with realism emerged. Realism highlights that the world is primary and theories are imperfect descriptions of the real world whereas constructivism holds that 'observers have more immediate access to thoughts than to the world of experience' [Umpleby and Dent, 1999, p. 95]. Constructivism is a major contribution to the philosophy of science [Umpleby, 1997].

Bertalanffy established *General Systems Theory* in the 1940s as a counterbalance to reductionism in a Variety of fields of system theory applications as well as to unify organization sciences in a holistic manner [Capra, 1996]. Bertalanffy was an Austrian biologist who used systems theory to provide alternatives to conventional models of organization; specifically he became famous for his idea of 'open systems'. Contrary to the traditional view, an open system is not in a steady state, but dynamic. He showed the limitations of the conventional models and also applied systems approaches in the social science, specifically in regards to the concepts of feedback, information loops and communication.

As the pioneers were followed by second and third generation practitioners, five main streams developed, as already noted above. *General Systems Theory* developed further in the 1950's at the University of Michigan's Mental Health Research Institute (MHRI) where the yearbook 'General Systems' of the Society for General Systems

Research is published. In 1954, Anatol Rapoport cofounded the Society for General Systems Research, along with the researchers Ludwig von Bertalanffy, Ralph Gerard, and Kenneth Boulding. Today the organization has the title International Society for the Systems Sciences. James G. Miller applied General Systems Theory on a broad scale to describe all aspects of living systems and developed his 'Living Systems' [1978], which focused on matter, energy and information processes.

The *Systems Approach* originated at the University of Pennsylvania by E.A. Singer and his student C. West Churchman, whose first student was Russel Ackoff. Singer suggested that a producer-product relationship exists when X is necessary, but not sufficient, to cause Y. All the other mentioned researchers but Ackoff remained mainly in a philosophical mindset. Ackoff took the approach and applied it to management and organizations, and eventually, he established with Churchman the field of *operations research* in the United States. They focused on management and the effectiveness of organizations, but others used different concepts in operations research and practiced it as a branch of applied mathematics to arrive at optimal or good decisions to improve or optimize the performance of a system. Another strain of operations research emerged from the British (calling it *operational research*) who had operated a global empire, since the mid-19th century. For its management they developed a Variety of methods to optimize their resource allocation and to improve their logistics. The British introduced the Americans to their concepts and together they solved the most pressing problems in operations research during World War II to design the optimal size of a convoy to cross the North Atlantic. During the Cold War, the military was successfully supported by think tanks using operations research, such as the RAND Corporation and the Research Analysis Corporation. Operations research is now well established in both the field of industrial engineering and business management. Related to operations research, but much more broadly and thus making use of its methods, is *systems analysis,* which analyzes systems of any kind as an interdisciplinary science. Systems engineering is very close to operations research, but systems analysis is much broader.

System Dynamics was founded at the Massachusetts Institute of Technology by Jay Forrester, who also invented the magnetic core memory for computers. The milestone in this school of thought was Meadows and Meadows's 'The limits to growth' [1972]. This book discussed global trends in population, natural resources and pollution using an integrated simulation model to project the future of humankind. The key is that System Dynamics is limited to a particular kind of simulation modeling used to assess and learn about the qualitative characteristics of system behavior.

Organizational Learning resulted from Peter Senge's 'The fifth discipline' [1990]. Before, Chris Argyris and Donald Schoen focused on double-loop learning where different values than in conventional management are emphasized [Argyris, Schoen, 1978]. These academics have extensive management consulting experience working with corporations and government agencies. Robert Putnam, Diana McLain Smith and Nancy Dixon are leading the next generation of organizational learning research.

Total Quality Management (TQM) did not emerge from academic circles. W. Edwards Deming, Joseph Juran and Phillip Crosby are key figures. Deming is particularly noteworthy. He had a long history of consulting with Japanese organizations and their most prestigious industrial award was named after Deming in 1950. Later, by 1980, when Japanese levels of productivity overtook American levels, this led to a near panic by American executives [Umpleby, 1999]. Thirty-five years later the United States followed Japan creating an award for corporate excellence named after Malcom Baldrige. TQM's connection to cybernetics is to be emphasized, since the principles have common ground, e.g. increasing the autonomy of workers, reducing hierarchical relationships and measuring results.

2.1 The Viable System Model's core concepts

The VSM was invented to manage complex problems, which arise from the way a system behaves and interacts with its Environment. In Beer's terms, any single, possible state of a system is the basic unit of complexity. For example, in nature, the complexity of the system 'tiger family' increases the more animals this 'family' system interacts with, the food sources it has available, the size of the area it lives in, and so on. The task of a system's management cybernetician is to regulate and control this complexity in an organization.

The main concept of the VSM is viability, which is the ability to maintain a separate existence within a turbulent Environment [Beer, 1994a, p. 199]. The VSM demonstrates how complex systems maintain internal stability in the case of external disturbance, such as a hurricane event. The aim of the VSM is not single-goal oriented, e.g. maximizing profits, but viability and survival. In essence, the VSM emphasizes the means for survival. Its concepts and language are hard to understand because they are abstract, but this way it can be integrative and also holistic, which makes its use in the field of Geography explicit. Moreover, viability depends on a number of necessary and sufficient conditions, specifically the functioning of five subsystems, which he devoted many papers and three books to identifying and explaining. System 1 stands for implementation, System 2 for coordination, System 3 for control, System 3* for audits, System 4 for intelligence, System 5 for policy and the Environment constitutes not only the natural Environment, but all that is outside of the System as a whole. Overall, the VSM does not offer a normative model, but is a diagnostic tool and it requires working with people from within the System using their subjective input.

Another important concept is Variety, which is the number of distinguishable states of a system and a measure of complexity. The Environment is bombarding the coping system with threats, stresses, pressures and the art of managing all of this is called Variety Engineering. Further, recursive structures are central to understanding the VSM. It says that every viable system entails and is entailed in a viable system, like Russian Dolls [Beer, 1979, p. 118]. This concept is needed to handle Variety and complexity through redundancy. Recursion is the iterative application of the same principles or structures to different organizational levels and implies that the structure is self-referential. This enables one to investigate a problem of natural and human systems as one complex system of interactions on different Levels of Recursions. Those rules or cybernetic laws assert themselves naturally, according to Beer, but to do so in the most efficient way the system needs to be designed.

Beer points out that, since the Industrial Revolution we have lived in a hierarchical culture and hence the notion of Recursion is foreign to our ways of thinking [Beer, 1994a]. The VSM challenges this, arguing that the rapidly changing Environment of today requires response from autonomous units; otherwise the system cannot be viable and will fail. Within any system, there must be a balance between autonomy and control, as discussed later in 'Freedom, Autonomy and Cohesion within the Viable System'. To achieve this, functional decentralization and cohesion of the whole are fundamental within the VSM, and its recursive structure is contrasted with the concept of hierarchy. It is evident that there is a managerial hierarchy in an organization, but the higher levels are characterized by their 'ability to perceive the situation and to articulate what is to be done in comprehensible language, not by its capacity to command' [Beer, 1994a, p. 68]. Parallel thoughts are recognizable in other thinkers such as Abraham Lincoln – the sixteenth President of the United States – who did not rule by command, but by example and eloquence [Sandburg, 1954].

2.2 Am I me? – On subjectivity and identity

One of Beer's many innovations is to employ biological cybernetics to illuminate managerial cybernetics [Beer, 1994a]. The most important of these biological principles is Maturana's observation that, 'life is not primarily characterized by the process of self-reproduction, but by the process of self-production' [Beer, 1994a, p. 405] and Beer states that this is also true for organizations. 'As long as the living organism can maintain its organization, despite the living death of its cellular elements, and the behavior of its parasites, through lice, amoebae, and viruses to its pathological protein chains, then 'I' am still 'me'' [Beer, 1994a, p. 405]. 'The Viable System is directed towards its own production' [Beer, 1994a, p. 405] and even though every kind of change occurs within the organization it remains recognizably itself. For example, employees come and go, but the organization keeps its identity.

To characterize this biological-managerial principle, Beer coined the term, autopoietic, deriving from the Greek poio (to make). An autopoietic organization 'makes itself' continuously being concerned primarily with the preservation of its own organization. Even if the purpose and identity of a system is in doubt, autopoietic organization can still remain viable because it is able to keep its identity, as all biological organisms do. But, in general, the purpose of a system is what it does.

This biological example can clarify the identity of an autopoietic organization and the underlying concept of different Levels of Recursions [Beer, 1994a, p. 404]:

'Death does not matter to the individual E. Coli in our gut. Our birth and death is recognizable at another Level of Recursion where criteria of 'being alive' have been agreed by the Metasystem. Analogically, cells in our body die and are born continuously during our lifetime. Life and death of the cellular elements do not concern the living being as long as it maintains its organization. If there is a cancerous outbreak, that might well constrain the system's viability and eventually lead to the death of the whole system. Overall, the 'me' is just an arbitrary selection from the infinite Recursion'.

The cybernetician's most fundamental question is: Whatever else may happen, am I, the organization, me? Beer emphasizes that 'the point of self-consciousness is reached by a system that has developed the power to recognize itself at the infinite Recursion' [Beer, 1979, p. 373]. Consequently, 'of all observers of that Viable System called the organization, the most significant is inevitably itself. This is because of the reflexive nature of the affirmation of identity' [Beer, 1979, p. 114]. Logically, infitity needs to be understood as a process and Beer asks to understand infinity without going there.

Accordingly, picking the Level of Recursion for analysis, the System in Focus, is arbitrary, since the Recursions are infinite on both sides and there is no closure to Recursion. The cybernetician needs to understand this infinity of processes in order to understand the self-consciousness of an autopoietic organization, recognizing that identity and being aware of its purpose.

Beer's VSM seems very much based on easily to define and quantifiable functions, but its value lies in its qualitative capabilities to diagnose systems. Identity shapes the system, first of all giving it its purpose. Just as with identity, the purposes of a system are also subjective. The initiators of the organization – owners, employees, customers or observers – formulate these purposes. The subjectivity of a system, however, turns out to be problematic, since in practice these purposes are inconsistent. The most fundamental inconsistency is due to what Beer believes to be the autopoietic nature of a Viable System – that the system produces itself. But, a system's overall purpose can only be its own survival. Other purposes, such as maximizing profits or market share, are only recognized as a monetary constraint on this primary goal. Maximizing profits is only one of several subgoals, and there are plenty of other such constraints on an organization.

Beer's thinking on the subjectivity of purpose and identity has many parallels to Jean-Paul Sartre's existentialist metaphysics. Beer seems to follow Sartre's ideas of self-determination, self-consciousness, reflexive self-awareness and identity in the way they emphasize the freedom and consciousness of the human being. For Beer, the subjectivity of any organization is reflected in a subjective management style and also in the subjective choice of the purpose of the system as a whole.

The boundaries and priorities of the system are based on the values and norms of the party inventing this system. Since measures have to be objective, this seems like a paradox, but the subjective nature of a system is requiring just that! Beer therefore asks the manager of a system to set his or her own measurement parameters, depending on the system's intended purpose.

2.3 The structure of the Viable System Model

The Viable System Model consists of five systems: System 1 (implementation) through System 5 (identity). The term in parentheses following each mention of a specific system states the purpose of that system. System 1 (implementation) produces the whole system in a subjective, autopoietic manner and is a Viable System in itself at one Level of Recursion lower than the system in focus. Systems 2 (coordination) through 5 (identity) are the support systems of System 1 (implementation) and it is important to note that there is no seniority (Figure 27) [reproduced from Espejo et al., 1996, p. 119].

· The five Systems were later renamed by Espejo et al. [1996].

2.3.1 System 1 (implementation)

The three elements of System 1 (implementation) stand in contrast to the senior management, also referred to as the Metasystem, containing System 3 (operational control), System 4 (intelligence), and System 5 (identity). System 1 (implementation) is treated from the Metasystemic perspective as a Black Box. The discussion of how to handle a Black Box in that context is found in the last chapter. System 1 (implementation) produces the system and consists of three elements: local management, local operations and a lo-

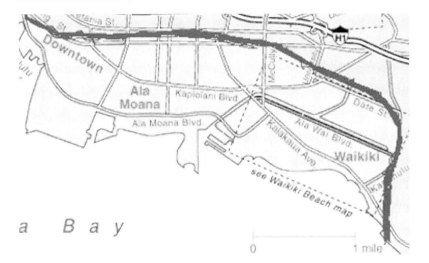

Figure 26: Approximate area of Honolulu below 10ft elevation

cal Environment. These three 'local' elements are connected on a horizontal axis (Figure 28) [reproduced from Beer, 1994a, p. 125] and will be called 'System 1 (implementation) management', 'System 1 (implementation) operations' and 'System 1 (implementation) environment'. When 'System 1 (implementation) is used by itself, it refers to all those three elements.

All System 1 (implementation) environments are encapsulated in the System 4 (intelligence) Environment, also named the 'envelope environment'. The system as a whole interacts in a defined way with its Environment through Systems 1 and 4.

From an analytic point of view, a management cybernetician is faced with the hard task of identifying those System 1 (implementation) elements that produce the system. Naturally, several System 1s (implementation) exist in an organization. First of all, the System 1s (implementation) have to be Viable Systems in themselves if the system is to survive. The cybernetician chooses the appropriate Level of Recursion for the System in Focus. This is an iterative process and the choice is the most useful application. Cybernetically sound systems generally have seven plus or minus 2 elements [Beer, 1985, p. 19].

The System 1s (implementation) are not isolated, but interact with each other. This is performed along the vertical connections between the System 1 (implementation) elements, the squiggly lines (Figure 29) [reproduced from Beer, 1994a, p. 126].

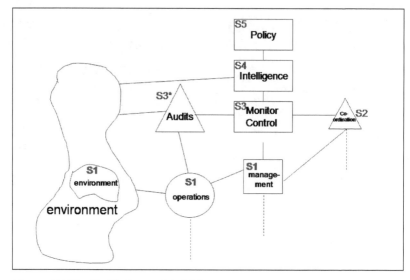

Figure 27: The Viable System Model I

For example, disaster impacts and necessary resource requests in Environment A dealt with by operation A influence Environment B. In biological terms, it is represented by the natural balance of predator-prey and predator-predator relationships. Operations would mean 'to hunt'. If two predator groups (operations A and B) hunt the same group of prey, soon this resource would become exploited and the decreased availability of food would affect the population numbers of both predator groups – the degree of reduction depending on a Variety of factors. Overall, the demand of both groups of predators influence each other regarding their food availability and consequently and ultimately their survival.

The squiggly lines between System 1 (implementation) operations can represent weak or strong connections. A weak connection would exist if the System 1 (implementation) operations would compete for resources such as money or resource supply, which is obtained from the Metasystem. A strong connection would exist if completely different System 1 (implementation) processes were strongly dependent on each other. The squiggly lines represent the interdependency and the preciseness of actions of the System 1s (implementation). The more precise and well defined, and also the more interdependent the action is, the stronger the connection. To return to a biological example, a weak connection would be represented by a predator-predator relationship where the survival of both depends on a readily avail-

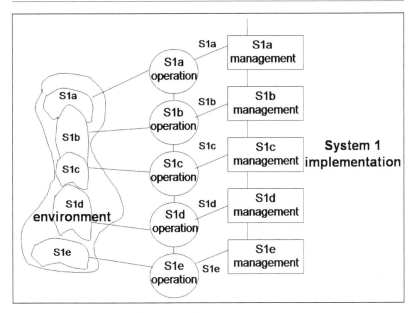

Figure 28: System 1 (implementation)

able Variety of prey. For example, if both cheetahs and lions hunt antelopes, zebras and much other prey, their dependency is relatively low and the connection of the squiggly lines between System 1 (implementation) operations ('to hunt') would be weak. If there were only antelope in the hunting area, the connection would be strong.

System 1 (implementation) is a necessary, but not sufficient component of the Viable System. The supporting Metasystem, namely System 2 (coordination) through 5 (identity), fulfill together with the System 1 (implementation) the necessary and sufficient conditions of viability. Those will be explained after the elaboration of Variety Engineering, which is essential to controlling complexity.

2.3.2 Controlling the complexity of a system

Control, Homeostasis and the stability of a system are reached through Variety Engineering. Variety is the 'number of distinguishable states of a system and is a measure of complexity' [Beer, 1985, p. 21]. However, control and the stability of systems is not achieved by measuring complexity and

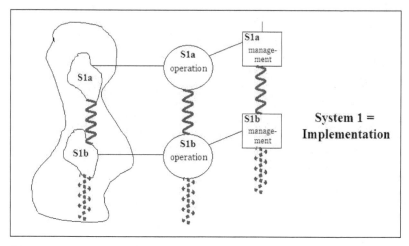

Figure 29: System 1 (implementation) connections

counting all distinguishable states and reaching balance or Homeostasis, but by matching or counter-balancing Variety. In Japan's multi-scale disaster, what complexity means becomes clear in one second: not only do we have a tsunami disaster, but a nuclear havary and consequences of strong earthquakes and their aftershocks to deal with. Government officials, TEP-CO leaders and the population itself are facing a highly complex situation – a mess in essence.

But, under the systemic lens, the complexity of the universe is only chaotic subjectively, in our eyes. The nature of any system is proliferating Variety, but, if nature is organized that way, there must be a natural answer to this perceived chaos. Beer finds this natural answer in the fundamental principle of *Ashby's Law of Requisite Variety,* which states that 'only Variety can absorb Variety' [Beer, 1989, p.17], that 'control can be obtained only if the Variety of the controller is at least as great as the Variety of the situation to be controlled' [Beer, 1981, p.41]. Cybernetic management has as its purpose, then, that of designing systems in a way that leads to a most effective matching of Variety with Variety at minimum cost. Obviously, in Japan, many red flags that in times of 'peace' – compared to the current situation – would have alarmed the disaster management system of Japan were ignored. This entails the building codes for nuclear plants and the intensity of possible seismic activity in the region (Japan is one of the most at risk regions on the Pacific Rim of Fire that surrounds the Pacific Ocean). Many more examples can be found. Another messy situation is also information management, which is currently observed by other countries as not as efficient as it should be in Japan, for the sake of Japan's affected population. 'One lethal Variety attenuator is sheer ignorance' [Beer, 1985, p. 25]: by ignoring different aspects of a problem situation the Variety is greatly reduced, but either the efficiency of the organization might suffer or essential aspects of viability, e.g. in form of devastating vulnerabilities, might be missed. Instead of 'applying' ignorance in high-Variety situations, management meetings can solve or overcome this Variety Engineering problem and create Homeostasis. Ashby's law though cannot be ignored: 'Only Variety in the control system can deal successfully with Variety in the system to be controlled' [Beer, 1989a, p. 18].

To jump back to the cybernetic manager: Getting the complexity of the Environment within the organization's response range, the cybernetician must use leveraging strategies to minimize this Variety imbalance through processes of Variety attenuation and amplification. Again, Beer emphasizes that Variety amplifiers and attenuators are subjective, but a disaster manager has ample information and is able to perform this thinking and management process. Generally, by principle and nature, the inner complexity of an organization is far less than the complexity of the Environment. Through Variety Engineering, management techniques are directed to reducing operational Variety within System 1 (implementation) so that the operation managed contains more activities than the management unit itself. As Beer observes, the *First Principle of Organization* says: 'Managerial, operational and environmental varieties, diffusing through an institutional system, tend to equate; they should be designed to do so with minimal damage to people and cost' [Beer, 1979, p. 565]. In this way, Homeostasis should be established through the Requisite Variety between the three elements of System 1 (implementation): local Environment, operations and local management, as shown in Figure 30 [reproduced from Beer, 1994a, p. 96].

The lines between the circles, squares and the envelope in the figures always represent and replace the arrows in both directions for graphical simplification.

Ultimately though, the environmental complexity threatens to overwhelm any system. In the end, this observation expresses Darwin's concept of 'survival of the fittest'. In the case of the Federal Emergency Management Agency (FEMA), one principal mechanism for Variety Engineering is the Incident Command System (ICS). In a disaster, the Variety of the ICS must match the Variety of the disaster event. That means that all activities of the disaster management cycle need to be able to cope effectively with the negative impacts of that event. If a hurricane destroys 90 % of residential housing,

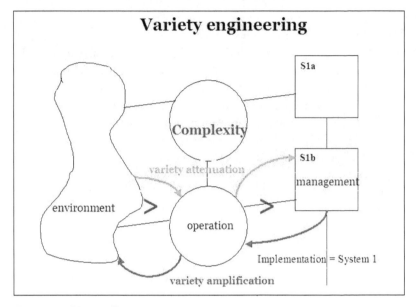

Figure 30: Variety Engineering

for example, FEMA needs to stand up enough shelter spaces – mobile homes, for example – as Variety attenuators to resolve this environmental complexity. Basically, what Beer's idea of Variety Engineering represents is that a solution has to be worked out for every possible situation – Variety amplification – or that the solutions found need to be able to cope with any possible situation – Variety attenuation. Critics find this law to be tautologous and Beer states in reply: 'but all mathematics is either tautologous or wrong' [Beer, 1989a, p. 18]. In practice, Variety Engineering workshops are hold to get the system in question under control. All Variety drivers are identified and coping strategies developed, as being implemented at Malik Management Switzerland.

2.3.3 System 2 (coordination) through System 5 (identity)

System 2 (coordination), 3 (operational control), 3* (audits), 4 (intelligence) and 5 (identity) define the necessary and sufficient conditions of viability and support System 1 (implementation) in a non-hierarchical setting. Systems 2 (coordination) through 5 (identity) are by themselves not Viable Systems and should not show autopoietic behavior; if they did, it would be

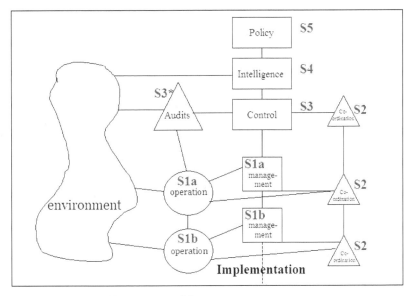

Figure 31: The Viable System Model II

pathological autopoiesis and would be a cancerous growth of that system. Those systems are 'services to the autopoiesis of System 1' (implementation) [Beer, 1994a, p. 411].

The vertical axis in Figure 31 connecting System 1 (implementation) with the Metasystem – System 3 (operational control) through 5 (identity) – is the central Command Axis. A certain level of command is executed here while balancing the autonomy of System 1 (implementation) units and the coherence of the system as a whole, as will become clear in the following.

System 2 (coordination) serves as a Variety attenuator by setting norms, ethics and 'common knowns' that are assumed in a society or group of people. System 2 (coordination) of an organization reflects their style on letterheads and newsletters, housekeeping (computer manuals), and accounting practice (conformity, legislation), actuarial damping (professional rules), and is represented by secretariats or management accounting, for example. System 2 (coordination) elements can produce either high Variety attenuation, e.g. a weekly newsletter, or low Variety attenuation, e.g. a quarterly Journal. As a service to System 1 (implementation), System 2 (coordination) represents rules of coordination to simplify processes to control complexity, which are set by System 3 (control) in accordance to the overall system's purpose (System 5 (identity)). System 2 (coordination) also serves as the channel between different Levels of Recursion [Beer, 1994a], which will be explained later.

A biological example would be the rank system in the wolf pack. Without it, fights might emerge in situations that might threaten the pack's survival, such as the loss of food after a kill where another stable pack steals food while the unstable pack is occupied with a rank-determining fight over the recently-acquired food resource.

A traffic jam is another example of a System 2 (coordination) failure. Radio stations, policemen, helicopters and engineers – namely the interacting elements of System 1 (implementation) at the lowest Level of Recursion – were not designed to dampen the oscillations caused by individual driving behavior on the road. The Variety that all individual drivers create cannot be matched by those System 1 (implementation) elements such as traffic lights or policemen. On the command channel, System 2 (coordination) (traffic) regulations – put in place by System 3 (operational control) – are enforced to maintain cohesiveness: drive on one side of the road, observe traffic lights, etc. The System 2 (coordination) task is to warn drivers (System 1 (implementation)) and dampen the traffic oscillations by advising motorists on different routes that they might take to avoid the traffic jam. If System 2 (coordination) were designed effectively, one vehicle (one System 1 (implementation) element) might get from place A to B much sooner, though by a longer route. If the warning system fails, and individual drivers just follow their chosen route, Variety explodes and traffic jams result [Beer, 1985]. In a disaster situation, all citizens should tune in to the radio (System 2 (coordination)) to follow orders set by the government (System 3 (control)) to keep the system in Metasystemic Calm.

System 3 (control) lies orthogonal to System 1 (implementation) to examine the connectivity of the System 1 (implementation) elements [Beer, 1994a]. This is also the connection to the next higher Level of Recursion in which System 1 (implementation) is embedded. Figure 32 [reproduced from Beer, 1994a, p. 321] shows that System 1 (implementation) represents operations, and System 3 (operational control), 4 (intelligence) and 5 (identity) represent management of the System 1 (implementation) of the next higher Level of Recursion.

System 3 (operational control) has a synoptic view of the system as a whole that the embedded System 1s (implementation) cannot have. Its core function is strategic planning for all System 1 (implementation) activities, for example the best allocation of resources [Beer, 1994a].

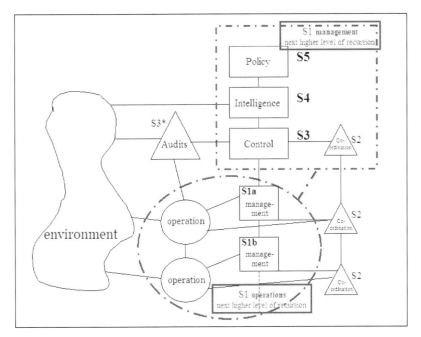

Figure 32: Two Levels of Recursion

It connects to all System 1s (implementation) on the vertical central command channel via the Resource Bargain – the deal by which the maximum cybernetically sound degree of autonomy is agreed upon – and via the Accountability Loop – the responsibility for received resources – and is responsible for the day-to-day operation of the organization. System 3* (audits) connects through sporadic audits with the System 1s (implementation), as shown in Figure 33 [reproduced from Espejo et al., 1996, p. 119].

System 4 (intelligence) deals with the larger Environment, called the 'envelope environment'. It represents strategic foresight and surveys for opportunities. In disaster management, System 4s (intelligence) handle forcasting, Research and Development, long-term mitigation planning. In business terms, those functions are for example market research, corporate planning and economic forecasting [Beer, 1994a]. System 4 (intelligence) has its own Environment contained in the larger Environment and also deals with an unknown future, called the 'problematic environments' (see Figure 34) [reproduced from Espejo et al., 1996, p. 119]. For the Asian Tsunami in 2004, there was almost no possibility to foresee the extent of that disaster and prepare for it. Certainly, the affected states could have had better forecasting

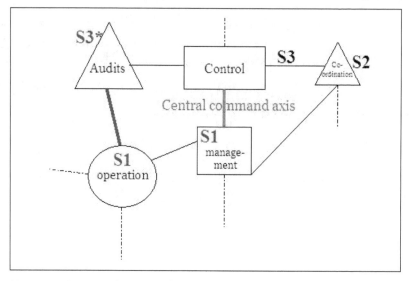

Figure 33: System 3 (operational control) and System 3* (audits)

and warning system, but people tend to forget or ignore risks that exist and always have been there, sometimes out of ignorance and sometimes because a disaster is so un-imaginable that it cannot be foreseen. What is important: System 4 (intelligence) activities are disseminated all over the system and cannot be identified in one spot. The responsibility of a well-functioning of System 4 (intelligence) on all Levels of Recursions lies within all units. Therefore, two core concepts, that of Self-organization and self-regulation, have to be induced into the system through System 2 (coordination).

System 4 (intelligence) fulfills an important task by creating alternatives for the organization. System 4 (intelligence) acquires degrees of freedom by simulating the amplification and attenuation of Variety 'to promote mutation, learning, adaptation and evolution – or survival-worthiness, which ultimately defines viability' [Beer, 1994a, p. 230]. In other words, System 4 (intelligence) can invent a Variety of scenarios for the organization to promote adaptability to an increasingly changing Environment. To return to the chain of biological examples, an analogy could be given with genetic mutation. Many unfavorable mutations might evolve, but this way – as in trial and error – new and better adaptations to optimize a species' survival develop. Because the organization's future depends on System 4 (intelligence), it possesses much power and consequently power struggles emerge with System 3 (control). In Japan, those struggles are manifested in discussion of where to direct resources – in immediate disaster response (System 3) or long-term efforts in mitigation (System 4). Those principles need to be designed beforehand and in place so no time is lost in such discussion in a cybernetically sound way – this is vital to viability.

System 4 (intelligence) activities are in danger of failing if regulatory processes – such as professional or governmental rules that prohibit the evolution of the organization – are too restricting. System 4 (intelligence) has to tackle these problems by inventing new strategies. Governmental rules can prohibit necessary investments or put up 'red tape' and make necessary action inoperable. System 4 (intelligence) must wrestle with constraints like these and should never accept them. It also must spend time to understand the regulatory system of the outside [Beer, 1994a].

System 5 (identity) represents the will of the whole and sets the direction for the organization. Its cybernetic function is closure, essential for the organization's identiy and the monitoring of Homeostasis between System 3 (operational control) and 4 (intelligence) (Figure 35) [reproduced from Beer, 1994a, p. 261]. System 5 (identity) listens to the 'I am OK'-messages confirming Homeostasis flowing through the system and basically sleeps until it gets a warning from the System 3–4 loop that the system has become unstable. In nature, this task and role would belong to the pack leader.

The only task of System 5 (identity) is to detect System 3–4 instability and then act on instability when it sets in. The power to balance the System 3–4 investment resides in the Variety equations between those two systems [Beer, 1994a].

System 5 (identity) does not give instructions, but it does 'give feedback to questions like 'Is this idea a starter?' [Beer, 1994a, p. 354]. It also has a normative and ethical role – what should be done. Its ethos pervades the whole of a Viable System. In practice, a System 5 (identity) can be elected – as in a Board of Directors that represents the interest of shareholders – or non-elected – as in the case of a dictatorship where control is gained while the will of the whole is not embodied. What is beyond System 5 (identity) is the next Level of Recursion, of which this Viable System as a whole is an operational element (System 1 (implementation)).

Overall, Systems 3–2–1 compromise the 'Inside and Now' of the organization, while Systems 3–4–5 are the 'Outside and Then'. This non-hierarchical structure presents itself in the fact that the System 3 (operational control) in practice runs the organization. System 5 (identity) is not the actual 'boss' and is run by System 3 (operational control), since System 3 (operational control) controls System 5 (identity) access to information about internal Variety.

2.3.4 The Russian dolls – controlling complexity through Recursion Levels

Recursivity is a major element in dealing with complexity due to its redundant structure. Figure 32 shows one Viable System – System 1 (implementation) through 5 (identity) – embedded in System 1 (implementation) management and System 1 (implementation) operations of one Level of Recursion higher than itself. System 2 (coordination) to System 5 (identity) represents the System 1 (implementation) management of the next higher Level of Recursion and the whole System 1 (implementation) represents the System 1 (implementation) operations of this next higher Level of Recursion.

System 3* (audits) is not depicted as part of the square due to graphical limitations, but it belongs to System 3 (operational control). System 1 (implementation) represents the System 1 (implementation) operations of the next higher Level of Recursion.

2.3.5 Details of Variety Engineering: The three Axioms of Management

Beer states *The First Axiom of Management* as 'the sum of horizontal Variety disposed by *n* operational elements equals the sum of vertical Variety disposed on the six vertical components of corporate Cohesion' [Beer, 1979, p. 566]. That means that the sum of the Variety disposed by all System 1s (implementation) lying on the horizontal axis must equal the sum of the Variety disposed by all elements on the vertical axis, namely System 2 (coordination) through 5 (identity). In short: $V(h)=V(v)$. This way, balance within the Viable System is established. Overall, these processes of Variety balancing occur on the System 1–3 level, on the System 4–5 level and the System 3–4 level, with certain distinctions discussed here.

Figure 36 reproduced from Beer, 1979, p. 323] shows Recursion *w*, which is to be viewed under a 90-degree rotation, with only Systems 1 (implementation) and Two (coordination). Recursion *y* is fully represented in the diagonal as well as the horizontal Recursion *x*. The whole diagram represents *one circle* (System 1 (implementation) management) of Recursion *v*.

These distinctions are found in *The Second Axiom of Management*: 'The Variety disposed by System 3 (operational control) resulting from the operation of the First Axiom equals the Variety disposed by System 4 (intelligence) [Beer, 1979, p. 298]. This means that Variety between System 3

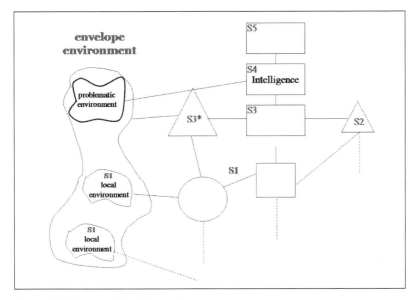

Figure 34: System 4 (intelligence) environment

(operational control) and 4 (intelligence) needs to be matched. Within the Metasystem, System 5 (identity) is itself Metasystemic and monitors the System 3–4 Loop. It is necessary that Systems 3 (operational control) and 4 (intelligence) absorb each other's Variety.

The *Third Axiom of Management* says that 'the Variety disposed by System 5 (identity) equals the residual Variety generated by the operation of the Second Axiom' [Beer, 1979, p. 298]. This means that the System 5 (identity) Variety and the Variety of the System 3–4 loop need to match. As for System 2 (coordination), it functions to dampen oscillation, in essence to attenuate Variety, as already noted above.

2.4 What a heart needs to be whole – understanding VSM in depth

2.4.1 Freedom and autonomy

'Only agreement of the heart will justify a given level of Cohesion in any institution' [Beer, 1994a, p. 159]. This is one of Beer's core concepts, since

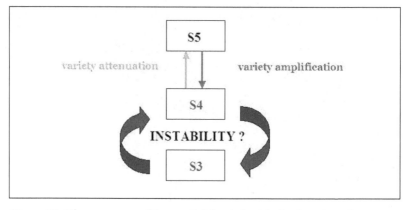

Figure 35: The emergence of System 5 (identity) with the detection of instability

this lies at the heart of any organization. From this core concept, Beer concludes: 'Therefore: freedom is in principle a computable function of systemic purpose as perceived' [Beer, 1994a, p.158]. The interaction between the horizontal and the vertical axis defines freedom for the whole organization. System 3 (control) must give System 1 (implementation) the maximum autonomy and minimum intervention as along as its identiy is not at risk. The *Law of Cohesion for Multiple Recursions of the Viable System* shows that the Variety equation is what stops the organization from blowing apart: 'The System 1 (implementation) Variety accessible to System 3 (operational control) of Recursion x (must equal) the Variety disposed by the sum of the Metasystem of (the lower) Recursion y for every recursive pair' [Beer, 1994a, p.355]. In other words, the *Law of Cohesion* restates the fact that System 1 (implementation) is the Metasystem of the next higher Level of Recursion (Figure 32). This Law follows from the *First Axiom of Management* $V(h)=V(v)$. It recognizes that cohesiveness is the glue of an organization, where 'Cohesion balances freedom and constraint to provide a workable level of autonomy' [Beer, 1979, p.289]. Cohesiveness is a function of the purpose of a system, which is subjective, as argued earlier. Being subjective, Cohesion is achieved through the information flow between all five systems.

Beer develops this diagram to show that System 3 (operational control) does want to know System 1's (implementation) intentions and therefore requires System 1 (implementation) to generate data; what data is being generated depends on the purpose of System 1 (implementation), which is autonomous in choosing those data and acts as aVariety attenuator. This enquiry runs from System 3* (audits) directly to System 1 (implementation) operations, circumventing the command channel between System 3 (operational control) and System 1 (implementation) management. It is important to note that this action is sporadic, in contrast to the constant information flow between System 3 (operational control) and System 1 (implementation) management along the Command Axis. The enquiry also causes System 1 (implementation), which is the Metasystem of the next lower Level of Recursion Y, to change state: information has arrived, and 'it changes us' [Beer, 1994a, p. 343].

To this end, two forms of vertical intervention on horizontal autonomy exist. First, operations of all System 1s (implementation) intervene to a certain degree on each other along the squiggly lines (Figure 29). Second, the Metasystem intervenes on the System 1s (implementation) through System 3* (audits) (Figure 33). By vertical intervention, Variety is attenuated because constraints are established. But this interferes with the cybernetic argument of System 1's autonomy or freedom. In the disaster manager's world, let the department of Emergency Management Services act independently of other departments, which it sometimes might do, they are uncoordinated with the hospitals – effective and efficient resource allocation is impossible, System Cohesion lost and disaster management functions rendered dysfunctional.

2.4.2 The usefulness of uncertainty – planning by no plans

Beer recognizes a large gap between the many false beliefs of what planning is and the reality of planning as the organizational glue of the organization. In management terms, planning is a continuous process. In theory, a plan is set to be accomplished in arbitrary time epochs where interacting elements are often unpredictable. In sum, a manager is in a continuous decision process because rational expectations and probable scenarios are constantly changing. More information arrives continuously, and information is what changes us. Hence, 'planning is a continuous act of adaptive decisions that continually aborts' [Beer, 1994a, p. 338]. Since contemporary management is used to thinking in time epochs, deadlines, etc., the dynamic aspect of planning is difficult to understand. Beer though looks at planning as a balancing process, operating against adaptive criteria according to *Ashby's law*. Ultimately, the manager's only interest is to detect instability in the system and act upon it. If a system is set up accordingly, planning by no planes becomes the new strategy naturally. Just because conventional thinking does not allow for this mindset valuing the great advantages of this concept, does not mean it is not favourable. 'Plans are the embodiment of the intentions subscribed to at each Level of Recursion: since these intentions are constantly changing, and not in a homogeneous way with respect either to time or to probability, they must continually abort' [Beer, 1994a, p. 342]. Still, continuous planning is the cohesive glue of the Viable System embedments and is represented by the *Law of Cohesion*.

The manager's job is to set the criteria of stability, to detect instability and if appropriate change the criteria. Consequently, 'the manager's requirement for measurement is that it should measure stability and instability in the system that he (this being his role) has subjectively defined'[Beer, 1979, pp. 286]. Overall, the stability of the system depends on the ability of its subsystems to absorb each other's Variety. Intuitively, we think 'to know something properly, you must measure it' [Beer, 1979, p. 279], but Beer asks us to be alert to what we count as a measurement and how we measure it. Criticizing the subjectivity of measurements and the personal factors hidden behind figures, he argues that the Variety of the measures we use does not equal the Variety of what we measure – and that Requisite Variety is therefore not established. To add to the predicament, computers, that we think help us greatly in these matters, attenuate inappropriately the Variety of what is presented [Beer, 1994a]. It is key here, to set the data filters appropriately so that data is lost, but not the relevant information.

To obtain 'a new vision of the arena of management information', Beer introduces the following cybernetically relevant terms [Beer, 1979, pp. 282]: A 'fact' is defined as 'that which is the case'; 'noise' as 'a meaningless jumble of signal', 'data' a 'statements of fact' and 'information' 'that which changes us'. By definition, 'noise becomes data when the fact is recognized. Data becomes information if a person changed his or her state and when the fact in them is susceptible to action' [Beer, 1994a, pp. 282]. The core of the cohesive glue that holds organizations together is a change of state due to information, not due to edict. To deal with noise in the system, redundancy is needed, which is cybernetically given through the organization's recursive structure. For example, the imbalance between the Variety of a frog's Environment and its brain's ability to process that Variety is resolved by its visual system. The massive Variety of the Environment is cut down to only that information that evolution has decided the frog needs. Something moved – food? A predator? The frog sees and acts. The vast majority of its

Environment is not registered by its eye. Cybernetically, the noise has been cut, data received and information used for survival.

Often in a disaster, it is an ethical System 5 (identity) question, as to what to react or set a response: for example setting up shelters for people with animals to be evacutated. Sadly, in Japan, pets are left tied up in the evacuated zones close to the Fukushima Nuclear Plant and left to starve to death. Journalists passing don't untie them because they hope the owners return. In Hawai'i, many residents will not leave without their pets and evacuate and the pet-density per household is high. The Deparmtent of Emergency Management of the City and County of Honolulu took that serious and are prepared to set up pet-friendly evacuation shelters, even though the shelters overall are not sufficient for the whole population. So, it is left up to the disaster managers and their System 5 (identity) identity and ethical stance if that data is cut out as noise or has to be taken into account as relevant information

Managerial measures are worthless in the actual task of managing, according to Beer. Instead, managers at all levels need to be alerted to any instability in any loops, which can set in at anytime, anywhere in the system and are signaled by a 'red flag'. This alerting signal is called 'Algedonic' – Greek for pain and pleasure [Beer, 1994a, p. 406]. In other words, 'Measures should be concerned with stability' [Beer, 1994a, p. 275]. Ideally, loops should display equilibrium or Homeostasis, but, when they do not, the manager must act. If stability is maintained, Metasystemic Calm of the system is secured. If an Algedonic is sent through the system, the system awakes from its Metasystemic Calm.

Contemporary managers are used to dealing with causalities and raw figures, instead of ratios. But, system failure happens due to instability, not due to causality. Beer exemplifies this in regards to Western and Eastern medicine: 'Western Medicine searches for the one cause for illness, whereas Eastern medicine tries to stabilize the total system through the harmonizing of relationships between the parts of the body' [Beer, 1994a, p. 290]. He promises that 'improvement in the management of complicated systems will not occur until managers give up the dysfunctional concept of causality and the search for the unique cause' [Beer, 1994a, p. 291]. Complex systems fail because they are potentially unstable, and because some concatenation of circumstances has made the Potentiality actual. No unique event is the cause [Beer, 1979]. This correlates with disaster management theory [Blaikie et al., 2004]: 'and when we look for one (cause) it often seems that if the total system had been in a different state, that event would not have led to disaster' [Beer, 1979, p. 290], as Japan clearly exemplifies: if the nuclear plants would have been built further inland or building codes would have been more strict, the severity of this disaster could have been averted.

2.4.3 Waking up from living in the past – the vital real-time alarms

The handling of time houses one of the major misconceptions in management. We cannot change the past, however much we may wish. The step into the right direction is rejecting causality, which means measuring instability in the 'here and now' and becoming aware that reports only contain data after the fact – past data. Consequently, the continuous flow of the management process is an essential characteristic of any Viable System. From this follows his Fourth Principle of Organization, that 'the operations of the first three principles must be cyclically maintained through time without hiatus or lags' [Beer, 1994a, p. 258]. Real-time data – or, as he called it, *bogus real time* data, is a continuous data stream measured instead of numbers per time epochs within a periodic reporting system. The data filing system cannot sense events in the organization in absolute real time, 'but it can be made aware of updating of its indexical file and rise to self-consciousness' [Beer, 1994a, p. 504]. This real-time data collection should be observed in an Operations Room or another establishment depending on cultural settings and style, which highlights the VSM's recognition of human and cultural issues.

When instability is signaled by an Algedonic Alarm, it will flow through all Levels of Recursion to alert the system and call for action. Beer states that if we can 'acquire data about stability that can be transformed into information about the possibility and likelihood of incipient instability, we can avert instability' [Beer, 1994a, p. 375].

Beer points out that 'the time base on which reporting is done is a function of the nature of the business' [Beer, 1979, p. 375]. For example, for a publisher of a daily newspaper the time basis would be a daily endeavor. For the Hurricane Hazard Management System (HHMS), the time base on the highest Level of Recursion is the interval between different hurricane events. Since the probability of a hurricane event for Oʻahu is not given – the calculation of statistically relevant data is not possible on the basis of the available data of hurricane events for the Hawaiʻian Islands – it is assumed that the HHMS for a major hurricane event on Oʻahu is not an effective system as of now. Many indicators discussed in Chapter 1.4.2 point towards that fact. So the time base for the HHMS would be the time of one hurricane season. This time epoch runs from June 1st to November 30th every year and expresses the idea on what time base this system is operating on.

2.4.4 What managers really need most – measurements of effectiveness

A major shift in thought is that survival – viability – needs to be ensured through effectiveness, not through single-goal orientation. There are three indicators of organizational effectiveness: (1) Actuality, (2) Capability and (3) Potentiality. These three parameters can be also combined to form three different indices of performance measures: Productivity, Latency and Performance.

'*Actuality*' is what we manage to do now, with existing resources and under existing constraints – we can provide 10'000 people with shelter spaces over the next three months, for example. *Capability* is what we could achieve now, if we really worked at it, with existing resources and under existing constraints – for example, we can do this over the next six months. *Potentiality* is what we could be doing by developing our resources and removing constraints, although still operating within the bounds of what is already known to be feasible' [Jackson, 2003, p. 99] – in this case, we could house 20'000 people for six months. Actuality refers to System 3's (operational control) activity such as the allocation of resources for System 1 (implementation) activities. Capability refers to System 4's (intelligence) Development Planning, and Potentiality describes System 5's (identity) Normative Planning [Beer, 1994a]. In practical terms, *Actuality* represents the status quo, *Capability* the intention and *Potentiality* the will to advance [Beer, 1994a].

In Figure 37 [reproduced from Beer, 1994a, p. 288], the square represents System 1 (implementation) management, the circle System 1 (implementation) operations and the loosely-defined local Environment.

As one might suspect, the management task in all this is to declare the subjective values for Actuality, Capability and Potentiality. Once this is done, the role of the Black Box (BB) is to filter the information produced by the meter (M), which measures the messages between System 1 (implementation) operations and the local Environment and sends a continuous message to the Black Box (BB): 'I am OK' or 'I am not OK'. The disaster manager decides that ten people per tent are OK in the given situation, which might change later on due to chaning environmental constraints:

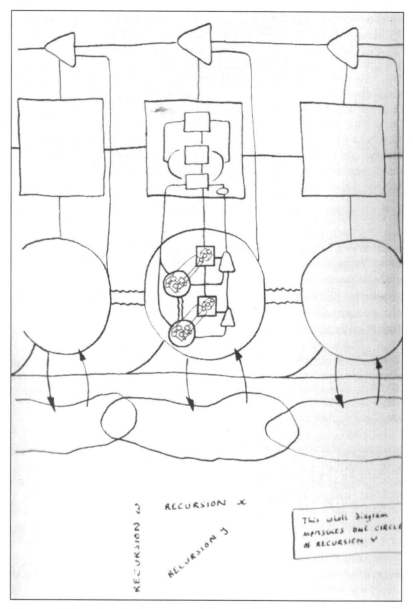

Figure 36: Three Levels of Recursion of the Viable System

maybe the situation is so severe that putting 15 people in one tent becomes necessary. This flexibility is often not regarded but put in firm rules where disaster managers might face legal consequences if decided differently. Red tape often becomes a major issue in such situations. Generally, the manager does not need to know the details – the names of the people in the tents; he only needs to know that what he manages is 'OK' or 'not OK'. Beer states this fact in The First Regulatory Aphorism 'It is not necessary to enter the Black Box to understand the nature of the function it performs' [Beer, 1979, p. 40].

For Actuality, the 'I am OK''-message means: 'I do x'; for Capability: 'My plan is to do y'; for Potentiality: 'I wish I could do z') [Beer, 1979, p. 292]. Other subsystems in the loop respond in an 'I am OK'-fashion in the following way: 'responding to your criterion of Actuality (or Capability; or Potentiality) to this extent (we have/ have not done it) [Beer, 1979, p. 292]. The meter then measures the ratio between the declaration and the response for each of the three criteria. If the meter measures '1', the situation is stable. The Metasystemic character of System 1 (implementation) management reinstates that System 1 (implementation) management must not dive into the 'muddy', not transparent box (BB) to receive the information needed for decision making. Overall, measurements to detect instability are needed, rather than parameters that track the muddy boxes.

An additional management task is to set the subjective criteria as to what instability means in terms of the mixture of *Productivity*, *Latency* and *Performance* [Beer, 1994a]. The potential imbalances in this mixture answer to statistical criteria as to how much *deviation* counts as instability and the *rate* of information. These two criteria are reflected in Beer's Second Regulatory Aphorism, 'It is not necessary to enter the Black Box to calculate the Variety that it potentially may generate' [Beer, 1979, p. 47].

When management assigns a precise rule set for *Productivity*, *Latency* and *Performance* into the Black Box, the Black Box becomes transparent, and no need exists for managers to 'dive into the muddy box'. This results in a holistic approach in contrast to the cause-effect concept: if the Productivity index for this loop, in this subsystem is running at (say) 74 – instead of 100, that means that 'Actuality' is not meeting the managerial criterion of Capability by 26 %' [Beer, 1994a, pp. 293].

The nature of this holistic measure is a gigantic Variety attenuator where data is lost, but no information is lost – and information is what changes us. 'Data in excess of information are irrelevant to the management process' [Beer, 1994a, p. 296]. Ultimately, statistical filtration should be used to report on the likelihood of incipient change [Beer, 1994a, p. 297]. This is a major insight of VSM logic.

In practice, however, managers try to dive into their muddy boxes. They set a percentage of deviation for a target to monitor the instability of their system. The point to understand does not lie in the numbers, but in likelihood: 'What is the likelihood that something has gone wrong?' [Beer, 1994a, p. 295]. Beer refers to this kind of forecasting as filtration. He supports Bayesian Statistical Theory and the techniques of Harrison and Stevens for 'short-range filtration' to handle the filtration problem in terms of likelihood and emphasizes that they detect instability earlier in time than the human brain [Beer, 1994a]. 'Managers simply do not have an implanted knowledge of statistical theory' [Beer, 1994a, p. 295]. While living in Chile, Beer used the Bayesian statistical theory and demonstrated that 'a probability-plus-computer monitoring system can detect change (i.e., information) in the movement of a performance index long before a human can detect it by eye in a graphical time series' [Beer, 1994a, p. 295]. He claims to have monitored 75 % of the social economy of Chile on a single IBM 360/50 down to plant level.

2.4.5 Cybernetic's communication principles

Channel Capacity is the measure of the amount of information transmitted in time X. *The Second Principle of Organization* says: 'The four directional channels carrying information between the management unit, the operation and the Environment must each have a higher capacity to transmit a given amount of information relevant to Variety selection in a given time than the originating sub-system has to generate it in that time' [Beer, 1994a, p. 99]. If the Channel Capacity is not designed properly to transmit the information, information will be lost or the recipient cannot receive the necessary information due to information overload: the papers and figures come in at a rate that cannot be processed. In disaster management, these channels of Variety transmission could be schedules for preparation efforts (amplifying Variety) and reports on those efforts (attenuating Variety). Channels between operation and the Environment, in which preparation is embedded, could be forecast information and its distribution system (amplifying Variety) and elements such as user knowledge and translation of scientific language into lay language (attenuating Variety).

It is important to note that the provision of Channel Capacity depends to a high degree on technology, which is a Variety generator. To print a letter repeatedly, for example, is much more effective than writing it by hand each time. Much more information can be transmitted during the time X and hence the time and effort saving effect gives a channel increased capacity.

Information needs to be translated whenever a boundary is crossed and this coding and decoding mechanism is called Transduction. This thought is captured in Beer's *Third Principle of Organization:* 'Wherever the information carried on a channel capable of distinguishing a given Variety crosses a boundary, it undergoes Transduction; the Variety of the transducer must be at least equivalent to the Variety of the channel' [Beer, 1979, p. 101]. Filters can be used to ensure proper transmission across boundaries. The input filter to a university could be a test to be accepted into a program and the output filter would constitute the final exams.

Soft factors such as trust, credentials, and credibility among others are incorporated into the Viable System Model through the processes of Transduction. For example, if a person serves as a transducer during a disaster, but the collegues do not trust this person, Transduction is not effective.

2.4.6 Higher consciousness and mathematical Buddhism – philosophical understanding of VSM concepts

Beer emphasizes the human condition in several aspects of the Viable System Model. Channel Capacity and Transduction is one way to incorporate and account for human and cultural factors. Equally so within System 5 (identity): If it is System 5 (identity) that brings closure to the Viable System and represents the will of the whole, how does it know what it is that it knows? Beer answers that 'by listening to itself doing the job, conscience is developed' [Beer, 1994a, pp. 298]. Within the concept of recursivity, this intuitive aspect is also explored: 'the point of self-consciousness is reached by a system that has developed the power to recognize itself at the infinite Recursion' [Beer, 1979, p. 373].

The ever-continuing self-generating aspects of the Viable System Model (VSM) can be interpreted as 'mathematical Buddhism' [Beer, 1979, p. 399]. The cybernetician aims at detecting instability, which is 'inimical to the contemplation of the infinite Recursion and therefore to corporate self-consciousness' [Beer, 1979, p. 374]. Managers must be alert to instability in real-time, as explained before, and measure it continuously. To not avert incipient instability, and let it become actual, is to ignore the pre-symptoms of psychosis and go mad. Further, measures of effectiveness can also be calculated mathematically, but the pure goal-oriented idea, e.g. making profit, is foreign to VSM concepts. At the VSM's core stands the reflexive self-awareness and the subjective purpose. The goal of self-awareness generates itself continuously and is ever-changing. Beer's time concept presents itself also in his idea of planning, namely planning by no plans, and incorporates Buddhist thoughts: reincarnation and samsara, the never-ending cycle of creation and destruction [Beer, 1994a]. As soon as a plan is developed, it must be aborted, since new information arrives constantly, and information is what changes us. This corresponds again with the VSM's concept of recursive structures. The 'highest' Level of Recursion is referred to as the level in which one has any power to 'affect outcomes by edict' [Beer, 1979, p. 373]. We could go to infinity and recognize the Earth as a possible System 1 (implementation) in the galactic system, but we need to accept that 'no finite model is possible, because we do not have Requisite Variety to make it' [Beer, 1979, p. 374]. One can only 'contemplate the process whereby such models are endlessly capable of generation', which is to define the infinite Recursion, which is to 'explode into self-consciousness' [Beer, 1979, p. 374].

Beer's thoughts have certain elements of Jean-Paul Sartre's existential metaphysics so a short excursion seems useful to understand Beer's model more holistically. One aspect is particularly interesting for decision making and the existence of systems. For Sartre, the past is fixed and unchangeable. The future is not connected to the past, but radically separated from the past by the present, which does not exist. Hence the past does not influence the future. Only mental processes by which a conscious decision is made determine the future. The present does not exist because the moment the present happens, it is already the past. Beer is not looking for the essence of a system, but for capturing it in the non-existent present where the gap between past and present introduces radical contingency or radical freedom into the system [Stanford Encyclopedia of Philosophy, 2004].

Within this gap between the past and the future created by the non-existent present, the space evolves that allows influencing the future through human agency, more specifically through decisions and through VSM. If the present existed, then it would provide an iron link connecting the past to the future and no human agency would exist; management of contingency would be impossible because no contingency would be possible. All would be determined. Consequently, the VSM does only exist in the non-existent present where free decisions are possible. The existentialist herewith underscores the dynamic aspect: everything is constantly becoming, being created and recreated, suspended in the non-existent present making itself ever new. In the VSM, this is reflected in the 'planning by no plans' concept. New information always arrives, and information is what changes us, and consequently the system. Hence planning is a process in which the manager plans by constantly aborting plans. Further, the ever new recreation of all systems is reflected in the VSM's recursivity. Thus, the fundamental reality of our human world is that systems must be constantly monitored and managed through various systems of systems because no system is ever stable; no system is ever what it strives to be or should be, because it does not really exist, although it is striving to exist in the non-existent present, where it cannot possibly exist. If existentialism is viewed philosophically with respect to other categories, it strikes that science distinguishes by truth, the moral category decides for the good and right, and the existential category has authenticity at its core. Beer also follows this concept by stating that the subjective whole only knows what it knows by listening to its intuition. Further, Sartre and Beer co-exist in the philosophical value of freedom as self-making and the resulting authentic existence [Stanford Encyclopedia of Philosophy, 2004].

Ultimately and indirectly, Beer asks the management cybernetician as well as the people of the system in focus to accept unknowability. By accepting the fact of the ever-changing and ever-becoming world, we become aware of and must also accept that there always will be surprises and that we cannot dominate the world through knowledge. To accept uncertainty is the first step into Beer's philosophy. His suggestion is to design systems that can adapt to environments we cannot control.

A reflection of the daoist idea of Wu-wei makes Beer's VSM concepts and meaning more recognizable. Taoism involves knowing when to act and when not to act. The System 5 (identity) incorporates this idea and sleeps until an Algedonic Signal arrives and it wakes up to act upon this sign of instability. The Wu-wei principle of 'effortless doing' can be seen as the ideal state of a Viable System. It is constantly producing itself, but is in perfect equilibrium and metaphysic calm, or in alignment with Tao. From the state of inner stillness, spontaneous actions in alignment with Tao evolve and hence all necessary actions happen effortlessly. Through this mindset, the right actions happen at the right time to achieve what should be achieved. This also corresponds with Beer's thought of the ever-evolving self-aware system and the non-goal orientation with the aim for viability and survival.

3. The Hawai'ian disaster management system – diagnosis and suggestions for redesign with the Viable System Model

As a first step, the elements of the Hawai'ian disaster management system need to be recognized and system boundaries established, which is not an easy task in itself. In disaster management practice, the disaster management cycle (Figure 38) is often described as the timeline of those elements: mitigation, preparedness, disaster impact, relief, recovery, rehabilitation and reconstruction. Other terms in use are response or recovery, for example.

It is difficult to distinguish between the different and often overlapping terms for these activities. It is more appropriate to speak of a continuum of activities, being conscious of the time overlap. For example, a clear distinction between relief and reconstruction efforts is not possible, since one could argue that rebuilding houses is as much reconstruction as it is relief work. Hence the various activities are best defined along a timeline with the disaster impact as a focal point.

'Mitigation' refers to all activities related to the prevention of negative impacts of a disaster and happens on a timeline of several months to years. 'Preparedness' differs from mitigation because it focuses on prevention of negative impacts within a timeline of several days to weeks before a disaster event. Those two activities are executed before the disaster impact and relate specifically to the disaster type 'hurricane' because a warning time of several days or more exists. In contrast, earthquakes have to date no warning time and a disaster cycle should be defined along a different time line.

Disaster 'response' activities begin after negative impacts have occurred and are focused on immediate needs emerging from those impacts lasting up to several weeks after the impact. It is part of the rehabilitation process, but these two terms will not be incorporated. Instead, after the initial 'response' to the impact, 'recovery' efforts are executed within a timeline of several weeks to several months, followed by the 'reconstruction' phase lasting from several months to several years. 'Reconstruction' is a long-term process that can blend in with mitigation. A clear distinction between reconstruction and mitigation is difficult, and ideally mitigation will be incorporated into reconstruction to build disaster resilience and reduce the vulnerability to negative impacts of future events.

In this project, the 'Hawai'ian disaster management' system under investigation is defined as the Hurricane Hazard Management System (HHMS) and encompasses all hurricane hazard-management activities from mitigation to recovery of all involved departments, agencies, organizations or institutions. It involves the Federal Emergency Management Agency (FEMA) that developed the Concept of Operations (CONOP) for a catastrophic hurricane impacting the State of Hawai'i and includes all governmental departments and agencies, the National Incident Management System (NIMS) and the National Response Plan (NRP). It involves further a plethora of non-governmental organizations, e.g. American Red Cross (ARC) and the private industry, e.g. the Hawaiian Electric Company (HECO). Geographically, the HHMS is not confined to the island of O'ahu alone, since assistance might be provided from the neighbor islands, the west coast of the United States and Guam. The HHMS is constituted by all entities involved in hurricane hazard management for a catastrophic hurricane on O'ahu.

The data collection included conferences, presentations, interviews, email contacts, observations, mainly the State Civil Defense's Makani Pahili Exercise, FEMA's Region IX Regional Interagency Steering Commit-

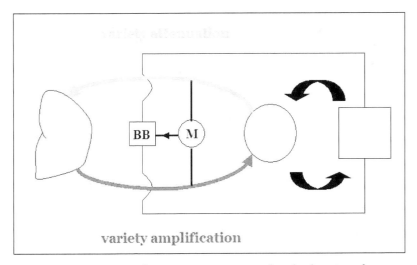

Figure 37: Measurement for management conceived as the detection of instability

tee Conference and the State Civil Defense's Debris Management Seminar. Further, books, grey literature, reports, websites were researched.

To start a VSM diagnosis a few essential aspects need to be considered. In usual management practice, the need for drastic action is often felt and a consultant hired to take responsibility for the drastic actions he recommends. But, a Viable System evolves over time. Beer emphasizes that no drastic actions should be taken when employing the Viable System Model (VSM) because they are mostly destabilizing. The aim of using the Viable System Model is to lead towards a 'framework for viability using the cybernetic language for discussions that usually revolve on the conflict of personalities and power struggles' [Beer, 1994a, p. 549].

'All Viable Systems are successful, and all successful systems are viable' [Beer, 1994a, p. 439]. The essence of viability is survival and is defined 'as the ability of a system to maintain a separate existence' [Beer, 1994a, p. 199] and its identity 'independently of other systems within a shared environment' [Beer, 1989a, pp. 21]. The assertion notwithstanding, it is clear that this is not true of every existing organization by itself, since organizations depend on other systems, e.g. legal or political, and are not viable by them-

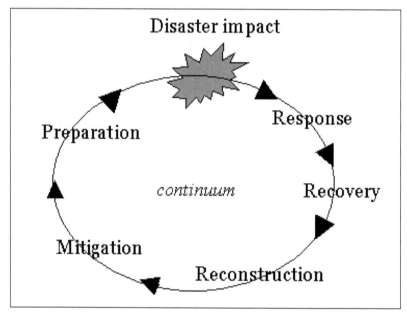

Figure 38: The disaster cycle (reproduced from the Pan American Health Organization [2006])

selves. Nonetheless, when examining an organization via the Viable System Model (VSM), it has to be assumed at the start of the diagnosis that the system is viable. For example, in financial terms, the system might seem perfectly viable to the managers, but in cybernetic terms disaster might be close. Often, managers 'feel that something is wrong', but cannot make out the pathology of their system. If that is the case, the Viable System Model has much to offer. Beer claims not to offer prescriptions, but only to 'elucidate how things are the way that we know them to be' [Beer, 1994a, p. 413]. Hence, the VSM is a diagnostic tool to map management capacities to promote viability [Leonard, 1999]. The VSM is a very subjective, interpretative and not solely structural analysis tool.

Since the nature of the application of the VSM is complicated, a topical map (see Figure 39) accompanies each section to clarify its relation to the other sections. After discussing the cybernetic aspects of time in relation to the Hurricane Hazard Management System (HHMS) in Part C1 of Figure 39, the VSM application will focus on the HHMS structure in Part C2, on the HHMS processes in Part C3, and on the HHMS viability requirements in Part C4.

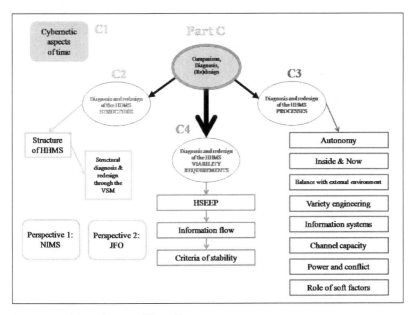

Figure 39: Topical map of Part C

3.1 Time – the vital factor to measure viability

Time is a most vital parameter of the VSM and the time-scale of managerial problems is essential to diagnosing and designing a Viable System. 'It does not help if the brain asks 'should I run for that bus?' and the parts need five minutes to answer' [Beer, 1994a, p. 508].

Three questions need to be answered (see Figure 40): is the HHMS stable in a sleeping mode, the Metasystemic Calm? Is the HHMS stable and viable when disaster strikes and environmental Variety proliferates? And, if the HHMS becomes unstable, how long before the system as a whole becomes stable again? Those limits need to be established so that measurements can be taken, statistical filtration be implemented and Algedonics set to alarm System 5 (identity) to wake up from its Metasystemic Calm, perform actions to make the system viable again and ultimately to define if the HHMS is a Viable System. A disaster manager is left to decide if the levees of the city to be managed by him will hold a 30ft tsunami, based on all the information he has, or if evacuation will run smoothly under given circumstances.

For the Hurricane Hazard Management System (HHMS), the hurricane season has an annual cycle and the timeframe of viability is chosen to

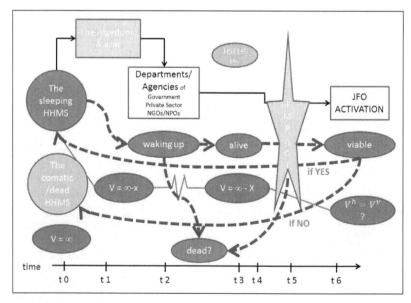

Figure 40: Cybernetic aspects of time

be from the point of instability to May of the following year – when another potential hurricane could threaten the island. If the HHMS has not reached stability by then, it is not viable. In general, the timeframe to fix instability varies and depends on the system's purpose.

3.1.1 A special case: hibernating systems

Generally, the cybernetic aim of a system is its survival. The HHMS is a special case, since practically it is a hibernating system, which turns on and off at certain points in time depending on when disaster strikes. It has to be underscored that the conventional (i.e., zoological) concept of hibernation differs from the cybernetic concepts of hibernation --- Metasystemic Calm, systemic death and alarm mode. Cybernetic hibernation has to be dealt with in terms of Variety Engineering, which the others do not require. The triggering criterion is not the hurricane hit, but any Algedonic Alarm sounding throughout the year due to structural or processual deficiencies within the system. At first glance, this might be an obstacle in diagnosing the HHMS with VSM, because it seems not to be definable as either dead or alive. The VSM is able to investigate any system though independent of its temporary active or passive state. A system is ideally in Metasystemic Calm and the System 5's (identity) Algedonic warning signal should let it wake up as soon as the system becomes unstable. Then, System 5 (identity) requests action to return it to a stable Homeostasis.

For the Hurricane Hazard Management System (HHMS), the VSM investigates business-as-usual in its Metasystemic Calm and checks if the system is capable of reacting to instabilities and to fix any problems in an appropriate and timely manner. A hurricane exercise such as the statewide Makani Pahili should be able to verify this but it is performed under unrealistic disaster conditions, e.g. landline phones are used. Its Metasystemic Calm implies that the people running the system throughout the year are busy in a business-as-usual mode doing non-disaster-related tasks. This is especially true in the many disaster support departments and agencies. For example, at the city Department of Planning and Permitting, 'business-as-usual' means reviewing building plans and issuing building permits. They are not disaster managers, but have to be trained to be able to turn into disaster managers when a hurricane threat becomes apparent. The trick is not to let the hibernating system become pathological and die while it is in Metasystemic Calm.

A soccer team represents a good analogy. The hurricane hit corresponds to the tournament with an unknown Variety explosion within the system, represented for example as an unknown game strategy of the other team. If the HHMS were viable, a hurricane hit would not matter; it would have Requisite Variety to counterbalance such environmental disturbance. A viable team would succeed with its goals. During the year, a soccer team is a 'sleeping system' since it does exist, even if only on paper, but through exercises it comes into existence regularly. Metasystemic Calm persists if no instabilities are detected. If some players are sick, for example, the system becomes unstable and the trainer has to proactively look for substitute players; otherwise, when a tournament is scheduled, the team is incomplete and not viable.

For the HHMS, this basic idea is found on paper in all emergency planning and preparedness documents. In a cybernetic sense, the HHMS is not really hibernating, but always in place, and ideally in Metasystemic Calm without any Algedonic Alarms sounding. This is exemplified in both the Federal CONOP and in the City and County of Honolulu Basic Plan, which states that preparedness 'is to be *integrated into the day-to-day management system* and overall planning process of each county department and agency and those designated supporting elements of state offices in the City & County of Honolulu. These offices shall ensure that disaster mitigation, emergency preparedness, and response and recovery plans are current and executable at all times. This responsibility may not be delegated nor disrupted due to reorganization or change in administration' [City and County of Honolulu, 2007, p. 7].

The crucial question must be, whether all departments and agencies of the HHMS are up to par and viable at all Levels of Recursion. Some Federal entities, such as the JTF-HD, are; they exercise all year and seem to be viable [Richards, 2007c]. The same can be said for other parts of the State and County HHMS that seem to keep the system in its Metasystemic Calm during the year. Private entities, such as HECO, also conduct disaster exercises throughout the year. Those include specific scenarios for hurricanes, earthquakes and tsunamis [Rosegg, 2007a]. These continuing activities to sustain Metasystemic Calm should be an archetype for all HHMS departments and agencies because these tasks lie within the day-to-day routine and are of major importance for the system to maintain its Metasystemic Calm and not to die. The large-scale coordination of catastrophic disasters is a different setup though, even if single sub-systems are themselves viable the system now contains all connections between those sub-systems, which need to be cybernetically sound designed for optimal functioning.

In the following, the structure of the HHMS will be analyzed (C2), followed by the diagnosis of the processes within the HHMS (C3) and its viability requirements (C4).

3.2 Structural diagnosis of the Hawai'ian disaster management

As Beer saw it, organizations of any form or size need to deal with an ever-increasing environmental complexity and hence their structure must adapt to this ever-changing Environment if the organization is to survive. Consequently, the increasingly complex Environment creates increasingly complex problems for an organization. The VSM identifies the most important structural aspects that lie behind system viability and performance in order to determine, at a deeper level, the issues that make the present functioning of the system ineffective. The understanding of cybernetic laws enables such diagnosis and highlight underlying factors that allow us to observe the system as it is.

In C2, 'Diagnosis and redesign of the Hurricane Hazard Management System (HHMS) structure' (Figure 39), an overview of the general four HHMS levels will be elaborated. With the full structure of HHMS in mind, a System in Focus will be chosen. Then, the importance of System 2 (coordination) will be explained for O'ahu before the core of the application: Two aspects of the HHMS will be investigated: First, the HHMS as NIMS framework prescribed by FEMA is elaborated and diagnosed along the VSM with remarks regarding its cybernetic requirement compliancy. The NIMS framework gives an overview of the HHMS structure as a whole and shows how all elements are plugged in. It shows the connections linking the federal down to the field level and among all the HHMS elements (Dimension 1 and 2 of Figure 41). Secondly, the System in Focus – the O'ahu Joint Field Office (JFO) alias the federal EOC – is diagnosed through the VSM in detail and prescriptions given based on cybernetics and the VSM. It is a special ICS application (Dimension 3 of Figure 41), in which the Emergency Support Functions (ESFs) are plugged in. This way, a thorough analysis of the HHMS along three dimensions can be accomplished: Horizontally along the geographical division of the various Command Posts as prescribed by NIMS (1), and vertically along the functional ICS (2), which is the basic structure for all Command Posts (see Figure 41). The Emergency

Support Functions (ESFs) in the diagram will be elaborated later and will add another layer. At the end, a summary of the whole elaboration will be given, before we set out to diagnose the HHMS processes in C3.

The HHMS is based on certain authorities detailed in the U.S. Department of Homeland Security [2004b]. The federal, state, and city and county levels of government and the private sector work together in an event of a catastrophic hurricane. Important players are FEMA, the County and State Civil Defense, the National Weather Service, the American Red Cross, the Hawaiʻian Humane Society, Tesoro, Hawaiʻian Telcom and Hawaiʻian Electric Company. Some examples of supporting organizations and agencies are shown in Table 7. According to the National Response Plan (NRP), only agencies receiving FEMA funds have to comply with NIMS. There are levels of accomplishments States and Jurisdictions have to rise in order to comply with NIMS and consequently have access to FEMA funding [FEMA, 2006]. But NIMS is only one part of the HHMS. Agencies that rely on different support, such as volunteer agencies (e.g. American Red Cross), are independent from NIMS, but are elements of the HHMS and are therefore incorporated.

AGENCY	LEVEL	ACTIVITY
DPS		Exercise communications, exercise operations in an isolated areas, review infrastructure
Joint Task Force – Homeland Defense	Federal	Exercise post impact activities, exercise sync-matrix, Validate communications plans
Department of Emergency Management	City	Validate TICP plan, conduct a CERT exercise, validate volunteer program
Civil Air Patrol		Exercise aircraft protection plans, exercise communications, exercise family preparedness
Federal Emergency Management Agency	Federal	Exercise regional interagency activities
HTA		Validate interoperability communication, discuss tourist evacuation
American Red Cross		Exercise shelter plans
Department of Human Services	State	Validate COOP Plan, discuss safe transportation of incarcerated youths, discuss evacuation & sheltering roles & responsibilities.
US Coast Guard		Exercise logistics section of UC.
Department of Health	State	Exercise communication equipment. Activate DOC.

Honolulu Police Department		Exercise HPD's shelter plans for personnel & pets.
National Weather Service		Press conference. Host workshops on general preparedness. Provide information or training to agencies upon request.
Center of Excellence		Exercise impact project models.
DOH –Rad		TTX environmental health assessment. Discuss debris management.
University of Hawaii	State	Stand up DOC. Exercise notification and recall plans. Provide a shelter simulation.
93rd CST		Integrate section personnel at various locations (SCD-EOC,C7C-EOC,DoD-JOC,DOH-DOC, JTF-HD-JOC). Exercise CST COOP plan.
USPS		Stand up DOC.
TAMC		Exercise TAMC shelter management plans. Exercise communications. Exercise healthcare hospice command system. Review infrastructure protection plans. Review MOAs/MOUs for evacuation.
DHRD		Discuss post impact roles & responsibilities.
Department of Transportation		Stand up DOC. Test communications. Review checklists, equipment, & location of area shelter locations.
Department of Education		Stand up DOC. Test communications. Test telephone tree. Discuss staff, family & pet sheltering. TTX post/recovery.
PACAF		Respond to DSCA requests. Conduct disaster response planning to ensure war fighting ability is maintained.
HI National Guard	Federal	Exercise command and control structure.
PACOM		Coordinate activities with JTF-HD.
PACFLT		Coordinate activities with JTF-HD.
PAC-Region		Coordinate activities with JTF-HD.
HAH		Selected hospitals and other agencies will participate in a CPX this week.
HHVISA		3 day exercise discussion on emergency/disaster planning
DCAB		Validate interagency action plan for special needs. Test Communications & sheltering.
State Farm	Private	Test communications. Exercise damage assessment process. Discuss issues related to accessing control area to complete damage assessments.
1st Insurance	Private	TTX Hurricane scenario the week of 5/7/07
Others		ACE, Humane Society, DoD, First HI Bank,

Table 7: Exercise Makani Pahili agencies and activities

3.2.1 The structure of disaster management in Hawai'i

In order to deal with Variety, the Federal approach to disaster management in the United States follows a strict structure, which is applied in all states and to all types of disasters. As its principal 'Variety Engineering' tool, the US Federal Emergency Management Agency (FEMA) has adopted the Incident Command System (ICS) [U.S. DHS, 2004a]. In accordance with the cybernetic laws of VSM, the internal Variety of ICS must match the Variety of any disaster situation, a hurricane event, in this case, and hence all activities of the disaster management cycle need to be able to cope effectively with the impacts of that event. For example, if a hurricane destroys 90 % of residential housing, there needs to be enough replacement shelter space available. This might sound logical and be a tautologous conclusion. Still, it gives us insights into small changes that the VSM identifies, the sum of which can make a big difference. The ICS analysis will be accomplished along the O'ahu JFO in chapter 3.2.4 and is the vertical aspect of Figure 41.

The large-scale coordination for all disaster management entities is in cybernetic terms ensured by System 2 (coordination), which is responsible for damping Variety – all regulations or rules belong here. It is steered by System 5 (identity), which decides on the system's identity and therefore sets the system's boundaries. System 2 (coordination) also attenuates Variety in the sense of 'coordination by mutual adjustment' between the System 1 (implementation) and the supporting systems (System 2–5). 'The more people can share common standards, approaches and values, the greater the chances that spontaneous lateral communication will occur. The stronger these lateral links the less control is necessary by management and the greater the sense of autonomy and empowerment experienced by the subsumed System 1s (implementation)' [Espejo and Gill, 1997, p. 3].

The basis of the interplay of all disaster management entities is laid out by the federal government in the National Response Plan (NRP) and the National Incident Management System (NIMS), both core System 2 (coordination) elements. The Federal Emergency Management Agency's (FEMA) top priorities for incident management and their mission – System 5 (identity) – is to 'save lives and protect the health and safety of the public, responders, and recovery workers, ensure security of the homeland, prevent an imminent incident, including acts of terrorism, from occurring; protect and restore critical infrastructure and key resources, conduct law enforcement investigations to resolve the incident, apprehend the perpetrators, and collect and preserve evidence for prosecution and/or attribution, protect property and mitigate damages and impacts to individuals, communities, and the Environment, facilitate recovery of individuals, families, business-es, governments, and the environment' [Emergency Management Institute, 2007c]. Systems 2 (coordination) and 5 (identity) are clearly defined here.

Through mission assignments the Resource Bargain and Accountabil-ity Loop is established. Lead agencies will then be responsible for 'sub-tasking' and managing the work of support agencies' [FEMA, 2007]. On the different Levels of Recursions, System 1 (implementation) autonomy is ensured. Further, FEMA mandates State and local governments to conduct collaborative planning with the federal government as a part of 'steady-state' preparedness for catastrophic incidents and mandates the City and County of Honolulu to follow the Emergency Operations Plan (EOP) that states 'the City immediately implements this Plan and ap-plies its emergency response and multi-departmental support resources as required to meet the specifics of the disaster/incident through the NIMS' [City and County of Honolulu, 2007, p. 6]. The Metasystem of the highest Level of Recursion is supposed to ensure the functioning of the System 1 (implementation) squiggly lines and their planning (System 4 of the lower Level of Recursion).

The structure of the HHMS (C2 in Figure 39) will be investigated on three levels. The third level does not represent yet the lowest level in the HHMS, but it is the lowest level in ICS terms. The HHMS structural levels are staffed with personnel from departments and agencies of all govern-mental, non-governmental and the private sectors. The lowest level of the HHMS involves everybody involved in hurricane hazard management, and while some details are given as examples, the Viable System Model will not be modeled at this level to anywhere near the full extent possible. In this sense, this dissertation also serves as a suggestion for further research in the application of the Viable System Model.

Figure 42 [based on U.S. DHS, 2004a] shows the hierarchical structure, with FEMA above the State of Hawai'i, which in turn oversees the four counties of O'ahu, Kauai, Maui and the Big Island.

The highest structural level of the Hurricane Hazard Management Sys-tem (HHMS) is represented by the federal EOC of the Federal Emergency Management Agency (FEMA), which is housed within the Department of Homeland Security (DHS) and is the agency with overall responsibility for coordinating the efforts of the federal government [FEMA, 2007]. A Joint Field Office (JFO) is established on O'ahu, which is the federal level EOC with representatives of all levels of governmental and non-governmental de-

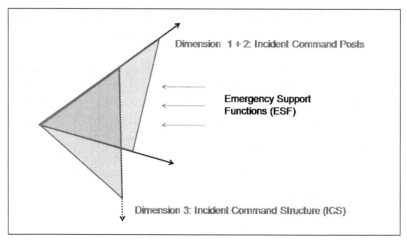

Figure 41: The multi-dimensionality of the Hurricane Hazard Management System

partments and agencies. Further, the State and County Emergency Operation Centers (EOCs) are activated depending on the development of the storm and the resulting needs. For the assumed case all of the above structures will be activated. Since the focus of this dissertation is the island of O'ahu, the description, diagnosis and possible suggestions for the redesign of the organizational structure will be limited to the island of O'ahu. In the assumed case, one JFO will be housed at Fort Shafter. Whether further JFOs would be established on other islands to support O'ahu, has not been discussed in detail, but is a possibility in case of incapability to establish a JFO on O'ahu, or for efficiency reasons.

Let us now look at the geographical division of the O'ahu JFO structure and its logic. The island of O'ahu is broken down into five divisions, as seen in Figure 43 [FEMA, 2007, p. 26].

Figure 44 [based on U.S. DHS, 2004a] shows an overview of the organizational structure of a JFO, the federal Emergency Operations Center on O'ahu with the Command Staff at the top and an Operations, Logistics, Planning and Finance and Administration Section, representing the ICS.

EOCs of all governmental levels are structured along the Incident Command System (ICS), administered by NIMS and the NRP and are each in one single location, called a Post. To understand Figure 44 and its organizational structure the ICS will be described briefly. Its diagnosis will follow along the O'ahu JFO as a special application for natural disasters.

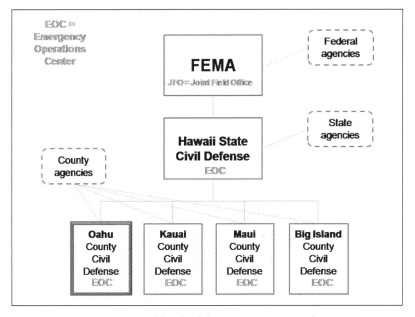

Figure 42: The governmental levels of the Hurricane Hazard Management System

The Incident Command System (ICS) structure represents a constantly adjusting organization and with it the parties involved. Its systemic quality supports VSM principles as its aim is to react flexibly to an ever changing Environment. All EOCs as are structured along this concept.

All federal departments and agencies, or agencies receiving FEMA assistance through grants, contracts, and other activities, will be using the proposed ICS, established in the National Incident Management System (NIMS) and implemented through the National Response Plan (NRP) [U.S. DHS, 2004b], which confirm the existence of a strong System 2 (coordination). It is a standardized, on-scene, all-hazard incident-management concept, uses a common terminology and has an integrated organizational structure to match the complexities and demands of single or multiple incidents without being hindered by jurisdictional boundaries. Its modular structure can be adjusted to any size and scale of an incident. Its flexibility makes it a very cost-effective and efficient management approach for both small and large situations [Emergency Management Institute, 2007b] and shows high cybernetic validity.

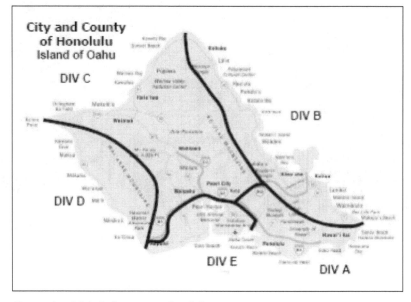

Figure 43: Oʻahu's five geographical divisions

Generally, for any incident type or scale, there is one Incident Command Post (ICP) established for each incident, located at its immediate vicinity. ICS organizations have five major functional areas: Command, Command Staff plus an Operations, Planning, Logistics, Finance and Administration Section (see Figure 45) [Emergency Management Institute, 2007b], but vary in application (Area and Unified Command).

According to NIMS, the Operations Section is used to divide the JFO geographically. Consequently, the island of Oʻahu with its five divisions is broken down into five Area Command Posts (ACPs) as shown in Figure 44 along the Operations Section. The dashed-lined box represents the island of Oʻahu and is extracted from Figure 42. Let us look now at the next lower structural level of the Hurricane Hazard Management System (HHMS).

Down the hierarchical chain, one Area Command Post (ACP) is described in Figure 46 [based on U.S. DHS, 2004a]. The ACP's Operations Section is divided geographically and its divisions are headed by multiple Unified Command Posts (UCPs), since the area covered by the ACPs would be too extensive to handle all the incidents. The number of UCPs will depend on the severity of the impacts within that area [U.S. DHS, 2004a]. This leads to the next lower Level of Recursion.

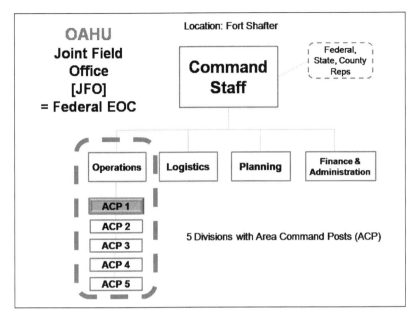

Figure 44: The highest level of the Hurricane Hazard Management System – the Joint Field Office on O'ahu

Figure 47 based on U.S. DHS, 2004a] shows one blue Area Command Post (ACP) on the upper left, which is divided into n UCPs. The exact number of UCPs cannot be planned, since it will depend on the situation; hence in all related figures the number of UCPs is given as 'n'. A UCP is again structured as an ICS. This figure points out the organizational structure of UCP 1 into the four ICS Sections. The National Incident

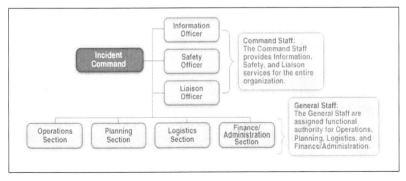

Figure 45: The Incident Command System (ICS)

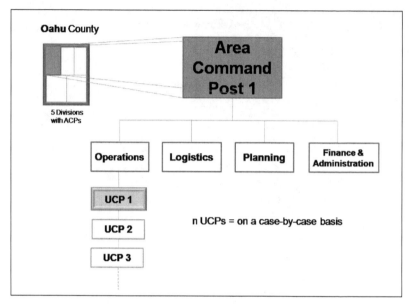

*Figure 46: The second level of the Hurricane Hazard Management System –
the Area Command Post (ACP) structure*

Management System (NIMS) prescribes a maximum of eight Posts as the
'manageable span of control', which goes in accordance with the VSM,
which prescribes exactly a maximum of eight. If that span is exceeded,
the Unified Command (UC) turns into an AC and is further divided geographically. Since this detail of application is as of now considered on a
case-by-case basis, no data could be collected. An overview of all levels
just described is given in Figure 48 [based on U.S. DHS, 2004a] with five
ACPs and *n* UCPs.

Only the first breakdown is pictured for the Oʻahu Joint Field Office
(JFO): ACP 1 and UCP 1. The ICS Operations Section is recursively divided
by geographic region. At the Unified Command level, the third level of the
HHMS, the actual System 1 (implementation) takes place to a major extent,
depending on the situation. If overwhelmed, the county assets are complemented by state and federal assets in a hierarchical manner.

3.2.2 Matching and diagnosing the Hawai'ian disaster management
       with the Viable System Model

The VSM enables the cybernetician to determine factors preventing viability
and suggests appropriate solutions with the aim of improving the viability of
their elements. So far, we've only given an overview of the HHMS. To start a
full diagnosis of a complex system, Beer prescribes choosing a System in Focus.

The mapping of the HHMS onto a VSM diagram can be done in a Variety of ways. This process affects the way of looking at the HHMS and must
be evaluated with respect to the principle of usefulness. A model can only
be as correct as it is useful. From a cybernetic perspective, a Viable System
Model is perceived along all levels of the Hurricane Hazard Management
System (HHMS). Table 8 shows the final VSM application and the clarified
choice of the System in Focus. The System in Focus in cybernetic terms is
chosen to be the Incident Command System (ICS) level, which regards the
federal Emergency Operation Center (EOC), the Joint Field Office (JFO),
because the most detailed information is collected on that level. The level
above, the NIMS framework, also will be analyzed in further detail, since
all EOCs are entailed here and the connection between those structures
is important. The Area Command Posts (ACPs) and Unified Command
Posts (UCPs) are included within the NIMS framework as well, but are not
diagnosed in as much detail because of insufficient data availability – their
structure is determined on a case-by-case basis [Rosenberg, 2007b], which
shows evidence of a missing System 4 (intelligence).

HHMS levels	Level of Recursion	Time of existence	Diagnosis
One department or agency	LoR 4	continuous	mentioned
Emergency Support Functions (ESF)	LoR 3	continuous	included in diagnosis
Incident Command Structure (ICS): IC plus Sections	LoR 2	hibernating	System in Focus
NIMS framework: EOCs, ICPs	LoR 1	hibernating	included in diagnosis

*Table 8: Matching all HHMS levels with the VSM Levels of Recursion under
aspects of time*

In Table 8, at the lowest Level of Recursion (LoR4) the individual governmental, non-governmental and private departments, agencies and entities are found, ideally resting in a Metasystemic Calm. Each of these should be a Viable System 1 (implementation) organization in its own right. Each department should have its own disaster management plan and take care of the safety of its own employees as well of its tasks within the HHMS. This dissertation did not concentrate on this Level of Recursion, because it lays two Levels of Recursion lower than the System in Focus. Instead, the analysis was concerned with the part that departments and agencies play in the HHMS through the ESFs of Level of Recursion 3 in the JFO, an ICS structure, of Level of Recursion 2. Before elaborating the details of the VSM application to the HHMS structure (C2 in Figure 39), we further explicate System 2 (coordination), as it entails all regulations and rules and is the base of the large-scale coordination level.

3.2.3 VSM Diagnosis along the National Incident Management System (NIMS) framework

The NIMS supposedly provides a holistic systems approach that integrates the best existing processes and methods. We want to examine this approach

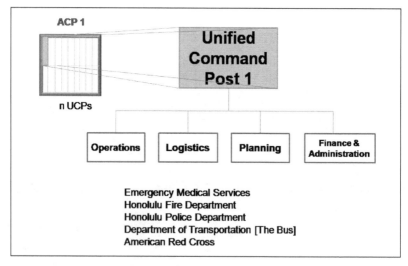

Figure 47: The third level of the Hurricane Hazard Management System – the Unified Command Post (UCP) structure

in detail next (C2 'Perspective 1: NIMS' in Figure 39). NIMS incorporates flexibility on one hand, but also standardization taking into account System Cohesion. Flexibility is given with the adjustable Incident Command System (ICS) for all government and private entities regardless of incident type. NIMS uses standardized processes and procedures to increase interoperability. NIMS does not impose a new system or organizational structure, it simply emphasizes the interrelated nature of the components in the creation of an integrated coordination and support system [Emergency Management Institute, 2007b]. This concept is parallel to Beer's ideas, but is based on best practices, not on cybernetics.

Figure 49 [U.S. DHS, 2004b, p. 19] represents a generalized framework that has not been fully applied yet in Hawai'i.

The first essential step to understand the HHMS from a cybernetic perspective is that it represents a multi-dimensional system as shown in Figure 41. Looking at Figure 42 the federal level Emergency Operation Center (EOC), the Joint Field Office (JFO), is based on the ICS and develops its systemic arms downward in the three-dimensional space along the structure shown in Figure 44. The state and local (county) EOCs analogously develop their systemic arms downward along the ICS. State departments are directed and coordinated by the state EOC, county departments by the county EOC. Their agencies and their disaster management personnel, again, are structured along the ICS. In the JFO, two to three representatives of the state and county agencies are present in a major disaster and hence, a JFO can house several hundred personnel. Overall, the NIMS framework is organized along the various Posts of all governmental levels whereas the ICS represents the organizational structure that fills these locations.

Figure 49 develops horizontally in two dimensions with all organizational units, or Posts, from the federal to the local level. This diagnosis is accomplished first. Vertically, the ICS a la NIMS develops under the JFO, under both state and county Emergency Operations Centers (EOC), the five Area Commands (AC) and the multiple Incident Commands (IC), which would be Unified Commands (UC) in the O'ahu case. This diagnosis follows secondly. The NIMS framework is staffed by all departments and agencies of government, non-government and private sector through the Emergency Support Functions (ESF). Hence, into ICS and consequently all Posts the ESFs are plugged in, which is elaborated then. The JFO is a special application of the ICS and exemplifies the diagnosis of the NIMS ICS. A detailed diagnosis of the Area Command Posts (ACPs) and Unified Command Posts

(UCPs), which follows the same principles, is therefore not accomplished, but is elaborated when appropriate.

Figure 49 relates to Figure 42, one representing the generalized NIMS framework version, the other its application in Hawai'i, respectively, with the JFO and both the state and county EOCs. It further relates to Figure 48 showing the JFO and the division of O'ahu into ACPs and UCPs. The other two EOCs are not shown, but are linked to the JFO because of the multi-dimensional quality of the HHMS, which forces the cybernetician to decide on how the VSM will be applied. Leonard reminds that the correct application is the most useful one and that Beer does not give a prescription on application style and choice [Leonard, 2006]. To give a thorough analysis of the Federal Emergency Management Agency's (FEMA) part of the HHMS, both the horizontal and the vertical structures will be diagnosed. Problems regarding the effective functioning of the HHMS are highlighted under cybernetic aspects. Beer points out that the application of the VSM is most difficult in this phase while picking the System 1 (implementation) and the appropriate Levels of Recursions. The multi-dimensional quality makes the VSM most useful if applied to both levels.

In general, EOCs are 'typically organized by major functional discipline (fire, law enforcement, medical services, etc.), by jurisdiction (city, county, region, etc.) or by some combination thereof' [U.S. DHS, 2006, pp. 17]. Jurisdictional translates to the concept of 'geographical' mentioned before. Overall, within the HHMS the breakdown is a combination of functional and jurisdictional division and is operationalized along the Operation Sections, as seen in Figure 48. The Operations Section of the JFO and the Divisions (Area UCPs) is broken down by geographical (jurisdictional) areas. Ultimately, the multiple (n) UCPs on the third level of the HHMS are organized by functional disciplines as indicated in Figure 47. The geographical division is represented by the horizontal dimension of Incident Command Posts, the functional division by the vertical division through ICS.

The terms 'national', 'regional' and 'field' refer to the operational level and have a geographical aspect and differ from the governmental levels. For example, a JFO operates on the field level, but houses representatives of all levels of governmental and non-governmental departments and agencies. Local (county) and state EOCs are also on the field level with the Area Commands – a special case of Incident Commands – on the lower structural level, in the case of Hawai'i five Area Commands (see Figure 44).

The organizational structures are differentiated regarding 'coordination' and 'command'. Except the five Area Commands for O'ahu, the structures are 'coordination' elements. A discussion regarding these two different types of organizational styles will follow in chapter 3.2.3 (Summary).

Federal, state and county Emergency Operation Centers (EOCs)

On the field level, a Joint Field Office (JFO) is established, which is the physical location of the federal EOC. The JFO would be completely activated for the HHMS [Gilbert, 2007a]. On lower levels of the HHMS, the state and county EOCs are established. In all of these EOCs, the officials responsible for responding to major emergencies and disasters assemble to direct and control the jurisdiction's response. In cybernetic terms, this represents the Metasystem, System 2 (coordination) through 5 (identity). The coordination of information and resources to support incident management activities takes place here, which is a System 3 (operational control) task and circumscribes the Resource Bargain. The JFO works in coordination with the state, county and local EOCs to support incident management efforts, which are all on the same Level of Recursion and can be seen in Figure 50 [based on NIMS, U.S. DHS, 2004b, p. 19].

Because the JFO is a state-federal partnership, no City and county liaisons are involved in decision making and resource allocation [Rosenberg, 2007b] and therefore, the county EOC is only represented in System 3 (operational control) of that Level of Recursion.

In cybernetic terms, the Environment entails the most Variety of all system elements. This Variety has to be absorbed by the Viable System in the ideal case. The JFO departments and agencies do this by ensuring that joint planning for tactical activities is accomplished in accordance with approved incident objectives, a reflection of System 3's Resource Bargain and Accountability Loop interaction along the Command Channel with System 1 (implementation) management. They ensure the integration of tactical operations as System 3 (operational control) task enabling synergies along System 1 (implementation) squiggly lines and approve, commit and make optimum use of all assigned resources through the Resource Bargain and Accountability Loop [U.S. DHS, 2004a].

In other words, the cybernetic requirement that all departments and agencies involved can have a say in System 5 (identity) in a participatory fashion is met and the JFO accomplishes all Metasystemic tasks. In the case of the Hurricane Hazard Management System (HHMS), where county and state resources will be depleted fast, federal support will come through the ESF structure that is plugged into the National Incident Management System (NIMS) and reflects dimension four, as explained later.

In Figure 50, the application of the VSM to the NIMS framework is illustrated. The Metasystem – System 2 through 5 – is represented by the JFO. It provides regulations for System 2 (coordination) by enforcing the National Response Plan (NRP) through the VMS Resource Bargain on the Command Channel; personnel and resource support for System 3 (operational control) to implement decisions in a coordinated manner; strategic warning, planning and coordination for System 4 (intelligence), and policy and identity for System 5 (identity). The *Environment* stands for the disaster situation that the vulnerability analysis discussed in chapter 1.4.2 describes.

At the level of the State Civil Defense (SCD), it accepts, coordinates and encourages ideas of all levels, which is a System 5 (identity) function. It further reflects System 4 (intelligence) functions by providing a forum with the Makani Pahili exercises to coordinate disaster management along the Homeland Security Exercise and Evaluation Program (HSEEP), which also reflects a System 3* (audits). Thus, SCD validates Department of Emergency Management (DEM) activities as FEMA validates SCD. As System 3 (operational control), the state EOC allocates funding across all county departments and agencies. Those departments and agencies are on the next lower Level of Recursion that is not investigated here.

The federal JFO and both the state and county EOCs represent System 3 (operational control) and 4 (intelligence) functions watching the larger Environment for warning signs and respond, e.g. through informing local hospitals about potentially necessary medical services. System 4 (intelligence) is also concerned with the future in regards to the recruitment and training needs of the HHMS team, keeping abreast of new techniques and equipment, working with others to plan for coping with carious contingencies, maintaining liaisons with hospitals, law enforcement agencies and other departments, devising means to shorten response times, lengthening of the life of equipment and developing new modes of public education, among others. Other System 4 (intelligence) functions of the state EOC are to handle media inquiries, to provide the wider world with public information and other media relation's responsibilities, e.g. how public opinion develops. FEMA is also part of System 4 (intelligence) through providing technical expertise [Hirai, 2007b], or, by planning to restore infrastructure requirements after impact. If Hawai'i lost all harbor capabilities, FEMA would provide for temporary haulers from the Navy, barges and mulberries to ship resources to the shore

[Richards and Tengan, 2007]. The National Weather Service (NWS), represented by a JFO Liaison Officer, also represents part of System 4 (intelligence) on the highest Level of Recursion because it assesses the hurricane risk.

The State of Hawai'i represented by the state departments and agencies is organized analogously. The county and state departments and agencies do not function under their routine agenda, but are organized in a fourth structural dimension, the Emergency Support Functions (ESFs), which are headed by federal departments and agencies. The federal departments and agencies staff the JFO Sections and are also organized through the ESFs. The ESFs are plugged into all Posts in Figure 49. The ESFs are shown in more detail in Table 9 and 10. It is task of the cybernetician to choose what is being modeled as System 1 (implementation) and it is more useful to go along the geographical, not functional division for the VSM application to the NIMS framework.

The five Unified Area Command Posts and Unified Command Posts

Relating to Figure 38, these most pressing first responders are the Department of Transportation (DoT), Honolulu Fire Department (HFD), the Honolulu Police Department (HPD), the Emergency Medical Services (EMS) and the American Red Cross (ARC) organized as ESFs. However, the cybernetic problem of the Metasystem diving too deep into the System 1 (implementation) is well illustrated by this Variety of governmental organisations executing the very System 1 (implementation) tasks at the UCP level. For example, during Hurricane Katrina, county level first responders were in need of the authority to implement action opposed by the federal level, which ultimately had the authority [Breakout Session Infrastructure, 2007]. Within the NIMS framework, another cybernetically unjustified example of Metasystemic intervention into System 1 (implementation) regards the UCP, the actual System 1 (implementation) as the functional elements shown in Figure 48. It should have sufficient autonomy. But, this cybernetic requirement is not fulfilled because it depends on the Resource Bargain with the highest Level of Recursion of the HHMS, the Incident Management Assistance Team (IMAT), creating a potentially unstable situation. On another note, the Commander may have up to six Unit Leaders who report to him, which is a cybernetically sound design. Still, the Resource Bargain needs to be contained on the local and state level – to have the federal level involved in that fashion causes too many intersection of management. That Variety cannot be handled in a disaster situation and should be newly designed. Questions of power conflicts are inevitable because federal, state, and local responders report in to UCP to receive an assignment in accordance with the procedures established by the Unified Command regardless of their agency affiliation.

A final area of concern is that the missing implementation of System 2 (coordination) makes the functioning of Channel Capacity and Transduction principles for liaising agencies hardly possible and risks system viability to a great extent. One could say 'we are doing something but if that adds up to disaster management, I don't know' – clear communication knowing the terms and meanings of technical language and what to expect within interpersonal relationships are key in the effective functioning of any management. The problem here is the weak link between the UC and the liaising departments and agencies. 'Agencies with jurisdictional responsibility join the Unified Command, while agencies that lack jurisdictional responsibility, but are heavily involved in the incident are defined as supporting agencies and are represented in the command structure and effect coordination on behalf of their parent agency through a liaison officer attached to the Unified Command' [U.S. DHS, 2006, p. 21a].

Summary: A Viable System Model application to the National Incident Management System (NIMS) framework

The Area Command (AC) of the generalized NIMS framework is a cybernetically sound concept. When stood up, the ACs add a management level between the Incident Command Posts at the lowest Level of Recursion and the Joint Field Office (JFO) so that residual Variety can be dealt with and does not become unmanageable at the JFO level. Moreover, from FEMA's perspective, as found in its online courses, the advantages of the NIMS framework are principally that the organization is relatively simple, with straightforward lines of communication and chain of command. All key decision-makers and representatives of participating agencies are included, as appropriate, within the organization, and all can contribute as needed. In VSM terms, this is also an advantage as it ensures System 1 (implementation) autonomy as well as the system's Cohesion because a clear identity is maintained.

The cybernetic problems at the Area Command level are, first, that of 'commanding' rather than of 'coordinating'. The VSM prescribes that intervention along the Command Channel is only acceptable if System Cohesion is at risk. The general setup of a command structure at the lowest level of the

Hurricane Hazard Management System (HHMS) contradicts VSM concepts. The local level within HHMS should have more autonomy and the federal level decision makers should incorporate the ideas and application of NIMS given by the local level on O'ahu. The top-down approach of NIMS has to be adjusted to the local settings where it is applied and local decision makers should have the final word. Second, because there is no match between independent organizations that do not have to comply with ICS at the local level, such as the American Red Cross, and the JFO Coordination Group, at the federal level, disadvantageous linkages may appear and cause problems [Emergency Management Institute, 2007b]. Differences in communication and organizational structures hinder an efficient and fast information flow between them. On O'ahu, it is helpful that some employees at the local level have worked at the state level before and that they are familiar with the processes of both organizational structures. As a large-scale organizational coordination tool, the Syntegration invented by Beer to solve the System 3–4 balance could improve the effectiveness and efficiency by a great factor. Similarly, right after a catastrophic event, as seen during Katrina and in Haiti, resources poor in and much efficiency and effectiveness is lost in the beginning due to coordination and information failures. This unique tool comes to solutions with enormous speed and implementation power to coordinate organizational networks. The Syntegration, as being performed at Malik Management and its partners, has proven successfully in over 500 applications without failures, in the business and non-business sector. I am proposing to use this tool as a setup to coordinate disaster management efforts and enhance resource (time, money, manpower) efficiency by a great deal to help victims more quickly and reduce vulnerabilities on all scales (Reissberg, 2011).

Within the Area Command (AC), there may also be confusion about who does resource ordering: the Operations Section or the Resource Unit? From a VSM perspective, these are System 2 (coordination) errors that often lead to inefficiencies and time lags. The appropriate communication channels are simply not established and roles and responsibilities are unclear, an indication of a missing System 2 (coordination). Cybernetically, the Levels of Recursion are 1) not organizationally separated and 2) the Metasystem is diving too deep into System 1 (implementation). Those tasks need to be set clearly, which would become apparent when the CONOP would be applied down to the local level before a hurricane hit. This is cybernetically a System 4 (intelligence) failure on the lowest Level of Recursion. It also means that the local level organizations would need enough autonomy to apply the

CONOP with their knowledge appropriately. This chaotic setup can be put in order through Variety Engineering workshops as conducted by Malik Management in Switzerland, for example.

The VSM clearly identifies vital functions because persons or groups mostly have more than one role and communicate on many channels, which are occupied in a complex pattern. The JFO as the highest jurisdictional level organization houses FEMA representatives as well as 'state, local, private-sector and non-governmental organizations' who 'are encouraged to assign liaisons to the Joint Field Office (JFO) to facilitate interaction, communication, and coordination' [U.S. DHS, 2004b, p. 28]. In cybernetic terms, the liaisons should provide for effective Channel Capacity and Transduction and also take part in and influence all JFO activities. That means e.g. that military jargon must be understood by e.g. American Red Cross employees, which is not the case. Additionally, 'encouraged' means that sending a liaison is voluntary. Under the stress of a disaster, insufficient liaison personnel risks reducing Channel Capacity and Transduction, which may lead to the System Cohesion falling apart. Communication and decision making processes will fail because the liaisons under stress will not work, either because they don't exist or if they exist they do not communicate in the same jargon or are not familiar with the other organizations structures and information channels. To fix this System 2 (coordination) issue, the Syntegration would accomplish an organizational change in a relatively short time. The Syntegration will be explained in chapter 3.3.10.

Decision making is another potentially conflictual aspect of this same situation. Two or three representatives of the county and state EOCs are located in the JFO as counterparts to channel information and perform Transduction functions between their EOCs and the JFO in strategic coordination or decision making processes as System 4 (intelligence) and 5 (identity), shown in Figure 50 [Richards and Tengan, 2007]. Ultimately they all have to follow the federal lead but the local level is most accustomed to the local conditions and has a better grip on the situation at hand – System 1 (implementation) on the local level needs more autonomy here. On the same note, regarding the Resource Bargain, a clear indication of too little System 1 (implementation) autonomy is evident: Preliminary Damage Assessments (PDA) and Rapid Needs Assessments (RNA) are accomplished with teams composed of county, state and federal representatives – most effective data sharing [Richards, 2007f] at first sight. In cybernetic terms, Channel Capacity and Transduction can be ensured, but, with the greater legal power of the federal representatives, the situation endangers

System 1 (implementation) autonomy as prescribed by the VSM, a cybernetic drawback. The Metasystem – the federal level – has reached too deep into System 1 (implementation) activities. State Civil Defense (SCD) and FEMA should let the local level county EOCs determine their own damage assessments, which can be 'proof read' later in the process ensuring System 1 (implementation) autonomy at the lowest level and not cutting through several Levels of Recursion. Hierarchical structures in general are cybernetically inacceptable. Overall, with as many intersections of management, there is too much effort to coordinate all System 2s (coordination). It causes these disagreements and inefficiencies reducing Channel Capacity and Transduction, because every department or agency currently uses a different language, forms and definitions of damage categories (e.g. FEMA, SCD, DEM, Small Business Administration). Insufficient NIMS training within Hurricane Hazard Management System (HHMS) during the research period existed, even though NIMS prescribes a common language, as does the VSM. Variety attenuation is intended but not in effect.

The Resource Bargain organized through the Emergency Support Functions (ESFs) [Richards and Tengan, 2007] representing System 1 (implementation) functions also poses cybernetic problems. The ESFs are coordinated on the principle that first county assets and resources are used, complemented if necessary by state, and finally federal assets and resources. The higher governmental level steps in when the lower level has exhausted its resources. Knowing that in a catastrophic disaster all resources will be depleted [Richards and Tengan, 2007] a System 4 (intelligence) functions needs to be placed specifically for this type of planning, which is not performed. One reason is ignorance out of knowing that a catastrophic disaster would have such bad consequences that it is simply unthinkable to manage it – a lethal Variety attenuation. The complexity of the situation forces to simplify, but unfortunately on the subjectively not cybernetically chosen ends.

Obvious cases of accountability of resources provided not being ensured are evident during the annual hurricane exercise, Makani Pahili, organized by the State Civil Defense (SCD) and mandated by the Homeland Security Exercise and Evaluation Program (HSEEP), a federal level program that is required for continued federal funding. The purpose of Makani Pahili is to test the preparedness level as well as disaster response capabilities of all departments and agencies. It is documented in After Action Reports (AAR) written by each separate entity. Since AARs are published by each participating agency, they potentially lack objectivity and the information contained can cover up potential inefficiencies. Cybernetically, the System 3* (audits) is missing, the audit function to ensure efficiency. It is the SCD Training Officer function to ask for the departments' and agencies' update and status, but he does not check on it. The System 3* (audits) function is conducted too loosely and no incentive exists to really accomplish it and so it fails. System 2 (coordination) again is voluntary. Another example of this non-enforced function was the cancellation of the US Coast Guard's Incident Action Plan (IAP) training due to no interest in 2007. Such training is important because IAP is the core concept of NIMS processes and ensures the daily operations of plans. However, since training and exercises are voluntary without external checks, no NIMS compliancy can be guaranteed. The system blows apart due to lack of System 2 (coordination), and due to a lack of System 3* (audits), which lets System 1 (implementation) and System 3 (operational control) fall into coma.

The physical location of disaster management entities is also problematic: System 3 (operational control) functions reside within the county, state and federal EOCs but are geographically separated which hinders System 3 (operational control) tasks. A system can only be viable if System 3 (operational control) has a synoptic view. A plan exists for a new hurricane-proof building where DEM, SCD and FEMA would collocate in a Joint Transportation Management Center (TMC) but has yet to be realized [Richards and Tengan, 2007].

After having diagnosed the HHMS along the NIMS framework on Level of Recursion 1, we will now look at Level of Recursion 2, where the JFO and the functional analysis of the Incident Command System (ICS) will be diagnosed.

3.2.4 Diagnosing the Oʻahu Joint Field Office (JFO) structure

The CONOP divides the State of Hawaiʻi into four Branches representing the counties of the State of Hawaiʻi (Oʻahu, Big Island, Maui, Kauai) (Figure 51) [FEMA, 2007, p. 25]. Branch I, Oʻahu, will be supported by five Divisions (Figure 43) providing federal assistance to support state and local operations. Those Divisions will be organized through Area Command Posts (ACPs) and have operational boundaries that are defined by geographic features and major infrastructure [FEMA, 2007]. Big Island and Maui have three divisions. Branch IV Kauai would have no further subdivisions according to the CONOP. The JFO will be a Unified Command on Oʻahu [FEMA, 2007], which is a special application of the Incident Command

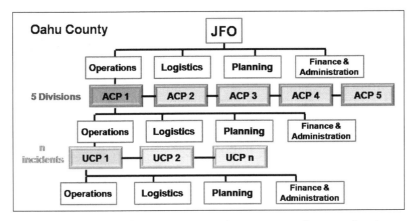

Figure 48: Overview of Hurricane Hazard Management System as Incident Command System (ICS)

System (ICS). First of all, the JFO's structure will be investigated in a functional analysis followed by the diagnosis of the JFO Sections. Secondly, the O'ahu JFO, its five Divisions in Area Commands (AC) and the multiple Unified Commands (UCs) will be investigated adding the geographical (jurisdictional) aspect for the O'ahu JFO application of NIMS, the third dimension. This analysis (C2 'Perspective 2: JFO' Figure 39) regards the vertical aspect shown in Figure 41 along the ICS (Figure 45). Figure 52 [U.S. DHS, 2004b, p. 29] illustrates the generalized full-fledged JFO structure according to the National Incident Management System (NIMS) for natural disasters, which is a special elaboration of the JFO ICS and has not been applied in the State of Hawai'i to the full extent.

Personnel from all governmental departments and agencies and private-sector and nongovernmental organizations provide staffing for the JFO, through their respective Emergency Support Functions (ESF) [U.S. DHS, 2004b, p. 28]. Finally, those Emergency Support Functions (ESFs) – the fourth dimension – will be analyzed under VSM aspects.

Figure 51 combines Figure 42 and Figure 44. The dashed lines around the Operations Section of Figure 44 are analogous to Figure 51. Branch I identifies the O'ahu JFO and the Divisions with the Area Command Posts (ACPs). Figure 43 shows FEMA's geographical divisions (A through E) along which the five of Area Command Posts (ACPs) on O'ahu were designed in the CONOP [FEMA, 2007]. This varies from statements of one O'ahu County Emergency Operation Center (EOC) representative [Gilbert, 2007b], who said there might be as many as eight ACPs. Cyberneti-

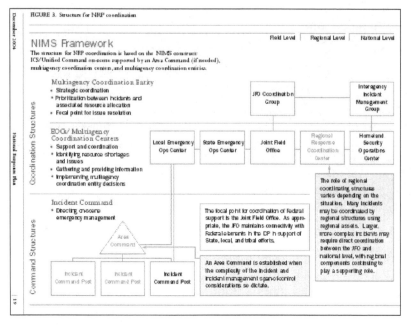

Figure 49: National Incident Management System (NIMS) framework

cally, this is a System 2 (coordination) oscillatory problem and should be agreed upon and clear before a hurricane event, plus planning is missing (System 4 (intelligence)). The argument was here, that it cannot be planned and actions will be situation-based. But since the HHMS assumes maximum use of all assets and resources in a catastrophic event, the planning of organizational structure scenarios should be accomplished by System 4 (intelligence) on the level of divisions of Oʻahu, even if the numbers and locations of UCP cannot be absolutely pre-determined.

Figure 53 based on Figure 51 and Figure 52 shows the Metasystemic Coordination Group and Staff as well as its Sections.

The Joint Field Office (JFO) Coordination Group represents the Incident Command of Figure 45 and the JFO Coordination Staff represents the Incident Command Staff, respectively. The four Sections – Operations, Planning, Logistics and Finance and Administration are reflected both on the ICS and JFO.

In general, the Coordination Group sets the incident objectives, strategies, and priorities and has overall responsibility at the incident or event site [Jones, 2006] in the roles of Systems 3–4–5. It also assigns tactical resources and oversees operations [Jones, 2006] as System 3 (operational

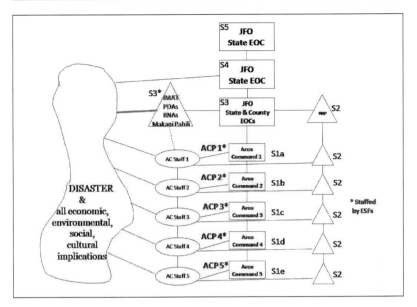

Figure 50: A Viable System Model application to the National Incident Management System (NIMS) framework

control). In this function, the JFO Coordination Group sets the Resource Bargain, the Accountability Loop keeping the synoptic overview. As System 2 (coordination), the JFO Coordination Group ensures adequate safety measures. As System 3 (operational control), the JFO Coordination Group is 'responsible for the assessment of the incident priorities established by the National Preparedness Goal' [U.S. DHS, 2004b, p.19]. It manages the Resource Bargain with all involved agencies through assessing resource needs and orders, approving requests for additional resources and approving and ensuring incident funding and expenditures and ordering the demobilization of resources when appropriate. As System 4 (intelligence), the JFO Coordination Group tasks include further 'collecting, analyzing, and interpreting information from a Variety of sources' [U.S. DHS, 2004b, p.19]. It also authorizes information release to the media and informs System 5 (identity) as it subjectively chooses and consciously influences its identity through information management. All meta-systemic functions are in place. Let us now evaluate the System 1 (implementation) functions.

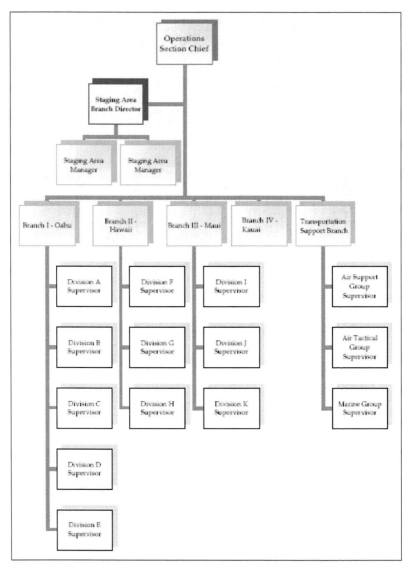

Figure 51: The CONOP Incident Command System (ICS) structure

The Joint Field Office sections

This structure includes the following Sections: Operations, Planning, Logistics, and Finance and Administration. These sections are spread all over the VSM and will be diagnosed in the following.

The Operations Section at the JFO level is the functional element that breaks up the ICS geographically into five Divisions as Area Command Posts (ACPs) at the next level and finally multiple Unified Command Posts (UCPs) at the incident level. The five divisions of the Operations Section on O'ahu will be headed by a Division Supervisor to coordinate field operations in their area. The System 1 (implementation) produces the system at this level. The Planning, Logistics and Finance and Administration Section would not be so divided [McCoy, 2008].

Although the JFO uses an Incident Command System (ICS) structure, the JFO does not manage on-scene operations, and hence has no System 1 (implementation) tasks. This ensures in this case that the Metasystem does not impinge on System 1 (implementation) autonomy several Levels of Recursion further below, a cybernetically sound concept. Rather, incidents are managed at the scene through the Unified Command Post (UCP) on the lowest level of the Hurricane Hazard Management System (HHMS) where System 1 (implementation) takes place, not on the JFO level.

Generally, the NIMS states that a mix of functional and geographical approaches may be appropriate for the Operations Section at the JFO level and up to 25 divisions can be applied. Cybernetically, the breakdown into five branches, as in the O'ahu case, would be justifiable; a breakdown into 25 divisions would call for intervention, since the VSM prescribes a maximum of seven elements within System 1 (implementation). In Louisiana and Mississippi during Hurricane Katrina, the span of control was exceeded by the sheer size of the event and the number of counties involved. This led to a Variety explosion of unmanageable magnitude. Some Variety can be attenuated if a high level of redundancy is given within the organizational structure at hand, but this is highly case-dependent and the breakdown into 25 divisions would need a cybernetic inspection.

On the UCP level, the Operations Section coordinates operational support to on-scene incident management efforts as System 1 (implementation) management and is responsible for coordination with other federal Command Posts that may be established to support incident management activities [U.S. DHS, 2006a] representing the System 1 (implementation) squiggly lines. Especially for a large event, the coordination between the System 1s (implementation) along the squiggly lines is vital. For example, in 1992, after Hurricane 'Iniki hit Kauai, emergency workers cut up utility poles with chain saws to open roads and, consequently, later ran out of poles for reconstruction. There was no coordination between certain System 1 (implementation) elements, specifically between the System 1 (implementation) for immediate response and reconstruction. The System 1 (implementation) squiggly lines are cybernetically intact now after this experience, since the Department of Emergency Management (DEM) plans to order their volunteers to move the poles gently to the side, open only a single pathway with contra flows and to reuse the poles, a Variety amplification of the System 3 (operational control) coordination [Gilbert, 2007a]. On Oʻahu, only a limited number of replacement poles exist and consequently, large parts of Oʻahu would remain black until the pole supply would come to Oʻahu. DEM plans to reuse utility poles but they might be buried or saturated with rain water and not be reusable. The only alternative, to burry more of the utility lines, faces problems regarding costs, political issues and the coordination between the agencies using the poles [Gilbert, 2007a]. The way Variety has to be attenuated for System 3 (operational control) to be able to get into Homeostasis fast would have to be discussed and managed in detail by the involved departments and agencies. Those utility poles do not only carry power lines, but are owned by different stakeholders – electric, cable and telephone companies. Consequently, the responsibilities and assignments are unclear and not explicit; a coordinating System 2 is missing. The mitigation issue of putting poles underground remains unsolved since responsibilities are pushed away. Long-term mitigation efforts only impose costs for these private companies with no immediate economic advantage. The government, State or County Civil Defense as System 3 (operational control) might be able to motivate them (part of System 1 (implementation)) through incentives, which is one way to strengthen System 2. The VSM prescribes that System 3 (operational control) looks for synergies between System 1s (implementation) – the importance of this task is currently underestimated.

Another important aspect is the fact that 80 % of the critical infrastructure in Hawaiʻi belongs to the private industry, such as HECO [Rosenberg, 2007a]. Cybernetically, the train of thought for the problem solution is such that first, two systems have to be distinguished based on time. In a business-as-usual situation, 80 % private ownership of critical infrastructure makes those private businesses clearly the dominator of System 3 (operational control). But, in a disaster situation, the County and State Civil Defense take over the lead. This system hibernation and related problems might not be regarded as a big deal, but the lens the VSM points out identifies the 'start' of a problem chain – an Algedonic Alarm would sound here while the system as a whole seemingly is in Metasystemic Calm, but is on the verge of falling into coma if this problem is not recognized. While there is still no actual hurricane on the horizon, there is enough time to

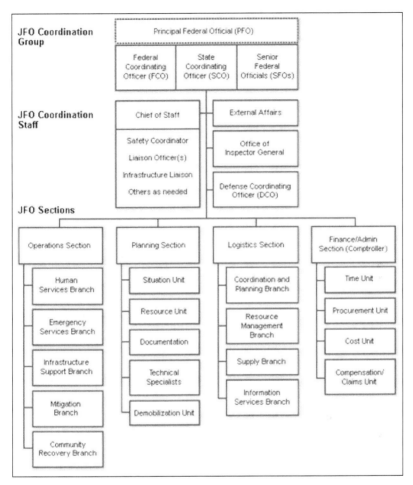

Figure 52: The Joint Field Office (JFO) structure for natural disasters

reduce vulnerabilities here and to set the HHMS up to be viable once a catastrophic hurricane is brewing up. There would need to be a law, System 2 (coordination), in place for the business-as-usual situation, where the government has the System 3 (operational control) lead and this part of the hibernation is excluded. As a consequence, the private industry would have to prepare for a worst-case scenario of a Makani Pahili situation and would be obligated to, e.g. put 80 % of all utility poles underground. The financial cost could be divided by profit-per-pole calculations, for example. Consequently, the government would not be restricted anymore regarding planning and mitigation measures and would no more depend on the goodwill and consensus of private companies. Equally, such problems of red tape also concern the transportation system. For example, H3 is state-owned and in case of a disaster the state is responsible for its repairs, but many of the roads are owned by the City and County [Romaine, 2007]. These inconsistencies also flag an Algedonic Alarm well before any disaster strikes and if taken care of in advance less money is wasted during a disaster and can help to save life and assets on grand scale. The complaint, that money and funding is the issue is called off if looking at the HHMS through this lens.

The Operations Section shown in Figure 52 entails a Human Services Branch, an Infrastructure Support Branch, a Mitigation Branch and a Community Recovery Branch, which are not further explained in the Federal Emergency Management Agency (FEMA) Concept of Operations (CONOP) for a catastrophic hurricane impacting the state of Hawai'i [FEMA, 2007]. Its diagnosis will only be possible to the generalized extent as given by NRP Section 5 [U.S. DHS, 2004b]. Branches are internally divided by geographical area along five Area Command Posts (ACPs), e.g. the Human Services Branch has five geographical divisions. On Level of Recursion x, shown in Figure 53, the Operations Section reflects System 1 (implementation). The different Branches are part of the next lower Level of Recursion. At this point, the Viable System Model (VSM) suggests the identification and modeling of different Levels of Recursions. Figure 54 [Beer, 1994a, p. 321] shows two Levels of Recursion embedded within each other to demonstrate these circumstances.

Beer demonstrates the higher Level of Recursion as Recursion x, the lower as Recursion y in the diagonal. In Figure 36 it became clear that all System 1s (implementation) are contained within one System 1 (implementation) operations of the next higher Level of Recursion, which is crucial for diagnosing and modeling the VSM [Beer, 1994a, p. 323].

In Figure 55 the VSM is applied to the Joint Field Office (JFO) on the next lower Level of Recursion y where the System 1s (implementation) are divided geographically into five Area Command Posts (ACPs).

Three Levels of Recursion are shown: in blue the System 1 (implementation) of Recursion x, in black the VSM of Recursion y and in red the VSM of the next lower Level of Recursion z. The following diagnosis will include the Levels of Recursion x and y.

On Recursion y, the Human Services Branch reflects System 3 (operational control) and coordinates assistance programs to help individuals, families, and businesses meet basic needs and return to self-sufficiency. As

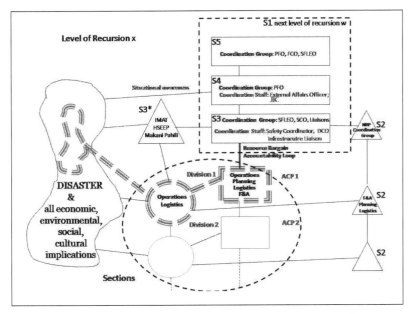

Figure 53: A Viable System Model application to the Joint Field Office (JFO)

System 3 (operational control) it also coordinates with volunteer organizations and is involved in donations management, and coordinates the need for and location of Disaster Recovery Centers (DRCs) with local and tribal governments. DRCs are staffed by federal, state, local, tribal, voluntary, and nongovernmental organizations as needed, with knowledgeable personnel to provide recovery and mitigation program information, advice, counseling, and related technical assistance. The Infrastructure Support Branch reflects System 3 (operational control) and coordinates 'public assistance programs' authorized by the Stafford Act to aid state and local governments and eligible private nonprofit organizations with the cost of emergency protective services and the repair or replacement of disaster-damaged public facilities and associated environmental restoration. The Mitigation Branch reflects System 4 (intelligence) and works with the other Operations branches (System 3 (operational control)) to promote the use of recovery activities that will reduce or eliminate risks to persons or property or to lessen the actual or potential effects or consequences of future incidents. The System 3–4 power struggle will be discussed in the summary of this chapter. The Community Recovery Branch reflects System 4 (intelligence) and works with the other Operations branches and state and local officials to assess the long-term

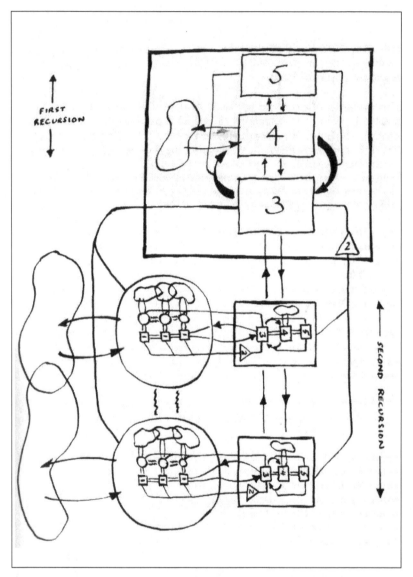

Figure 54: Two Levels of Recursion of the Viable System Model

impacts of an incident, define available resources, and facilitate the development of a course of action to most efficiently apply available resources to restore and revitalize the community. The power struggle just mentioned is also of high importance in this context.

The above branches coordinate with one another along the System 1 (implementation) squiggly lines to identify appropriate agency assistance programs to meet disaster management needs, synchronizing assistance delivery and promoting synergies and encouraging incorporation of hazard mitigation measures where possible in a proactive manner. This incorporates System 1 (implementation) of the lowest level into the whole. Variety explosion should be constrained here by restricting System 1 (implementation) voice up to the highest Level of Recursion. The data collection revealed a perceived problem with Variety proliferation because 'everybody is talking to everybody' [Latham, 2007]. It is a clear task of the System 3 (operational control) to filter the noise into data and into relevant information that then is given to the Metasystem of the next higher Level of Recursion, which it is a System 1 (implementation) of – otherwise Variety cannot be controlled and Homeostasis is lost from the start. System 4 (intelligence) is reflected in the mitigation framework, since they analyze hazard mitigation risks, provide technical assistance to state, local, and tribal governments, citizens, and businesses and grant assistance. Additionally, these branches work in tandem to track overall progress of the recovery effort, particularly noting potential program deficiencies and problem areas as System 3 (operational control) with System 2 (coordination) [U.S. DHS, 2004b].

Further, the JFO Planning Section prepares and documents the Incident Action Plan (IAP) to accomplish the mission objectives set by the JFO Coordination Group. This is both a Metasystemic task on the Level of Recursion y involving Systems 3–4–5 and, for implementation, a System 1 (implementation) management task on Recursion x. The IAP could be designed as a measurement tool. In greater detail, the Planning Section 1) collects and evaluates information, a System 4 (intelligence) tasks, 2) maintains resource status, a System 3 (operational control) task, 3) maintains documentation for incident records, a System 2 (coordination) task, and 4) develops plans for demobilization, a System 4 (intelligence) task [Emergency Management Institute, 2007b].

At the highest Level of Recursion x, the Planning Section also provides current information to the JFO Coordination Group to ensure situational awareness, which is a System 1 (implementation) management – 3 (operational control) interaction, as well as anticipating cascading effects, identifying national implications, determining specific areas of interest requiring long-term attention, and providing technical and scientific expertise, which are all System 4 (intelligence) tasks. Preliminary Damage Assessments (PDA) as System 3* (audits) tasks are organized in the Planning Section [Richards, 2007f].

Investigated functionally, the Planning Section houses a Situation Unit, a Resource Unit, a Documentation Unit, Technical Specialists and a Demobilization Unit (see Figure 52). The Resources Unit plays a significant role in writing the IAP, a System 3 (operational control) task because it conducts all check-in activities and maintains the status of all incident resources, a System 2 (coordination) task.

On Recursion y, the Situation Unit collects and analyzes information on the current situation, a System 3 (operational control) task, and also develops maps and projections, a System 4 (intelligence) task. On Recursion x, it prepares situation displays and situation summaries, a System 1 (implementation) task, to facilitate System 3 (operational control) on the same level, Level of Recursion x.

The Documentation Unit provides duplication services, maintains and archives all incident-related documentation, a System 2 (coordination) task and assists in ensuring that resources are released from the incident in an orderly, safe, and cost-effective manner, a System 3 (operational control) task.

As an illustration of the unsettled nature of the HHMS, the Logistics Section of the JFO for natural disasters (Figure 52), entails a Coordination and Planning Branch, Resource Management Branch, Supply Branch and Information Services Branch, which are not further explained in the Federal Emergency Management Agency (FEMA) CONOP [FEMA, 2007] and differ from the description in the National Incident Management System (NIMS). Consequently, the branches cannot be diagnosed in more detail and the analysis will only be possible to the extent that data allow.

Logistics can make or break an incident response. The Coordination Group establishes mission priorities as System 3 (operational control) on Recursion x, e.g. what resources can come to Oʻahu via ports and airports, and following that the Logistics Section executes the plan as System 1 (implementation) on Recursion y. On Recursion y, the Logistics Section also fulfills Metasystemic tasks by coordinating logistics support including control and accountability for federal supplies and equipment, a System 3 (operational control) task. Bridging Recursions x and y, the Logistics Section takes care of facility location setup, space management, building services, general facility operations, transportation coordination and fleet management services as System 1 (implementation) operations on Recursion x, again reflecting System 3 (operational control) tasks on Recursion y. It also provides information and technology systems services as System 4 (intelligence) on Recursion x and administrative services such as mail management, reproduction and customer assistance as System 2 (coordination) tasks of Recursion y [U.S. DHS, 2006a]. Based upon mission objectives, the Logistics Section also develops several portions of the

Incident Action Plan (IAP) and forwards them to the Planning Section as System 1 (implementation) on Recursion x along the squiggly lines. Further, as System 1 (implementation) on the Level of Recursion x, NIMS prescribes that the Logistics Section work closely along the squiggly lines with the Finance and Administration Section to contract for and purchase goods and services needed at the incident, thereby fulfilling the Resource Bargain. For example, the Logistics Section is responsible for ordering, obtaining, maintaining, and accounting for essential personnel, equipment, supplies, providing communication planning and resources as System 1 (implementation) management on Recursion x, setting up food services, setting up and maintaining incident facilities, providing support transportation and providing medical services to incident personnel as System 1 (implementation) operations on Recursion x. In sum, on Recursion x, the Logistics Section provides support, resources, and all other services needed to meet the operational objectives of the JFO Coordination Group, e.g. arranging for vehicles, fuel, lodging or food [Emergency Management Institute, 2007b]. These are System 1 (implementation) tasks.

The Finance and Administration Section monitors the costs related to the incident, provides accounting, procurement and cost analyses [Emergency Management Institute, 2007b]. This Section houses a Time Unit, a Procurement Unit, a Cost Unit and a Compensation and Claims Unit (see Figure 52) which are not further explained in the National Response Plan (NRP) nor in the FEMA CONOP [FEMA, 2007]. At Recursion x, it reflects System 1 (implementation) management and is bound to the Resource Bargain through System 3 (operational control) (see Figure 55). It is responsible for the financial management as System 1 (implementation) on Recursion x, for monitoring and tracking all federal costs relating to the incident within the Resource Bargain and the functioning of the Joint Field Office (JFO) while adhering to all federal laws, acts, and regulations as System 2 (coordination) on Recursion x [U.S. DHS, 2006a].

On Recursion y, the Procurement Unit is responsible for administering all financial matters pertaining to vendor contracts, leases, and fiscal agreements. The Time Unit is responsible for incident personnel time recording as System 2 (coordination). The Cost Unit collects all cost data, performs cost effectiveness analyses, provides cost estimates, and makes cost savings recommendations as System 3 (operational control), and the Compensation and Claims Unit is responsible for the overall management and direction of all administrative matters pertaining to compensation for injury and claims related activities kept for the incident as System 2 (coordination) and 3 (operational control).

From Figure 54 and Figure 55 it can be concluded that all Systems necessary to fulfill the requirements of a Viable System are present. To comply with its sufficiency, the 'how' has to be investigated next. Before that task will be accomplished, the Emergency Support Function (ESF) structure has to be discussed. The next Level of Recursion lower, the Unified Command Post (UCP) level, will not be investigated further, but is shown graphically in Figure 56. Since that model duplicates the Incident Command System (ICS) on higher Levels of Recursion, its diagnosis would be redundant.

Emergency Support Functions within the National Incident Management System (NIMS) structures

On Level of Recursion 3, the ESFs represent the System 1s (implementation). They are plugged into the JFO in a certain pattern as will be shown. An Emergency Support Function (ESF) is a grouping of all levels of government and certain private-sector capabilities into an organizational structure to provide the support, resources, program implementation, and services (System 1 (implementation)) that are most likely to be needed to save lives, protect property and the Environment, restore essential services and critical infrastructure, and help victims and communities return to normal, when feasible, following domestic incidents.

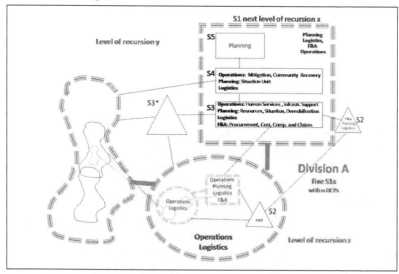

Figure 55: A Viable System Model application of three Levels of Recursion: Division A on the next lower Level of Recursion y

ESF	Scope
ESF #1 – Transportation	Federal and civil transportation support Transportation safety Restoration/recovery of transportation infrastructure Movement restrictions Damage and impact assessment
ESF #2 – Communications	Coordination with telecommunication industry Restoration/repair of telecommunications infrastructure Protection, restoration, and sustainment of national cyber and information technology resources
ESF #3 – Public Works and Engineering	Infrastructure protection and emergency repair Infrastructure restoration Engineering services, construction management Critical infrastructure liaison
ESF #4 – Firefighting	Firefighting activities on Federal lands Resource support to rural and urban firefighting operations
ESF #5 – Emergency Management	Coordination of incident management efforts Issuance of mission assignments Resource and human capital Incident action planning Financial management
ESF #6 – Mass Care, Housing, and Human Services	Mass care Disaster housing Human services
ESF #7 – Resource Support	Resource support (facility space, office equipment and supplies, contracting services, etc.)
ESF #8 – Public Health and Medical Services	Public health Medical Mental health services Mortuary services
ESF #9 – Urban Search and Rescue	Life-saving assistance Urban search and rescue
ESF #10 – Oil and Hazardous Materials Response	Oil and hazardous materials (chemical, biological, radiological, etc.) response Environmental safety and short- and long-term cleanup
ESF #11 – Agriculture and Natural Resources	Nutrition assistance Animal and plant disease/pest response Food safety and security Natural and cultural resources and historic properties protection and restoration

ESF #12 – Energy	Energy infrastructure assessment, repair, and restoration Energy industry utilities coordination Energy forecast
ESF #13 – Public Safety and Security	Facility and resource security Security planning and technical and resource assistance Public safety/security support Support to access, traffic, and crowd control
ESF #14 – Long-term Community Recovery	Social and economic community impact assessment Long-term community recovery assistance to States, local governments, and the private sector
ESF #15 – External Affairs	Emergency public information and protective action guidance; Media and community relations; Congressional and inter-national affairs ; Tribal and insular affairs

Table 9: The scope of the Emergency Support Functions (ESFs)

Table 10 presents a summary of the ESFs and the primary agencies fulfilling the tasks.

ESF #	Function	Federal ESF Coordinator	State of Hawai'i Primary Department
1	Transportation	Dept of Transportation	Dept of Transportation
2	Communication	DHS/National Communication System	Dept of Accounting and General Services (DAGS)
3	Public Works and Engineering	DoD/USACE	Dept of Accounting and General Services (DAGS) (Bottled / Bulk Water & Ice)
4	Firefighting	Dept of Agriculture / Forest Service	State Fire Council (DLNR)
5	Emergency Management	FEMA	Department of Defense (State Civil Defense)
6	Mass Care, Housing, Emergency Assistance and Human Services	DHS / FEMA	Department of Defense (State Civil Defense)
7	Resource Support	General Services Administration	DAGS / Dept of Human Resources Development
8	Public Health and Medical Services	Dept of Health and Human Services	Dept of Health

9	Urban Search and Rescue	DHS / FEMA	Department of Defense (State Civil Defense)
10	Oil & Hazardous Material Response	Environmental Protection Agency	Dept of Health
11	Agriculture and Natural Resource	Dept of Agriculture	Dept of Agriculture
12	Energy	Dept of Energy	DBEDT (State Energy Office)
13	Public Safety and Security	DHS / Dept of Justice	Dept of the Attorney General (proposed)
14	Long Term Community Recovery and Mitigation	DHS / FEMA	DBEDT (proposed)
15	External Affairs	DHS	Dept of Defense (State Civil Defense) proposed

Table 10: The Emergency Support Functions (ESFs) and performing agencies

At the federal level, ESFs are headed by an ESF coordinator and are carried out through the Joint Field Office (JFO). On the state level, the ESFs are headed by individuals of the state government drawing upon various state departments, as well as City and county departments, with the private sector for support and expertise [City and County of Honolulu, 2007]. Analogously, the county Emergency Operation Center (EOC) draws on its department and agencies [U.S. DHS, 2004b, p. 101].

Only the ESF structure within the JFO, the federal EOC, is diagnosed here along the ICS structure given by the NRP and NIMS. The state and county have their own individual setup along the ESF structure. The State Emergency Response Team (SERT) is shown in Figure 57 [City and County of Honolulu, 2007] to exemplify the setup within the State.

It is tempting to model the ESFs as the System 1 (implementation) elements of the EOCs of all governmental levels. This however would be cybernetically contradictory because the VSM prescribes a maximum of eight elements, whereas the ESFs as System 1s (implementation) imply that the JFO was trying to manage 15 System 1s (implementation). As mentioned before, if there is enough redundancy, the magic number seven plus/minus two as the number of elements cybernetically sound can be exceeded, but the ESFs show little redundancy at all (see Table 9 and 10). That Variety

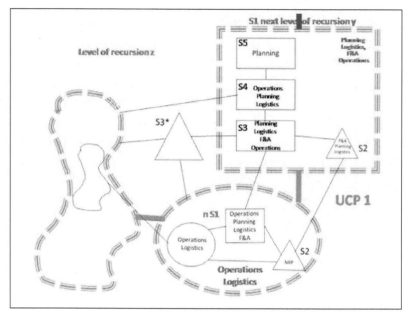

Figure 56: A Viable System Model application to the Unified Command Post (UCP) Level of Recursion z with n UCPs

must crash any organizational setup from a VSM perspective. Moreover, System 1s (implementation) are transformers of input into output producing the System. Thus, the ICS structure of Incident Command Posts is the element transforming the ESFs (input) into effective hurricane hazard management (output). The ESFs in that sense represent a resource and not a transformation of a resource – it could be argued. The VSM application always follows what is most useful and a different stance could be acceptable. In this viewpoint, the ESFs should not be modeled as system 1s (implementation). As a resource, it is plugged into the JFO structure as shown in Figure 58 [U.S. DHS, 2006a, p.16]. The resources provided by the ESFs reflect the resource typing categories identified in the NIMS, which belong to System 2 (coordination) [U.S. DHS, 2004b]. Each department or agency has tasks in a Variety of ESFs, creating a massive amount of interfaces – and Variety.

The federal, the state and the county EOCs are staffed by their respective departments and agencies, which are structured by the ESFs. This variation of VSM application should indicate the way of using the VSM as a diagnostic tool. The analysis of this Level of Recursion – at the ESF

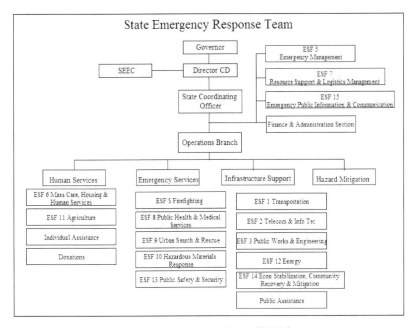

Figure 57: The State Emergency Response Team (SERT)

level – was not intended and therefore will be left open for discussion. Please also note that the ICS structure is diagnosed here, not the governmental levels. Overall, a firm System 2 (coordination) needs to be designed and implemented. For the HHMS, the implementation deficiencies are the major cause of ineffectiveness, which could be improved through a firm training program with a properly designed Accountability Loop and System 3 Star (audits) on top of the already mentioned Variety Engineering exercises. In the following, a summary of the VSM application to the JFO will be given.

Summary: A Viable System Model application to the O'ahu Joint Field Office

Each Emergency Support Function (ESF) is at first sight a Viable System in itself on Level of Recursion 3 and is structured through the ICS, a cybernetically sound concept. The ESF structure supports synergies, since departments and agencies of the same interest area are coupled within one ESF. This is Variety attenuating and therefore a desirable element. But, since the VSM prescribes no more than nine elements, it entails too many.

Cybernetics would suggest aggregating the existing 15 ESFs into five to nine activities. Another Level of Recursion could be inserted. An application where the ESFs are treated as a resource, not as the transformation of a resource as a System 1 (implementation) is a possibility to be discussed, not followed here. Redundancy is found in the ICS, but is lacking within the ESF structure itself and leads to Variety proliferation and ineffectiveness. Inefficiencies exist due to the ESFs hierarchical structure being plugged into a decentralized ICS structure. System 1 (implementation) autonomy is not guaranteed and power struggles evolve, also because local knowledge is more relevant than non-adjusted top-down instructions from the federal level.

Variety will proliferate when ESFs are plugged into the JFO in such a complex pattern with that many intersects and overlaps as shown in Figure 58. For example, overlaps exist between ESF 6 (Mass Care, Housing, and Human Services) and ESF 11 (Agriculture and Natural Resources), which also takes care of Food safety and security. Functions though have to be clearly designated. Regarding the disaster cycle, shown in Figure 38, the HHMS departments and agencies have different timelines and definitions of it, such that overlaps of System 1 (implementation) activities cannot be avoided. A firm System 2 (coordination) definition is needed for the schedule of disaster management activities. Either additional Channel Capacity and Transduction is needed at those intersections amplifying the internal Variety to match the own organization's Variety – which does not make sense because an organization should not proliferate its own Variety unnecessarily –, or a minimization of element interaction would lead to more effectiveness – that is the cybernetician's intention.

Interconnectedness, often proclaimed as the solution to complex problems, is too high – cybernetics gets at the right way and level of interconnections. With that many interwoven elements just described, the Variety explosion becomes quite evident. Take 15 ESFs alone. Those have 15 times 14 relationships with each other, a total of 210. If only assuming a binary situation here – that those relationships are either good or bad – we are dealing with 2^{210}=xxx relationships. Instead of controlling this immense complexity, the elements are left alone to deal with them on the go, and that also in a catastrophic disaster situation. That it will fail is more than clear. A Variety Engineering exercise on a grand scale would help identifying functions needed and then distribute them in orderly manner to units needed. That would establish Requisite Variety consciously. This can be accomplished in a Variety Engineering workshop series (see Figure 64 later in chapter 3.3.4).

Cybernetics also recognizes this circumstance as a System 2 (coordination) oscillatory problem because the ESF structure overlaps with responsibilities and functions of the personnel within the JFO structure. Further, Channel Capacity and Transduction are at risk and become hard to accomplish, especially when NIMS training for personnel is not accomplished as of now. As mentioned before as a problem within the NIMS application (see chapter 3.2.3), the different languages of governmental, non-governmental and military personnel and ruling concepts, such as consensus-based vs. command-and-control-based are the reality of this failure.

After having elaborated on the VSM diagnosis of both viewpoints, the NIMS framework on Level of Recursion 1 and the JFO structure on Level of Recursion 2, an overall summary of this detailed VSM application will be given. The status of the HHMS regarding the presence of all VSM Systems will be summarized and structural advantages and disadvantages explained under cybernetic aspects. Then, the VSM will be compared to the NIMS framework in a short structural analysis, the weaknesses of the NIMS framework investigated and finally the question will be answered, if the HHMS is a Viable System in Beers sense.

3.2.5 Complete summary of the Viable System Model application

The VSM demonstrates how complex systems maintain internal stability in the case of external disturbance, such as a hurricane event. Cybernetic laws prescribe how a set of five subsystems has to be designed through recursive structures and how complexity is managed holistically. By developing indicators of organizational effectiveness and indices of performance, as demonstrated later, the subsystems' feedback and communication loops can be designed to function most effectively and efficiently. These feedback loops are crucial for the best control of all disaster management activities. Overall, all system elements prescribed by the VSM are in place for the HHMS. However, existence alone is not sufficient, the quality is crucial. Moreover, the processes between the system elements also determine the viability of the system just as much. Those processes will be discussed in chapter 3.3. In the following, a summary of the structural deficiencies and redesign suggestions are given.

Overall, a specific application of National Incident Management System (NIMS) for the State of Hawai'i does not exist, with the argument that it will be developed as the incident occurs [Gilbert, 2007a]. This is a significant deficiency of the System 4 (intelligence) function. The case of Hurricane Katrina in 2005 where NIMS was applied and actively used provides some realistic examples for potential systemic deficiencies: on the ground, Louisiana was constituted of many under-resourced System 1s (implementation) that were unable to communicate sufficiently with each other and which had almost no support from Systems 2 (coordination) through 5 (identity). The System 2 (coordination) to 5 (identity) functions which did exist were out of touch with each other and incapable of deploying resources [Leonard, 2006]. Likewise, the State of Hawai'i will also be overwhelmed fast. The Fire and Police Departments disintegrated in New Orleans, as is probable in Hawai'i. The Public Works Department responsible for debris removal faces the same outlook, as well as Emergency Medical Services (EMS), Search and Rescue and the infrastructure of all ports and the power production [Rosenberg, 2007a]. Even worse, there is no on-island debris management infrastructure; therefore this will have to be sent out to Hawai'i pre-landfall. As of writing of this dissertation, no plans for pre-staging necessary for a catastrophic hurricane such as Katrina was in place.

In New Orleans, increased negative impacts resulted from the long years of apathy, the lack of city level capabilities and hence the inability of state and federal levels to rely on city level initiative. The System in VSM terms was literally dead. If the O'ahu Department of Emergency Management (DEM) should also fail, Hawai'i State Civil Defense (SCD) will be equally helpless. SCD cannot support agencies that are incapable to help themselves or only making demands. It can coordinate trucks, but cannot dig out the victims. It cannot help the Honolulu Police Department if it does not exist, as happened in New Orleans. Even if it has resources, if there is no structure to plug them into, the system will fail, as seen during Hurricane Katrina. In contrary, in the earthquake of October 2006, SCD helped agencies that were already able to help themselves. In sum, to avoid the disconnection between the federal and the county levels, strong interconnections of the Levels of Recursions are needed. The Federal Emergency Management Agency (FEMA) needs a structure to plug into [Richards and Tengan, 2007] and so does the State Civil Defense (SCD). The Viable System Model can show the tweaks and drivers regarding how to provide a functioning structure where the resources available can be used most effectively and efficiently.

Structural advantages and disadvantages under cybernetic aspects

The importance of certain elements on different Levels of Recursions changes over time, such as the emergence and demobilization of the Joint Field Office (JFO) or the Emergency Support Functions (ESFs). First-responders, such as the Honolulu Fire Department (HFD), the Honolulu Police Department (HFD) or the Emergency Medical Services (EMS), have a different 'life span' than personnel of the American Red Cross, who take care of sheltering, mass care, reconstruction or psychological services [Richards and Tengan, 2007]. The viability requirements on the lower Levels of Recursion vary therefore. Still, the System's viability depends on the liveliness of all Levels of Recursions. Structurally, the recursive and redundant structure of the Incident Command System (ICS) is a cybernetic plus, but since it is mixed with hierarchical and complex setups, it risks these viable aspects.

A complete analysis of all Viable System functions revealed that all system elements are in place, but that the balance, quality and importance of some need adjustments. Most importantly, it became obvious, that effectiveness can be enhanced through the VSM suggestions without more funding opportunities. Due to the hibernation of parts of the HHMS it is helpful to make comments on all Levels of Recursion 1 to 4 depicted in Table 8, but not all Levels of Recursion could be considered in the structural diagnosis with the same detail due to data availability and time constraints.

System 1 (implementation)

Structurally, all necessary System 1 (implementation) activities are present, but adjustments are needed. The System 1s (implementation) of all Recursions are designed to be viable, but due to practical system deficiencies they are allowed to fall into a coma because Recursion 1 and 2 only become fully active only when a catastrophic disaster strikes, instead of being exercised and practiced all year round. The annual Makani Pahili hurricane exercise is not sufficient for this purpose. This is a specific characteristic of a hibernating system.

On Recursion 3, the single departments and agencies of Recursion 4 represent the System 1s (implementation) and are organized as Emergency Support Functions (ESFs). The problem here is that the ESFs are organized in 15 segments which violates VSM rules prescribing seven (plus/minus two) System 1 (implementation) elements. This degenerates the HHMS into a non-viable form because System 3 (operational control) cannot cope with that Variety in an effective way. Therefore a different subsumption would be necessary to limit the number to eight ESFs; or one could add another Level of Recursion. Further, on Level of Recursion 3, synergies are needed along the System 1 (implementation) squiggly lines, in-between the ESFs, so that the different levels of government do not work in isolation. A common ground of expectation and appreciation between State of Hawai'i and federal level is needed as well as a single game plan [Breakout Session Infrastructure, 2007]. Keeping lively System 1 (implementation) squiggly lines means understanding each other's capabilities and limitations at all government levels as well as in the private sectors. A Syntegration would be one highly effective solution for this multi-stakeholder problem solving need [Beer, 1994b], of which an excerpt will be given later.

On Recursion 2, the ESFs are subsumed within the governmental EOCs: the county and state EOC, and the JFO, the federal EOC. Five Incident Command Posts in the HHMS are represented as Area Command Posts (ACPs). This division of O'ahu into five elements (ACPs) goes in accordance with cybernetic laws, which prescribe that the number of operational systems should be between five and nine [Beer, 1985]. Beer favors decentralization by territory, but only under the condition that each territory is an autonomous System 1 (implementation) [Beer, 1989b]. Only when System Cohesion is in danger should System 1 (implementation) autonomy be restricted. This is not always guaranteed in the Hurricane Hazard Management System (HHMS), e.g. the Preliminary Damage Assessments (PDAs) and Rapid Needs Assessments (RNAs) impinge too far on this essential characteristic.

Recursion 1, the federal NIMS Level, where all JFOs are be located, is cybernetically sound, since for O'ahu, only one JFO is planned. A second could be located on the Big Island, which still would not exceed the VSM prescribed number of eight.

In Japan, even though the earthquake risks are among the highest on the Pacific Rim of Fire, a nuclear disaster occurring simultaneously was seemingly not accounted for. The Fukushima Plant was built on the ocean without proper protection for the tsunami-type possible for this region, which includes building codes. Protection would have included a high level of training of disaster personnel and fast resource allocation capabilities, specifically energy and water. Reality shows currently the gaps in the lower level Recursions. Still, due to the frequent occurrence of earthquakes in Japan, the System 1s (implementation) are functioning more effective and efficient than in Hawai'i for a similar scenario overall. The System 2 (coordination) was not prepared though, a missing System 4 (intelligence) factor.

System 2 (coordination)

System 2 (coordination) deals with problems between the System 1s (implementation) and between all system elements. It provides for conflict resolution and stability. However, at the time of the study, System 2 (coordination) was missing in large part because the State of Hawai'i did not have an Incident Command System (ICS) plan, and HHMS personnel were not trained or applying ICS. This persists mainly due to a lack of full HSEEP implementation, where program evaluation is missing, a System 3* (audit) failure. The exercises are only evaluated internally by each department or agency. Further, those evaluations are not tied to the Resource Bargain between System 1 and 3. Unchecked, the exercises are often a voluntary part for many HHMS actors and are not taken serious. Imagine if the Japan Tsunami of March 10th 2011 would have arrived in Hawai'i: the evacuation ran smoothly, but the disaster after the disaster would have been catastrophic. Even though no deaths would have occurred due to the natural disaster, the human tragedy in the aftermath would have been tremendous with no plan for order of evacuation, without harbor facilities to support the population of over a million on Oah'u alone and Honolulu International Airport out of service. Most military airports lie also in the ocean's proximity. Given those constraints on physical infrastructure, it is absolutely mandatory and even more important to have the elements still in place working effectively and efficiently ensuring smooth processes. This regards specifically information and communication.

As stated before, the lack of training lies partially in the fact that the HHMS is only activated in catastrophic events and ICS is rarely used. The ICS functions on a small scale in local events, but in catastrophic events the integration of all governmental levels becomes difficult, especially if the single elements are unsure of how to play their parts. Problems stated by governmental officials are 1) the clear distinction of roles and responsibilities, which would be set up within the System 2 (coordination) and controlled by System 3 (operational control) and 2) the fact that personnel do not follow or are not trained in the Incident Command System (ICS). A federal official stated that, while NIMS training before hurricane Katrina in 2005 existed, the state and local leadership was not trained [Latham, 2007]. During 'Iniki in 1992, when helicopters were in the air, it was not clear who was responsible for them. Personnel were only reacting to events instead of taking control and using ICS principles [Richards, 2007f]. In times of stress, this system is highly likely to fall apart. 'Rapid homeland security mission expansion and the diversity of risks outpaced planning, and planning actions have outstripped planning documentation' [U.S. DHS, 2006b, p.xii] – Requisite Variety cannot be met. System 2 (coordination) – the documentation – is overwhelmed by the actions that are induced to counterbalance the Variety explosion.

Evidence of missing System 2 (coordination), in essence not knowing their roles and responsibilities, can be illustrated by those examples from Hurricane Katrina: In the evacuation process during the Hurricane Katrina event in 2005, agencies and organizations, including the American Red Cross, were often unaware of their responsibilities for such critical matters as facilitating long-term housing [ICCMA, 2006]. Nongovernmental organizations (NGOs), such as the Red Cross and the Salvation Army, play key roles in providing basic necessities to survivors. But if their responsibilities and reporting relationships are not clearly defined and managed, and if they don't have the funding to accomplish their objectives, they become ineffectual. This is a case where increased effectiveness is possible without more funding. Some, but not all, of the slow response to Katrina resulted from confusion about what qualifies as an 'Incident of National Significance' (INS) and in what form a request for federal assistance must be presented [ICCMA, 2006], a missing System 2 (coordination) case. Another challenge arose at the state level because state emergency managers in Louisiana and Mississippi were flooded with requests for help as well as with offers of assistance. The EMAC pipeline soon became backlogged due to lack of capacity to process requests [ICCMA, 2006], in cybernetic terms due to the incapability of proper System 2 (coordination) functioning. Modern Information Technology can easily handle this.

Some of the local government teams that received authorization to assist did not have the most targeted experience, a missing System 2 (coordination) element, e.g. training. And it took three weeks for some cities to receive any assistance, even though local governments that were prepared to help made heroic efforts to get teams into the region sooner. A proper System 2 (coordination) would not have bureaucratic restrictions in the way of effective functioning.

On Level of Recursion 4, System 2 (coordination) consists of System 1 (implementation) members who do mostly their own System 2 (coordination) activities in isolation from other departments and agencies. For example, the Civil Defense Coordinator of a department puts together the folder in which all of the requirements for a departmental disaster plan are set down. But without a higher-level System 2 (coordination) cooperation between and among other departments and agencies becomes more complicated within the HHMS, specifically if it is just on a voluntary basis and based on good-will instead of being controlled by a proper System 3 (operational control) setup.

Oscillations between System 1s (implementation) on all Levels of Recursion are plentiful: between the departments and agencies, between the Emergency Support Functions (ESFs) and the Area Command Posts (ACPs). Whose job is it to deal with conflict of interests between S1s? One participant at the RISC conference said: "Well, we are all doing something with our best intent, but if that adds up to disaster management, I don't know". The annual Makani Pahili exercise certainly does not provide the Cohesive Glue for the System to stick together and create the synergies and anti-oscillatory requirement between the System 1s (implementation). The necessity of having a problem exercise and implement ICS on a more frequent – ideally monthly – basis is clear. Again, a Syntegration is able to handle this complexity and can get the Variety exposed to the system into a manageable range. As mentioned before, according to the National Response Plan (NRP), only agencies receiving FEMA funds have to comply with NIMS, independent organizations do not. Consequently, their System 2 (coordination) on Level of Recursion 4 differs from governmental entities and inefficiencies emerge.

In sum, a large part of the System 2 (coordination) requires implementation of the NIMS framework and the National Response Plan (NRP). Both documents have to be a part of the HHMS's culture and have to be internalized, in cybernetic terms transduced, effectively. Channel Capacity needs to be appropriate for this process through training and certification standards. State Civil Defense (SCD) officials stated that, since the NIMS introduction, new concepts and language is used, but that they 'work like before' [Richards and Tengan, 2007]. A major problem. The Concept of Operations (CONOP) for a catastrophic hurricane impacting the State of Hawai'i draft still needs a lot of work [Rosenberg, 2007b] and Variety Engineering needs to be taken care of: workshops and concluding implementation of results are practiced by Malik Management Center Sankt Gallen, but publication of their consulting work is not available currently (also see Figure 64 in chapter 3.3.4).

Because it has that many implications, the System 2 (coordination) is analyzed here in more detail. First of all, 'the National Incident Management System (NIMS) provides a set of standardized organizational structures – such as the ICS, multiagency coordination systems, and public information systems – as well as requirements for processes, procedures, and systems designed to improve interoperability among jurisdictions and disciplines in various areas' [U.S. DHS, 2004a, p. 2] that is mandatory down to the local level. The Incident Command System (ICS) follows certain noteworthy principles [U.S. DHS, 2004a]: Most incidents are managed locally ensuring that System 1 (implementation) autonomy is preserved as prescribed by the Viable System Model (VSM). Hence, System 1 (implementation) autonomy is ensured on all Levels of Recursion, a cybernetically necessary condition. Further, 'the Incident Command System (ICS) is modular and scalable' [U.S. DHS, 2004a] and the 'ICS organizational structure develops in a top-down, modular fashion that is based on the size and complexity of the incident, as well as the specifics of the hazard Environment created by the incident. As incident complexity increases, the organization expands from the top down as functional responsibilities are delegated' [Emergency Management Institute, 2007b]. Being modular does not reject VSM principles, but the top-down, hierarchical approach is not cybernetically sound. If a hierarchical structure such as the ICS can extend arbitrarily, it risks the system's Cohesion. Additionally, the 'Chain of Command' approach establishes an orderly line of authority within the ranks of the organization, with lower levels subordinate to, and connected to, higher levels. Again, this hierarchical character is against VSM principles. The 'Unity of Command' approach means that every individual is accountable to only one designated supervisor to whom they report at the scene of an incident [U.S. DHS, 2004a, p. 10]. But what is needed, in contrary, is the focus of organization on the establishment ensuring necessary and sufficient viable functions, not a hierarchical structure. Consequently, the Resource Bargain and Accountability Loop stretch too far along too many connection points and causes the Metasystem to dive too deep into the System 1s (implementation) through different Levels of Recursion. Command should be limited to a great extend to one Level of Recursion.

On the positive side, the fact that the ICS 'should have a scalable organizational structure that is based on the size and complexity of the incident' [U.S. DHS, 2004a, p. 8] ensures that a flexible Hurricane Hazard Management System (HHMS) can adjust to a fast changing Environment. Overall, this design is cybernetically sound, but without System 2 (coordination) implementation, System Cohesion is potentially lost and the system too easily flies apart. 'The Incident Command System (ICS) incorporates Measurable Objectives' and 'Measurable objectives ensure fulfillment of incident management goals' [U.S. DHS, 2004a, p. 9]. But the devil lies in the detail: many organizations measure many different things in many ways – its coordination and implementation fails due to problems explained throughout this exploration.

It sounds ambitious when 'the Implementation of the Incident Command System (ICS) should have the least possible disruption on existing systems and processes' [U.S. DHS, 2004a], when it lacks deeper thinking. Important aspects of this coordination are not facilitated and are in reality a big obstacle to resource effectiveness and efficiency. 'This will facilitate its acceptance across a nationwide user community and to ensure continuity in the transition process from normal operations. ICS should be user friendly and be applicable across a wide spectrum of emergency response and incident management disciplines' [U.S. DHS, 2004a, p. 9]. Assuming that training is sufficient, a not necessarily valid assumption, this requirement would ensure that System 2 (coordination) did not fail. In order to make this a valid assumption, strong control mechanisms along the System 3* (audits) channel are needed, but are missing. Whenever these audit channels are missing, all hibernating systems, in general, and the HHMS, in particular, are at great risk of failure.

A System 2 (coordination) element ensuring Transduction and Channel Capacity is the Incident Action Plans (IAPs), which provide a coherent means of communicating the overall incident objectives in the contexts of both operational and support activities' [U.S. DHS, 2004a, p. 10]. The 'Span of control' principle stating that any individual with incident management supervisory responsibility should have three to seven subordinates [U.S. DHS, 2004a, p. 10] agrees with VMS concepts. It is stated that 'maintaining an accurate and up-to-date picture of resource utilization is a critical component of domestic incident management' [U.S. DHS, 2004a, p. 11] emphasizing real-time management but in exploring that system there were no effective means detected that would ensure it. The idea might be set on paper but is not realized. Integrated communications is based on a common communications plan and interoperable communications processes and architectures. Again, the lack of implementation and audits causes major systemic deficiencies.

The strongest and most effective part of the System 2 (coordination) is the local 'State of Emergency' proclamation – the legal declaration that authorizes extraordinary measures to meet emergencies. It has the force of law and supersedes any conflicting law. Pre-scripted Hurricane and Tropical storm Watch and Warning announcements exist [Department of Planning and Permitting, 2007]. HSPD-8 reinforces the provisions of the Stafford Act, a major System 2 (coordination) element. The President 'may direct any federal agency, with or without reimbursement, to utilize its authorities and the resources granted to it under federal law (including personnel, equipment, supplies, facilities, and managerial, technical, and advisory services) in support of state and local assistance efforts…'[The White House, 2003a]. FEMA has adopted proactive actions in 'FEMA's Concept of Operations (CONOP) for a catastrophic hurricane impacting the state of Hawai'i [Hawai'i State Civil Defense, 2007a, p.16]. To save time, pre-scripted mission assignments in cooperation with other agencies (ACE, CG, DoD) are increased, and paperwork, contracts and approvals are pre-scripted, so that ultimately only the final signature is needed for implementation [Fenton, 2007]. Further, a 'credentializing system' reflects Variety attenuation through System 2 (coordination) elements. It increases System 1 (implementation) integration by ensuring its autonomy in choosing appropriate personnel criteria. On paper, System Cohesion is kept; a measuring system is put in place, identity guaranteed, Channel Capacity and Transduction are all designed effectively.

Moreover, a specific System 2 (coordination) exception for the State of Hawai'i are the pre-landfall federal disaster declarations. Usually, FEMA processes a Governor's request for Presidential disaster or emergency declarations under the direction provided in the Stafford Act [U.S. DHS, 2007b]. Governors submit these requests to FEMA indicating the extent of damage and the types of federal assistance required [U.S. DHS, 2004b]. Hawai'i is exempt from these regulations of the federal Disaster Declaration process due to its extraordinary risk to catastrophic impacts in the face of a major hurricane [U.S. DHS, 2004b]. As a result, the Joint Field Office (JFO) stands up pre-landfall in Hawai'i even without a pre-landfall federal Disaster Declaration and the Federal Emergency Management Agency (FEMA) can pre-position assets pre-landfall [Breakout Session Infrastructure, 2007]. These are all steps in the right direction.

But, 'red tape' poses a major obstacle for effectiveness and consequently System 2 (coordination) elements are often incapacitated by law in *extreme circumstances*. Since those are not clearly defined System 2 (coordination) experiences heavy oscillations in Variety. A coordination example: NRP rules reaffirm that personnel and equipment should respond only when requested or when dispatched by an appropriate authority [Emergency Management Institute, 2007b]. Paradoxically, standard procedures regarding requests for assistance may be expedited or, under *extreme circumstances*, suspended in the immediate aftermath of an event of catastrophic magnitude. The NRP dictates that identified federal response resources should deploy and begin necessary operations as required to commence life-safety activities. Notification and full coordination with States should occur and the coordination process should not delay or impede the rapid deployment and use of critical resources [U.S. DHS, 2004b]. In real-life disaster situations it might look like this: The situation of people in acute risk of drowning in a flood prompts a disaster manager to order a helicopter right away without having the time to get through the procedures of ordering one, all red tape can be cut this way. When five minutes later it this helicopter is ordered by a senior unit, it is not available. The problem for the individual disaster manager is posed by the NRP stating that hierarchy has to be followed and could under certain circumstances have legal implications.

System 3 (operational control) and System 3* (audits)

In Hawai'i, System 3 (operational control) on Recursion 1 is in good standing since it looks for synergies and optimization: Joint education, research and development are in place and the Federal Emergency Management Agency (FEMA) has a training center with online courses. On Recursion 2, the Emergency Support Functions (ESFs) are distributed all over the Joint Field Office (JFO) and coordinated and centralized there showing a functioning System 3 (operational control), but only when activated. This hibernation causes control problems and the Metasystem becomes comatic during non-hurricane season. The JFO would have to be in place on a more regular basis because the ESFs departments and agencies are their own autonomous elements on Level of Recursion 3, which is cybernetically important, but in their roles on Recursion 2 need to be controlled by a sound and active System 3 (operational control) and System 3* (audits).

On Recursion 2 and 3, System 3 (operational control) is too weak to work properly in a cybernetic sense. The Makani Pahili exercised 2007 showed that information about the status regarding training, availability of resources and overall capabilities of the ESFs does not come in from a large enough Variety of resources and the Department of Emergency Management (DEM) and the State Civil Defense (SCD) have no synoptic view over that situation and its status quo, which the System 3 (operational control) function would require cybernetically. Since training is not required throughout the whole HHMS, the necessary audits are basically voluntary and System 2 (coordination) is in place on paper, but not implemented and both System 3 functions are hindered to develop properly. Overall, neither the annual exercises nor the summarized reports from the ESFs are cybernetically sufficient. It became clear in informal conversations that System 3 (operational control) of Recursion 2 that the SCD competes for the System 1 (implementation), the ESF's, interest in obtaining funding and complying with NIMS. So, in this case, the System 1s (implementation) have excessive autonomy in the HHMS and the single departments' and agencies' activity level and ambition in NIMS compliance other than on paper is not in check. The VSM helps here to find balance – freedom that is – regarding the best degree of autonomy without impinging too much on necessary freedom to be able to react to an ever-changing Environment.

On Recursion 3, the many interconnections with the private sector are problematic because this sector are not required to comply with National Response Plan (NRP) and the National Incident Management System (NIMS) standards and is therefore not a compatible system. Ensuring Transduction and Channel Capacity in System 2 (coordination) terms would be of high importance to minimize oscillations. Synergies are found during the Makani Pahili conferences and exercise, but the annual cycle is too long to ensure System Cohesion and System 2 (coordination) functioning. Overall, System 3 (operational control) is not alive and working well yet mainly due to System 2 (coordination) inefficiencies. Training and reports would have to happen in a more controlled manner on a shorter-time basis and incentives for the private sector to cooperate would be highly necessary. Cybernetic points out the importance of these steps.

On the other hand, the Metasystem of Recursion 1 has overdone the use of Central Command. The Metasystem operates at a fairly detailed level limiting its capacity to deal with strategic issues decreasing the system's effectiveness. Monitoring needs to happen on the right Level of Recursion between System 3 (operational control) and 1 (implementation), but if several Levels of Recursion are monitored, the intrusion of System 1 (implementation) autonomy will cost effectiveness of the whole. In the HHMS, the Preliminary Damage Assessments (PDA) and Rapid Need Assessments (RNA) are a sound concept as System 3* (audits), but the Channel Capacity and Transduction form loops through several Levels of Recursion interfering with Levels too far down. The effects on System 2 (coordination) were discussed in detail sufficiently before.

System 3 (operational control) should also check on connections between System 1s (implementation) (the ESFs in this case) and make sure that information lags and communications failures will not occur, which is not accomplished on any Level of Recursion of the HHMS. 'Collaboration requirements are not well-defined, fostering a tendency to plan internally' [U.S. DHS, 2006b, p. xii], which points towards a System 3 (operational control) failing to look for synergies between the System 1s (implementation) with the consequence of the System 1s (implementation) working in isolation. The System 1 (implementation) squiggly lines are not alive. 'The prevailing approach to planning emphasizes general roles and responsibilities over detailed procedures for specific hazards, scenarios, or thresholds of incidents' [U.S. DHS, 2006b, p. xii], but it needs to be emphasized that synergies are desirable as long as the roles and responsibilities are clear and the same task is not accomplished by several entities. On all Levels of Recursion, the System needs ways of generating synergy between the System 1s (implementation) to reduce the effect of self interest (boredom, disinterest, second job attitude) creating variances from the purpose of the system as a whole. Further, System 3 (operational control) intervention is weak and consequently there is no function to react to a falling apart of the whole organization.

With regards to communications, System 3* (audits) does not function, since it does not check on communication capabilities periodically. For example, the technical incompatibility of Web-EOC and e-Team is well known, but not resolved. Here, the system is not in a Metasystemic Calm, but dead. On this Recursion 2, the DEM and the SCD let the HHMS fall asleep, since System 3* (audits) are missing. Further, the control mechanism of System 3* (audits) needs to be an openly declared mechanism and a message of caring should be imposed so that defensive behaviors can be avoided. These conditions are partially present in the HHMS, specifically in Hawai'i where good inter-personal relationships are common [Richards and Tengan, 2007].

In Japan, frequent earthquakes give a perfect System 3* (audit) opportunity. The System is more conscious of itself than in Hawai'i, is better practiced but also shows a missing System 4 (intelligence) function regarding planning for a multi-scale event. In Hawai'i, the System 3* (audits) is present on Recursion 1 and 2, but since part of the HHMS is hibernating and not practiced sufficiently problems arise in the interaction between System 3 and other elements, the processes within HHMS: System 3 (operational control) has three communication channels with System 1 (implementation): the operational monitoring channel via System 3* (audits), the Command Channel along the Resource Bargain and the Accountability Loop and the anti-oscillation channel of System 2 (coordination). Those are discussed in C3.

System 4 (intelligence)

System 4 (intelligence) monitors changes of the external Environment and is responsible for adaptation and future planning. Planning budgets are often too tight and changes in resource allocation on Recursion 1, the federal level, also adjusting the System 5 (identity) and 2 (coordination) in that regard are needed so it can seep through the system. Here, efficiency can be enhanced despite the financial constraints. Most important, the lack of elaboration of the National Incident Management System (NIMS) application in Hawai'i down to the Area Command Post (ACP) level arguing that it can only be employed on a case-by-case basis is a source of non-viability. This weak System 4 (intelligence) needs healing by more frequent training and scenario applications to make the system as a whole fit to react to a fast changing Environment.

Observing the developments in Japan in March 2011 one might wonder if the maps of the Japanese nuclear power plants and earthquake probabilities ever been looked at – here the System 4 (intelligence) simply did a bad job – but why? It leads us to assume that their system's focus obviously was maximizing profits by conveniently overlooking safety concerns and measures instead of watching out for the overall system survival and viability, the core of VSM thinking. Unfortunately, the Japanese population has to pay the price for this unviable behavior. In a bionic and cybernetic sense, nature will get itself into balance; also if that means unviable elements will be eliminated. On the long run, natural laws will insert themselves in any given way unless designed effectively – for human kind's purposes.

The findings of the Nationwide Plan Review [U.S. DHS, 2006b] show that catastrophic planning efforts are unsystematic and uneven [U.S. DHS, 2006b, p. xii]. 'Planning processes are outmoded, current tools and guidance are rudimentary, and planning expertise is insufficient for catastrophic incidents' [U.S. DHS, 2006b, p. xii]. System 2 (coordination) and 4 (intelligence) are overwhelmed by the environmental Variety explosions. Real-time is not possible to process. As also stated in interviews repeatedly, NIMS has not been trained enough throughout all governmental levels. The training of personnel needs to be tightened in terms of System 2 (coordination), so that Channel Capacity and Transduction can function properly.

In sum, System 4 (intelligence) hardly exists for the Hurricane Hazard Management System (HHMS). On Recursion 1, the Federal Emergency Management Agency (FEMA) just started preparing the State of Hawai'i CONOP in 2007. It was at a draft level for the May 2007 Makani Pahili exercise. System 4 (intelligence) tasks performed are engaging in simulations and exploring different risks constituted of the National Weather Service (NWS), the Army Corps of Engineers and the NIMS training development by FEMA, for example. The NWS establishes the connection from System 3 (operational control) to the envelope Environment and represents System 4 (intelligence) regarding observations of climate change and implications of enhanced hurricane risks to Hawai'i over the long term. Strategic information from System 4 (intelligence) feeds into System 5 (identity), the policy system, which provides the vision of the system as a whole. For example, if hurricane risk increases due to climate change it will be on the NWS's monitor. But, holistic monitoring of the envelope Environment as identified by the vulnerability analysis is missing and emerging new vulnerabilities are not identified as they occur or even recognized, and if so often ignored due to the overwhelming complexity threatening O'ahu's viability. Some simulations are conducted and will be implemented in the planning process, but are not all-encompassing.

On Recursion 4 – the ESFs – the balancing of internal optimization and future plans – the System 3–4 homeostat – should be monitored by System 5 (identity). Currently that hibernating system has to be ensured on a constant basis. System 4 (intelligence) could be promoted on this Recursion as self-training and personal learning to improve effectiveness. Tests have to be mandatory though and maybe even linked to promotion to ensure their fulfillment, and not on a voluntary basis as of now. Or, incentives would be needed for this to occur. Cybernetically, the notion of Environment – the disaster scenario – must contain a regulatory model of the range of possible futures, a part of the vulnerability analysis. On Level of Recursion 2, these tasks would be taken over by the governmental EOCs that should stand up regularly during the year, not only once for the Makani Pahili exercise. On Level of Recursion 1, the HSEEP, as mentioned before, needs full implementation. This way, the HHMS could have the necessary and sufficient System 4 (intelligence) to become viable.

System 4 (intelligence) could promote its viability through an approach that Ackoff [1981] advanced: the idealized design. It invites one to envisage an organization as idealized without constraints and aids in rethinking the conditions and outcomes of dropping those constraints. The media could affect System 4 (intelligence) in a major way through influencing public risk perception and consequently public behavior on the long run, and so would educational programs of any kind. 'Help people that know how to help themselves' [Richards, 2007f].

Overall, some System 4 (intelligence) elements are in place, but only sporadic bursts of activity occur when the need becomes obvious. Politically charged activities will change perspectives once it is clearly communicated that survival is at the core, not maximizing short-sighted financial profits. Resources are lacking for a firm System 4 (intelligence) establishment, but an increase in effectiveness and efficiency as well as knowledge transfer and dispersion could improve the situation without more financial investment. A Syntegration would be of great effect in all resource regards and will be explained in chapter 3.3.10. It can also focus the given financial resources to a maximum effective and efficient extent to plan for the future uncertainties.

System 5 (identity)

A Viable System needs a commonly understood vision and identity for effective coordination. Culture and identity, System 5 (identity) elements, are powerful and necessary attenuators of Variety [Leonard, 1999]. System 5 (identity) is the ultimate authority, the policy provider and establisher of ground rules and identity. The HHMS has a strong self-awareness and focus given by the nature of the purpose of its organization – first, to save lives, and second, to protect property and assets. Hawai'i specifically has a strong System 5 (identity) based on its culture of the 'Aloha spirit'. It exhibits a very participatory approach where System 5 (identity) guarantees System 1 (implementation) autonomy. For example, a new ESF was created for special needs victims when the need was voiced [Fenton, 2007]. Mr. Teixeira, the State Civil Defense Vice Director, said 99 % of the county, state and federal departments and agencies involved in response efforts here understand 'how the system works'. Consequently, people would not be left dying due to red tape [Honolulu Advertiser, 2005b]. He showed a high level of trust in the HHMS personnel knowing the HHMS's identity. Still, a more frequent interaction would be desirable to ensure a cybernetically sound System 5 (identity). By making a contribution once a year has to be seen as a limitation on the System 1 (implementation) involvement in System 5 (identity) matters.

Even though the Aloha Spirit seeps throughout the HHMS, difficulties of shared identity on Recursion 1 consists of the different cultural and therefore social settings in Hawai'i compared to the mainland – Hawai'i is a very diverse cultural melting pot, from Asian to Latin-American and European origins, and different social behavior is abound. Since many elements in the HHMS are federally led, this is an important factor. Due to Hawai'i's isolation long-term and well established relationships and trust are common on the local level, but can differ greatly from the Recursion 1, the federal level, viewpoints. Besides socio-cultural aspects, economic and environmental settings also vary from the US mainland – a capitalistic attitude is not necessarily welcome and environmental values are high. Even on Recursion 4, where the HHMS personnel from the US mainland and local staff work together, those differences play a role in understanding this identity.

Viable System Model framework vs. National Incident Management System (NIMS) framework

The major difference between the VSM and the NIMS framework is the non-hierarchical structure of the VSM. Authority is used only as a last resort because the laws of Variety evidence that System 1 (implementation) cannot be handled by the Metasystem competently. Therefore, System 1 (implementation) needs maximal autonomy without putting the system as a whole at risk. In contrast, the NIMS framework is clearly hierarchical. In such an organization, everybody waits for initiative and change from the top [Holmberg, 1989]. Self-initiative and spontaneous reaction to a fast-changing Environment is hindered, but it is facilitated by the VSM as an essential requirement for a system's survival. Due to the System 2 (coordination) lacking implementation, the high complexity of NIMS and ICS has no chance for Requisite Variety to be established. This is accelerated by the unmanageability of informal and intangible networks of individuals of a Variety of agencies. Channel Capacity and Transduction is lost in this unusual combination of management aspects.

Ultimately, a well-designed information system can be used as an alternative to authoritarian control. It can enhance self-managed, autonomous individuals. That being said, there is certainly a need to control along the Resource Bargain and Accountability Loop through System 3* (audits). During non-disaster times, when the Metasystemic Calm needs to be ensured, the State Civil Defense (SCD) has few means of ensuring that the System does not become unconscious and dies. The problem is excessive autonomy, for example DEM deciding on implementing SCD preparation and mitigation measures during non-disaster time. Only under a State or Federal Disaster Declaration is the DEM required by law to comply [Richards and Tengan, 2007]. To cite one control mechanism that is in place, 'The DEM Deputy Director will cite departments or agencies delinquent in complying with the provisions of this Plan' [City and County of Honolulu, 2007, p.18], which ensures those relations on Recursion 4. This function must be executed more forcefully on all Recursion Levels.

A thought to be explored would be to change the management style depending on the timeframe of the incident. A hierarchical command-and-control structure could be set for actions due to the need to act consistently and immediately. Later on in the response, an increasingly nonhierarchical, more democratic approach could provide closure to the incident. In general, the approach to be applied could depend on time. For example, decision-making could be consensus-based when more time is available and authoritarian when time is limited.

The 'command-and-control' approach has significant shortcomings and changes and recommendations for improvements in the intergovernmental system are suggested [ICCMA, 2006] based on a network-centered approach with flexibility to move resources and assets where needed. A network of personal relationships can help expedite response and recovery efforts. Many local governments found ways to get help into the Gulf Region after Hurricane Katrina through their personal relationships with individuals in the communities affected by the disaster [ICCMA, 2006]. This networked solution includes a technology platform that consists of (1) a comprehensive database of human and physical assets from the public, private, and nonprofit sectors available for emergency response and recovery efforts and (2) a geo-mapping tool to identify, select, activate, track, and manage response assets. The database would accommodate the organization of human and physical assets available for rapid deployment. Participating local governments would use the database to maintain information about the availability of people, equipment, and technology that could be called upon in a disaster. Equipment and materials not in use could be stored in accessible locations, such as available military base facilities, which are well suited for this function. The network of relationships would need to include the military officials who have been tasked with support to local governments in disaster situations. [ICCMA, 2006]. This would be a sound, non-hierarchical System 1 (implementation) setup.

Is the Hurricane Hazard Management System a Viable System a la Beer?

The military, governmental and private sector communication and structural identities clash (System 5), a Variety of jargons and approaches are used (System 2) and the system is not aligned due to a missing CONOP application (System 4). Overall, the impact of the lack of an interrelated national planning system, inadequate national guidance, and outmoded planning processes was best summed up by one Peer Review Team member: 'They are doing a lot of things, but they are not sure they add up to catastrophic planning' [U.S. DHS, 2006b, p. 5]. This clearly signals the need for cybernetics: the single systems are in place, but fine-tuning is missing, hence a holistic approach is needed, since the whole is more than the sum of its parts.

This system cannot produce itself and talk to itself clearly due to too many structural differences. The self-producing property (autopoiesis) of a Viable System fails due to the failure of its Cohesiveness, which could be achieved by (1) the balance of System 3–4 by strengthening of System 4 (intelligence); (2) a Hawaii-specific CONOP application down to the local level, a firm System 2 (coordination) establishment; and (3) a proactive Algedonic red-flag system throughout all Levels of Recursion warning about inefficiencies when they occur, in real-time.

In structural terms, the Incident Command System (ICS) is a Viable System in Beer's terms. When examining practical examples such as hurricane events in Florida and comparing those to Hurricane Katrina 2005 it seems obvious that the ICS worked in Florida, but did not work in Louisiana and Mississippi. The missing System 2 (coordination) link – training and real application on a frequent basis – makes the difference on all Levels of Recursion. So even if structurally sound, the VSM only approves systems ultimately if they also function and regulate Variety in regards to the processes between the system elements. The VSM is often viewed as a structuralist approach, which is not only but actually requires that the complexity is also managed effectively and efficiently in their interplay and over time. On a day-to-day basis, the HHMS departments and agencies accomplish their job, but due to a lack of System 2 (coordination) implementation through all Levels of Recursion, the HHMS cannot work as an integrated whole when disaster is imminent and is overall not viable due to structural deficiencies. The system goes into coma in Hawai'i and alarms don't sound at all. The System 2 (coordination) is overwhelming System 1 (implementation), since the National Incident Management System (NIMS) and National Response Plan (NRP) are confusing and hard to understand. The Channel Capacity is not established here leading to Transduction issues and ineffectiveness. No county, state or federal official knows how NIMS is applied to Hawai'i in detail. The Concept of Operations (CONOP) for a catastrophic hurricane impacting the state of Hawai'i is not more than a table of contents of one possible application. The system is not ready to wake up even if Algedonic Alarms would be set and even though many theoretical aspects fit cybernetic requirements.

The HHMS is not viable at this point in time. The specific structural shortcomings were discussed in this chapter. For each structural deficiency an Algedonic Alarm would sound. So far, the many alarms sounding would constitute a constant alarm signal for the HHMS. The hurricane hit would make the HHMS's non-viability evident in a huge Variety explosion. Besides the structure of a system, the VSM prescribes 'how' the structure should function. In the following, a detailed diagnosis of the processes within the HHMS and the aspect of time will be elaborated.

3.3 Diagnosis and redesign of the Hurricane Hazard Management processes

Once structural problems of viability are dealt with, the question must be are their interactions adequate? In C3 of Figure 39, we discuss the processes of the Hurricane Hazard Management System (HHMS) ensuring that the whole works in a holistic and integrated form. The quality of system relationships is just as important as the systemic structures.

Enhanced effectiveness can be designed by giving the System 1s (implementation) the right degree of autonomy – how much can an Emergency Operations Center allow their performing units to be independent? How is that best coordinated (the Homeostasis of the 'Inside and Now')? The balance with the external Environment and Variety Engineering, the art of management is then followed by an excerpt on information systems. The relating Channel Capacity and Transduction highly influence the efficiency of information. Just as much, if not more important are issues revolving around 'soft factors', which will be elaborated in detail in the last section.

3.3.1 Autonomy

A major reason for ineffectiveness and inefficiency is caused by hierarchical and strong top-down approaches impinging on System 1 (implementation) autonomy (C3 in Figure 39) which must be guaranteed by System 3 (operational control) on the respective Level of Recursion.

The first step generating homeostatic balance consists of giving the System 1 (implementation) as much autonomy as the Hurricane Hazard Management System (HHMS) can handle without degenerating into separate and isolated parts disintegrating and losing Cohesion. Viability is enhanced when the ground-level operations have the maximum amount of autonomy consistent with their purposes because any intervention from above sacrifices some of the Variety. To justify intervention, pressing reasons need to exist for incurring the opportunity costs of not fully utilizing the lower Level of Recursion's greater familiarity with the immediate situation. In usual business operations, often a manager is appointed who enforces and ensures that problems are dealt with. The VSM advises letting the operational elements act in a proactive way, which needs to be induced by System 5 (identity) throughout – an attitude communicated and cherished – creating a culture of proactivity. This freedom leads to self-organized motivation and fulfillment. This interaction concerns the System 3–1 interaction along the Resource Bargain, the Accountability Loop and the Command Axis. Further, System 3 (operational control) monitors System 1s' (implementation) performance through System 3* (audits) and needs performance indicators as structured accountability system. Forms are provided by the National Response Plan (NRP), the System 2 (coordination) element, to document the status of the System 1 (implementation) activities. Specifically here, the limits of autonomy must be defined clearly so that Cohesion is ensured and to avoid one System 1 (implementation) threatening the Viability of the whole. It would state: 'you are autonomous unless the following occurs…'. For example a certain size power-outage, people in trainings pass tests with a minimum average score of 1,5 and so on. This way, the Resource Bargain and Accountability Loop can be ensured and the Command Axis is activated only when necessary.

For the HHMS, autonomy is recognized as an essential element of an efficient organization as part of the ICS concepts and principles. Accountability is discharged using the forms necessary for the Incident Action Plan (IAP) process [U.S. DHS, 2006a], which serve as daily performance indicators. When the JFO is not activated, new time-line dependent indicators need to be designed that indicate a particular standard that needs to be maintained in order to confirm the viability of the system as a whole. At times, autonomy of System 1 (implementation) is too excessive. At the Federal Emergency Management Agency Regional Interagency Steering Committees (FEMA RISC) conference, the non-viable character of these conflicts was highlighted: 'You can't get a single bottle of water here with one person – it takes a lot of logistics' not one functional agency [Breakout Session Infrastructure, 2007]. The VSM prescription requires the individual System 1 (implementation) to give up some of their autonomy in the interests of coming together as a coherent whole.

Overall, the System 1s (implementation) of Recursion 4, the single governmental, non-governmental and private-sector organizations now work in isolation with only loose cooperative links in the form of the annual preparatory conferences for the Makani Pahili exercise. System Cohesion is therefore lost. Coordination between them should be a System 3 (operational control) task. Ideally, the County and State Civil Defense, acting as a System 3 (operational control), should look for more synergies more often and give incentives to promote them.

3.3.2 The Homeostasis of the 'Inside and Now'

The 'Inside and Now' concerns System 3–2–1 as stabilizing and optimizing elements (see C3 in Figure 39). Instabilities are expressed by conflict, competition for resources, confusion and overlaps of tasks. The ideal design for those kinds of problems is to engineer Variety so that the environmental complexity, e.g. water and power systems requirements, that System 1 (implementation), some governmental and private entities, has to handle is compensated and balanced by the complexity of System 2 (coordination) and 3 (operational control). The complexity affecting System 1 (implementation) and the capabilities of System 2 (coordination) and 3 (operational control) need to be balanced by letting the System 1 (implementation) deal with as many problems as they can and increasing the capabilities of Systems 2 (coordination) and 3 (operational control) to let them deal with the remaining Variety competently [Walker, 2001]. Variety Engineering is treated in chapter 3.3.4 in more detail. How to deal with the human-induced difficulties is elaborated in the last chapter of this part (3.3.10). Self-organization is implemented here. Effective System 2 (coordination) would be, as stated before, clear terms, roles and responsibilities. In Hawai'i, this is not guaranteed: the IT capabilities do not match, departments use different damage assessment forms and divide the islands by different standards on their maps. A lot of effectiveness and efficiency is lost and the remaining financial resources could have a much better outcome. Instead, everybody is complaining about insufficient funding and ignores the fact that there is a lot of unused, tacit resources within the system. You just have to access it, and the Viable System leads one to those treasures showing their importance.

Further, tasks of the 'Inside and Now' are to gather information and pass it on to the Metasystem so that it can react to instabilities and send an Algedonic Alarm through the system. As a possible reaction, the higher Recursion can divert available assets (water, power) to areas in need.

Overall, there are six interactive elements: three Variety connections in the vertical plane of the local management, operations and Environment domains and three Variety connections along the Metasystemic intervention of System 3 (operational control), the operational monitoring channels of System 3* (audits) and the anti-oscillatory channels of System 2 (coordination). Figure 59 [reproduced from Walker, 2001] shows the environmental intersects (C1), audits and surveys as System 3* (audits) (C2), the

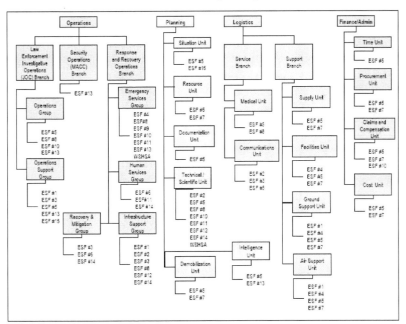

Figure 58: The Emergency Support Functions' (ESFs) positioning in the Joint Field Office (JFO) sections

operational interactions (C3), mandatory System 3 (operational control) information and prohibitions through the Accountability Loop (C4), negotiated System 3 (operational control) information through the Resource Bargain (C5) and System 2 (coordination) information regarding stability (C6).

With a focus on this massive 'Variety commerce' Beer reminds us of the *First Axiom of Management*: The sum of horizontal Variety disposed by *n* operational elements *equals* the sum of vertical Variety disposed on the six vertical components of corporate Cohesion.

Environmental interaction (Channel 1)

For the O'ahu HHMS, the (C1) interaction of environments is determined by the severity of the impacts, resulting needs and the quantity and quality of the resources provided by the individual ESF departments and agencies. This channel only regards the Variety caused by the interactions and interdependencies between all environments that the five Area Commands (AC) have to deal with (Figure 44). The impacts are uncertain, as well as interactions between those environments but it is a System 4 (intelligence) task to provide scenarios to simulate external interlinkages. Additionally, a database of experiences of those patterns and lessons learned can be developed. Assumptions can be incorporated: Catastrophic impact and total destruction for parts of O'ahu, including 80 % of O'ahu's infrastructure.

In sum, ignoring environment-Environment loops would be lethal due to the Variety proliferated by the Environment [Beer, 1994a]. For example, after the Kiholo Earthquake (October 2007), people bought generators to be self-sufficient regarding power generations – attenuating Variety from the viewpoint of the system and amplifying their own Variety. In case of a catastrophic hurricane, an island-wide problem will arise. If the Hawai'ian Electric Company (HECO) shuts down power in an area to have workers repair the system, they might be faced with a life-threatening problem: the generators' power back feeds into HECO's system, unless the house owner shuts off the house's main circuit from the main system. The power lines on the streets become energized even though the Hawai'ian Electric Company (HECO) has shut off the electricity. This knowledge is mostly not present, on both the HECO and the private side. Legal issues arise if one person gets electrocuted or hurt bringing everything to a complete halt. Oscillations need to be damped through System 4 (intelligence) research and implementing a strong System 2 (coordination). This is an environment-Environment Variety amplification for the HHMS. Before the earthquake, that problem was not known or thought about. The only way to control this situation is through education – the HHMS amplifying their own Variety to match the environment's (population's) Variety. In 2006, KSSK radio was broadcasting about the problem, and such radio broadcasts will be the way to tackle the problem in the future. If generators are on, people will have radio access [Gilbert, 2007a].

From a design point of view, the VSM would prescribe a System 4 (intelligence) task to research those environmental loops, their connections and interdependencies.

Interaction between System 3* (audits) and System 1 (implementation) operations (Channel 2)

What role the System 3*-1 interaction, Channel 2, plays within the HHMS should be elaborated in more detail here. This also regards Channel 5, the Accountability Loop. The serious issues begin on Recursion 2 where the System 3* (audits) monitoring channel should serve the State Civil Defense, System 3 (operational control) control function as an assurance that the accountability reports it receives from System 1s (implementation) are accurate in the form of After Action Reports following the annual hurricane exercise Makani Pahili. This function is the basis to evaluate the status quo of the System 1s (implementation) and is part of the federal Homeland Security Exercise and Evaluation Program (HSEEP), specifically the last step 'evaluation'. This Channel is not functional and System 3* (audits) cannot perform its role because the After Action Reports and Hot Washes tend to highlight the 'positive' side because no outside check is in action, no control mechanism from FEMA, SCD or DEM, the Metasystem of Recursion 2. The departments and agencies of the HHMS conduct internal reviews, the After Action Reports, and report to the SCD, the System 3 (operational control), but it is their decision what to report, what conclusions are drawn, what actions are necessary and implemented. The Metasystem knows this shortcoming, but does not give it much attention and essentially lets this part of the System die [Richards, 2007d]. The autonomy of System 1s (implementation) is too high and causes the System to fly apart – Cohesion is lost. One way to balance System 1 (implementation) autonomy, but make System 1 (implementation) agree is through incentives and promoting a proactive attitude. A firmly implemented culture of a system is capable to maintain systemic Cohesion. Mechanisms are needed where everyone is more concerned with the good of the whole than the individual, which is created by System 5 (identity).

The need for a System 3* (audit) mechanisms can be shown: State, local, tribal, private-sector, and nongovernmental organizations are 'encouraged' to assign liaisons to the Joint Field Office (JFO) to facilitate interaction, communication and coordination [Emergency Management Institute, 2007c]. Cybernetically, the definition of 'encouragement' poses a major problem; it is not ensured, but voluntary. In general, the relationships to other departments and agencies and their activities – the squiggly lines between all System 1s (implementation) – are equally loosely defined, since they are only encouraged. The function's importance for the system's viability is underestimated and an Algedonic Alarm would sound here, if a full-fledged VSM would be in place. Analogously, the Makani Pahili exercises are insufficient: trainings and workshops were offered on a 'if interested, contact me" – basis and were by invitation, but also voluntary [Richards, 2007b]. This causes a centrifugal effect for the Viable System as a whole.

This System 3* (audits) failure has consequences in terms of the System 3 (operational control): it does not ensure the Accountability Loop through coherent reports, but is necessary to complete the Resource Bargain. A cybernetically sound design of information flow through all Levels of Recursion should be ensured, e.g. through monitoring training stati. In sum, System 3* (audits) in terms of audits needs to be implemented, which does not exist for the Hurricane Hazard Management System (HHMS) on any Level of Recursion, to continuously monitor System 1 (implementation) to be able to send rescue to the system when it shows incipient instability.

Operational interaction along the squiggly lines (Channel 3)

Channel (C3) regards the interaction of operational units. Here, System 3 (operational control) searches for both synergies and oscillations created at the intersections between all System 1s (implementation), which System 2 (coordination) has to monitor and dampen. Those synergies and oscillations concern, for example, the practicalities of movement and distribution of goods and resources between the HHMS's departments and agencies organized as ESFs on Recursion 3, between the Area Command Posts (ACPs) and between the governmental Emergency Operation Centers (EOCs) on Recursion 2.

The principal Channel 3 issue is that Recursions 2 and 1 are hibernating and only active under a hurricane threat or impact. But, those Recursions are based on Recursion 3 and can only be viable if Recursion 3 is alive and able to awaken from its Metasystemic Calm in times of instabilities. On the positive side, Recursion 4 is the part of the Hurricane Hazard Management System (HHMS) that is not hibernating and is kept alive through the year. The Homeland Security Exercise and Evaluation Program (HSEEP) on Recursion 1, the federal level, which is implemented with the annual Makani Pahili exercise on the state level, showed a living C3 channel where synergies are actively pursued, but only annually, which lets the system fall into a coma.

Resource and information flow (Channel 4, 5)

In cybernetic terms, Channel 4 represents the Resource Bargain, Channel 5 the Accountability Loop. On O'ahu, 'the National Response Plan (NRP) Catastrophic Incident Annex (NRP-CIA) and Catastrophic Incident Supplement (NRP-CIS) addresses resource and procedural implications of catastrophic events to ensure the rapid and efficient delivery of resources and assets, including special teams, equipment, and supplies that provide critical lifesaving support and incident containment capabilities. These assets may be so specialized or costly that they are either not available or are in insufficient quantities in most localities' [U.S. DHS, 2006a, p. 18]. The HHMS has been stated to be underfunded from a Variety of departments and agencies on all governmental levels [Richards, 2007f]. Even with a perfect cybernetic structure, ultimately, without resources to plug into this structure the system will fail. Still, the VSM can increase resource efficiency with given resources and strengthen its viability in any kind of disaster.

The non-functional System 1–3 link is evident and the following example should give an idea of how operational efficiency can often be enhanced without increasing financial support. When FEMA officials came to the Big Island after the October 2006 earthquake, they started to look for the best location of the Disaster Recovery Center (DRC) in Waimea, inland on the Big Island. These FEMA officials talked to the City of Hilo Civil Defense about the DRC location ignoring both Mr. Tengan, their SCD counterpart, and SCD whose task it is to choose the DRC location. Due to this confusion, credibility issues arose. SCD promised the local population that support was under way and identified the YMCA as the DRC. When FEMA arrived and wanted to set up the DRC elsewhere, confusion arose among the population towards SCD and FEMA. Ultimately, the problem lay with FEMA trying to apply their processes to a structure that was not built to deal with the local conditions due to different infrastructure and system style [Richards and Tengan, 2007]. Being out of touch with the local scene caused another problem. Their damage assessments were superficial because the FEMA teams assessed not-damaged areas. But, FEMA is only supposed to validate SCD's findings, a System 3* (audits) task only. Time and resources were lost – several days of work could have been used for increased effectiveness and efficiency without needing more funding.

In management situations, it is essential that people can shift resources around to respond quickly to opportunities or threats – the System 1 (implementation) requirement of autonomy. The alternative is that opportunities come and go while awaiting an answer from the Federal Emergency Management Agency (FEMA). In disaster response, when quick action is necessary, waiting for communications to be set up or authorizations approved can be costly in terms of damage to both victims and the reputation of the responders. The hierarchical setup within the HHMS is especially problematic in this regard and cybernetically wrong, as stated earlier. To start the problem solving process, Variety Engineering must be the focus (see chapter 3.3.4).

Looking at the HHMS, one question might arise: Is there a point where the governor of a system has grown so large, and so many of its own resources are being used to govern itself, that a limit on the size of the system to be managed is effectively reached? But, for a cybernetician, infinitive Levels of Recursion exist in any system and if (s)he would have Requisite Variety to explore them all, he would reach full consciousness. In that sense, Beer never elaborates on limits of a system. It is the skill of the cybernetician to decide on a System in Focus to then draw the conclusions the VSM can provide. Ultimately, the clear conclusion must be: in the United States, there are enough resources; it's a matter of system effectiveness rather than resource constraints if resources are not in place where they are needed.

Interaction based on System 2 (coordination) (Channel 6)

At first sight, the National Response Plan (NRP) provides a strong, legally founded basis for the Hurricane Hazard Management System (HHMS) System 2 (coordination). In practice, System 2 (coordination) implementation is missing in many instances. System 2 (coordination) failures influence all Systems 1 to 5 on all Levels of Recursion. Due to this immense systemic impact, a separate section was warranted for its elaboration in regards to structure in chapter 3.2. Here, the implications on Variety Engineering aspects, the processes, are the focus with an aim on design.

Factors within the HHMS too often lead to Variety amplification rather than attenuation. A big part in preventing efficiency plays legal issues. Currently, parts of the National Response Plan (NRP) are a malignant cancer of bureaucracy. The problem of 'red tape' is a System 2 (coordination) induced Variety proliferation instead of a counter-balancing of Variety oscillations. For example, if the Federal Emergency Management Agency (FEMA) sent resources before a Presidential Disaster Declaration, they would sit unused because legally the first responders were not allowed to distribute them. The State would have to sign an agreement for replacement if a Presidential Disaster Declaration was not issued, trusting that there would be one [Fenton, 2007]. The State amplified its Variety to match a problem in their direct Environment caused by a Recursion higher – this is unnecessary. Similar issues arose during Hurricane Katrina: local governments across the country were ready to assist, but few of them were able to get through the state and federal governments' red tape to get into the region. In general, local government employees, always part of the rescue and recovery work, brought a sense of dedication and experience to the job and were the most cost-effective resource for assistance. But in some cases, such as debris removal, FEMA regulations increased costs because they allowed full reimbursement for contract labor, but not for local government personnel [ICCMA, 2006].

A major problem of the Incident Command System (ICS) according to State Civil Defense (SCD) officials is the lack of clear understanding of the HHMS personnel's roles and responsibilities (lack of System 2 (coordination)) causing power struggles down to the lowest Level of Recursion. This problem would be enhanced by the communication breakdown due to a storm's impact. At times, the Incident Command (IC) is populated by several departments and agencies where the process to compromise does not work or is very time-consuming [Richards, 2007f]. In the Public Health Service, a problem existed in defining the term 'special need patient'. Clarity on the term was lacking and hindered cooperation between agencies [Bryce, 2007]. Cybernetically, better System 2 (coordination) is needed.

How a change of System 2 (coordination) can influence effectiveness shows the following example: Standard Operational Procedures (SOP) is a term that FEMA changed after Hurricane Katrina in 2005. Now, they are termed Standard Operations Guidance (SOG). The change from 'procedures' to 'guidance' was induced because employees who did not follow the SOPs were liable for mistakes. In the case of Hurricane Katrina, certain actions were repressed by those SOPs. The change in terminology and its liability consequences is supposed to lead to more efficiency [Gilbert, 2007b], cybernetically a System 2 (coordination) change.

The incompatibility of communication technology, as well hardware as soft-ware problems, cause another slow-down in disaster response in terms of System 2 (coordination) processes. For example, the county Emergency Operation Center (EOC) uses software named e-Team and the state EOC uses Web-EOC, which are not fully compatible. Those are System 2 (coordination) obstacles to an efficient System 3 (operational control) functioning and can greatly diminish the System 2 (coordination) anti-oscillatory function. If System 2 (coordination) is not working efficiently, System 3 (operational control) may not be able to concentrate on its most important tasks, such as coordination and executive decisions, because it will waste time responding to management crises on the System 1 (implementation) level.

A source of great coordination failure and unnecessary Variety amplification if not explosion is the inconsistencies regarding FEMA's Concept of

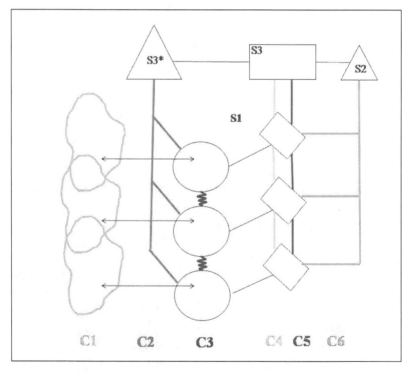

Figure 59: The six vertical channels of the 'Inside and Now'

Operations' (CONOP) and internal HHMS's assumptions, also a System 2 (coordination) implementation failure. A major misjudgment regards Honolulu International Airport (see Figure 60) [US Army Corps of Engineers, 2007]. At the FEMA conference, it was assumed that Honolulu International airport could be used, but the US Army Corps of Engineers showed an airport scenario from before and after the landfall of a catastrophic hurricane at the Debris Management Seminar, which made clear that its usage would be impossible. Consequently, how can you effectively plan, if some HHMS key personnel assume that Honolulu International airport is available if it will be impossible?

A most serious issue is that most county departments and agencies, the Coast Guard, the Honolulu Police Department, the Emergency Medical Services and the Honolulu Fire Department and several private sector agencies such as the Hawai'ian Electric Company (HECO), have different geographic references. Their functional jurisdictions differ from each other [Breakout Session Infrastructure, 2007]. How can you possibly plan together if O'ahu is divided by each entity in a different way? The cost for this cybernetic problem is the loss of effectiveness and ultimately money is

Figure 60: Honolulu International Airport scenario

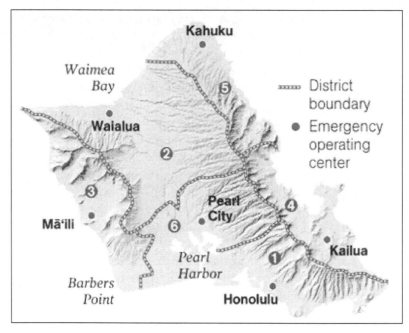

Figure 61: Oʻahu districts and planned Emergency Operation Centers (EOCs)

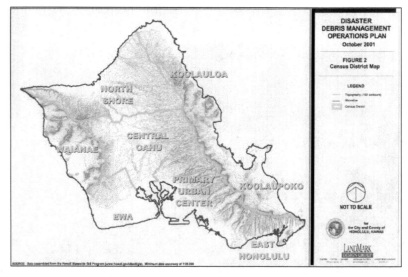

Figure 62: Census district map

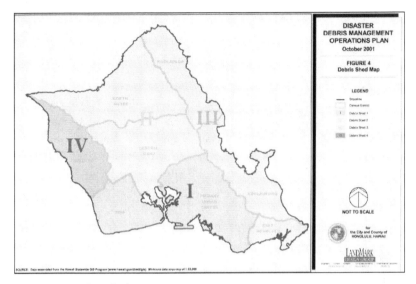

Figure 63: Debris shed map

wasted. The Department of Emergency Management (DEM), also valid
for the Disaster Debris Management Operations Plan, has six districts
as shown in Figure 61 [Gilbert, 2007b], but there are eight census districts shown in Figure 62 [Hawai'i State Civil Defense, 2007a] and the
Emergency Medical Services (EMS) operates with two districts. Figure
63 [Hawai'i State Civil Defense, 2007a] shows the planned divisions by
FEMA [FEMA, 2007].

More problems of geographical division emerge regarding the Flood Insurance Risk Maps (FIRMS) and State Civil Defense (SCD) evacuation
maps for the designations of coastal high hazard areas on tax map keys
(TMK) because the scales of existing hazards, land-use and zoning maps
are not compatible. The inundation lines on the state TMKs are generally
much further inland than those on the federal FIRMs. Further, there are
concerns about how new high-hazard area maps would be used by insurance
industry and whether they would simply stop selling insurance [University
of Hawai'i at Mānoa , 1993].

Contracts can also pose a problem even though they could greatly reduce Variety. The ARC has always worked closely with state and local government as a mass care service provider [Shigetani, 2007] but the coordination with Emergency Support Function 6 (ESF6) (Mass Care, Emergency
Assistance, Housing, Human Services) is not in balance due to different

standards between ARC and government agencies. Set and implemented standards can reduce Variety greatly.

High autonomy on the System 1 (implementation) level should be contained through a firm System 2 (coordination) design based on System 5 (identity) on Level of Recursion 2, the State of Hawai'i – because it is the purpose of the System to save lives as the highest priority. Fact is that 45 % percent of the Hawai'ian electricity system is currently underground. The remaining 55 % appear to be difficult to upgrade because of conflicts of interests: esthetics and secure transmission. Besides the financial effort, which would be about $11 billion according to a recent study, the problem lies in the fact that the poles are shared by telephone, cable and television companies and there is no agreement on investment in putting the lines underground. The phone company loses money currently due to the increase of cell phones and therefore will not take the lead in coming to an agreement. Further, it would take 30 to 40 years to put all the lines underground [Rosegg, 2007a].

As a last example of System 2 (coordination) Variety amplification, the statement 'all clear' is used to give disaster first responders the order to start the response, but the meaning of this phrase varies from agency to agency: The O'ahu County EOC's 'all clear' means that emergency workers can go out in not damaged areas. HECO's 'all clear' statement implies a different situation: it means that no downed lines will put emergency workers in danger and that the damage assessments can start [Gilbert, 2007b]. This is an immense System 2 (coordination) failure that makes Transduction impossible and will cause chaos in any disaster situation.

As being demonstrated, seemingly small issues can develop into a disaster through the concatenation of many small events. Alone, they would not matter, and pointing them out as the cause of the problem might seem ridiculous. But the cause-and-effect thinking needs to be abandoned and the 'domino-effect' accepted that can be induced by small events. Variety could be handled much more effectively and efficiently without more financial resources. Variety Engineering a la Beer's Chart IV [Beer, 1979] would be the answer (see Figure 64).

Beer also introduces the Regulatory Center. System 2 (coordination) can be divided into four realms that run between System 3 (operational control) and 1 (implementation): Materials and machine resources, money resources, people resources and time resources [Beer, 1994a, pp. 469]. NIMS complies with this idea of System 2 (coordination) division. But Beer also states that often System 2 (coordination) overloads System 1 (implementation). For example, the head of the Department of Transportation admitted that their Emergency Operations Plan with over 300 pages is overwhelming [Romaine, 2007]. Cybernetically, Variety explosions hit System 1 (implementation) from both sides, the Environment (disaster impacts) and System 2 (coordination) through information overload. The information filter that turns raw data into relevant information is missing – a System 3 (operational control) task – and the single person implementing NIMS is simply overwhelmed by the Variety generated in its own system – a suicidal setup. A 300 page Emergency Operations Plan only satisfies the subjective need to put certain data on paper, but is just noise for the single entities if relevant filters are not in place.

Beer warns that the appropriate design of System 2 (coordination) – as well as System 4 (intelligence) – is a major source of failures in his experience. First of all, System 1 (implementation) should configure a full-time team to design System 2s (coordination) since it is essential to the viability of the whole system. For the non-hibernating part of the HHMS that should be accomplished by the Metasystem of Recursion 4, of all governmental, non-governmental and private sector organizations. Second, the ESFs, System 1 (implementation) should ask the Metasystem to help design System 2s (coordination) since it is an operational element of the next higher Level or Recursion. It was stated in the Federal Emergency Management Agency Regional Interagency Steering Committees (FEMA RISC) conference that FEMA implements suggestions of the lowest-level elements and takes advice from the local level, but this needs to be greatly enhanced for System 2 (coordination) design.

3.3.3 Balance with the environment

System 4 (intelligence) must balance the internal and external world while ensuring the systems adaptability (see C3 in Figure 39). To adapt to environmental change and to produce strategies, System 4 (intelligence) needs an appropriate model of the capabilities of the 'Inside and Now' so it knows what tools it has at its disposal.

The envelope Environment is the larger Environment that the System 4 (intelligence) has to deal with (see Figure 34), which encompasses the physical, socio-cultural and economic Environment. What part of the infinite envelope Environment is of direct relevance? The physical Environment can be monitored, for example by the National Weather Service (NWS), and social trends can be identified and reactions devised through scenarios and experiments. An overall vulnerability analysis is essential (see chapter 1.4.2).

A GAP analysis by FEMA in collaboration with the State at the RISC conference is an example of System 4 (intelligence) activities as well as the elaboration of the Concept of Operations (CONOP) for a catastrophic hurricane impacting the State of Hawai'i [Fenton, 2007]. FEMA plans to sign concrete agreements pre-landfall, establish partnerships and reduce vulnerability in general by securing the requirements for a sustainable power supply in case of a catastrophic hurricane on O'ahu [Rosenberg, 2007a]. Each System 4 (intelligence) needs to do enquiries on its Level of Recursion, not on another Recursion, which is a common error.

Communicating with the public is an important aspect of attenuating external Variety and should therefore be given special attention. In VSM terms, two aspects need consideration regarding the public: First, the public is part of the envelope Environment outside of the HHMS System 1 (implementation) through 5 (identity) overwhelming the system with Variety. A well-prepared citizen can attenuate System 1 (implementation) (at the Area Command Post (ACP) level) Variety by being informed and prepared and taking part in System 1 (implementation) tasks, or (s)he can amplify Variety by being an obstacle to System 1 (implementation) operations. The public can be influenced by System 1 (implementation) and 4 (intelligence) through public education and related planning, for example, and its Variety can be attenuated. Secondly, the public can be part of System 1 (implementation) and 4 (intelligence) on the lowest Level of Recursion (the single individual responding to an incident) by actively mitigating (System 4 (intelligence)), preparing and responding on the short term (System 1 (implementation)). Hence, depending on the Level of Recursion, the public as a whole or the single individual is part of the HHMS. ESF 15 'Public Information" represents the structure's front operation to communicate with the public to direct a consistent message with confidence to the public [Teixeira, 2007b].

NIMS provides several public information systems such as the Public Information Officer, the Joint Information System, the Joint Information Center and the National Weather Service. 'Public information must be coordinated and integrated across jurisdictions and functional areas. Organizations may retain their independence, but each should contribute to the overall unified message for maximum effectiveness' [Jones, 2006, p. 12]. This complies with VSM communication requirements of consistent and accessible information: Transduction and Channel Capacity has to be ensured and comply with System 5 (identity). The Public Information Officer has the task to ensure Requisite Variety between the System, the HHMS, and the envelope Environment.

The 'Joint Information System (JIS) is an organized, integrated, and co-ordinated mechanism to ensure the delivery of understandable, timely, accurate and consistent information to the public in a crisis' [City and County of Honolulu, 2007, p. 15]. Channel Capacity and Transduction is therefore required but how effective this information flow would be for a catastrophic hurricane has not been tested. A test should be part of the Makani Pahili exercise for it to be a real-time and realistic scenario.

'NOAA Weather Radio All Hazards (NWR) is the prime National Weather Service delivery system of alerts and critical information directly to the general public. NWR broadcasts warnings, watches, forecasts and other hazard information 24 hours a day. The NWR network has more than 950 stations, reaching over 97 % of the population of the 50 states' [U.S. Department of Commerce, National Oceanic and Atmospheric Administration, National Weather Service, 2006, p. 18]. Overall, the NWS as an information breaker to the public deals with the high Variety of weather conditions threatening the system through amplifying its Variety in effective ways through research, monitoring and broadcasting tools.

The influence of the media needs to be emphasized. When inconsistent and wrong information reaches the public through the media, it leads to a distortion of public perception and behavior representing a high potential for Variety proliferation. Requisite Variety must be kept by sending out consistent information to not cause oscillations that flood the system and lead to instabilities. Information has to be managed and disagreements resolved internally, before sending it to the HHMS personnel and the public to attenuate this Variety. To gain Requisite Variety a System 2 (coordination) is in place using prepared press releases and briefings with government officials are prepared with up-to-date disaster information. To keep and maintain positive connections with the media, it is recommended to work with the media personnel throughout the year to enhance a good working relationship that facilitates positive exchanges during an emergency [Emergency Management Institute, 2007a].

Highly volatile rumors are a potent cause of Variety proliferation and are sometimes as dangerous as the emergency itself. The control of rumors is essential if the public is to remain accurately informed and as cooperative as possible with the emergency recommendations issued by public officials. The media can also be useful in dispelling rumors, thus attenuating Variety. Creating a rumor-control center could also achieve Requisite Variety: The public should have a number to call for confirmation or refutation of information. Further, well-known community leaders can aid in rumor control and their credibility serves well as Variety attenuators.

Overall, public education can greatly improve the HHMS's effectiveness and Variety Engineering capacity through on-going educational programs. Different HHMS departments and agencies have handbooks and guides for public education and hurricane warnings are posted in the communities. Overall, those activities either reduce the environment's Variety by increasing the public's capability to respond or increase the public's Variety to match the Variety exposed by the disaster.

As a vivid example, I recall the evacuation of March 2011 after the Japan Earthquake causing the Fukushima disaster. Since a 8.9 Earthquake is about the maximum measurable, Hawai'i took full precaution and all coasts were evacuated. This was the most serious evacuation in decades and the performance was excellent. As the situation developed, the Tsunami Watch switched to a Tsunami Warning at about 9pm and the sirens went off several times from then until 2am. My neighbors, military folks left their homes around 9pm to be stationed for the worst and the Emergency Operation Centers were in gear. Police went through the neighborhoods to evacuate people. I talked on the cell to Teixeira, Vice State Civil Defense, who confirmed that it was a very serious situation and waves were estimated at 4 meters. I knew from my research that the tsunami height cannot be determined exactly because it takes up to 24 hours to locate the epicenter of an earthquake. Consequently, it is a measure of good judgment in the end. An estimate is necessary for public information to make an evacuation go into gear. Packing up my disaster kit, several large bottles of liquor to trade in the aftermath, warm clothes and all IT equipment I headed up Pūpūkea Hills at about 110 meters height to join the tsunami party along the road, radio on. We were invited in a house for convenience - the Aloha Spirit helps in times of need. At 2am the tsunami was supposed to hit and at 1am police officers came up the hill calling all roads down from there closed. One friend was deep asleep and his wife called me from Miami to get him off their beach-front property - she heard about the Tsunami Warning on the news. After we both could not get a hold of him we drove down with a police officer and caught him in time. Other people refused to evacuate and stayed at their beach-front homes trusting buoy readings they used for surfing – just that a tsunami wave on the open ocean is mostly just half a meter in height, but about 500 km in length causing its enormous strength – this kind of wave just keeps on coming. At 2.15am the State Civil Defense announced that even though the waves have not been hitting as predicted, they are still due but at this time exact time their height is unknown. Now, while everybody was prepared, evacuated and as save as they wanted to be, officials stated the truth – that they do not know.

The waves hit between 3.30am and 8am with a maximum height of 1 meter causing minor damage on O'ahu. The Big Island was hit harder – several houses were swept out to sea. At 9 am the evacuation was called off and people returned to their homes. But even days later, all of a sudden, the ocean on our door-steps pulled out hundreds of meters uncovering the reef and slowly came back in, just like a slow-motion body of water in a huge bath tub swinging back and forward. This was observed for several days after the quake. A japan-like tsunami would have left us with severe problems for months and even years, due to Hawai'i's dependence on imports of food and water with one Million people on O'ahu alone. Having harbors and the main airport destroyed make resource provisions very difficult. Month-long power outages would have put at jeopardy the life of people in hospitals and the entire population without refrigeration necessary for food and other life-sustaining elements. The smaller military airports would have been the only life-sustaining veins of the islands for some time. Without power, water supply would have become difficult fast due to the failure of pumping systems and an outdated supply of generators on the islands. The aftermath of a tsunami would look very similar to a post-hurricane situation described in the vulnerability analysis in chapter 1.

In contrast, 'Iniki appeared to head away from the Big Island and then suddenly turned back toward Kauai. On the morning of September 10, 1992, 'Iniki passed 300 miles south of South Point on the Big Island moving west and slowing and strengthening [Browning, 2007c] to finally make a big turn, hovering an hour and a half West of Honolulu to then go for Kauai on a direct hit. So, when should a Tsunami Warning be sent out? When should this Hurricane Watch become a warning? The issue of credibility loss due to wrong forecasting is a difficult issue and has high damage potential for any future disaster. You can only scream 'wolf' so many times and will be heard, but if it is 'sheep' one too many times, your warning will lose effect exponentially.

Dependent on the system in place, more or less congruent information is transferred to the public. There is a high level of complexity in climate information and forecasting, which is not easily understandable for the general public and it is not practical to have the public match their Variety, their actions, to the scientific information. Information brokers such as the State

Civil Defense or other disaster management agencies do their best to protect the public and filter the relevant information acting as a Variety reducer. There are two filters: the scientists with probability models, climatologic experience and a high level of estimation capability that is necessary to a fast changing development of storm conditions; and the information brokers who need to give the public access to necessary information. If a warning is not communicated early enough, the population might not be able to prepare adequately for a coming storm.

In contrast to the envelope Environment, the local Environment is represented by the Environment the single System 1 (implementation) has to deal directly with and which is part of the larger envelope Environment. System 4 (intelligence) is connected to the 'Inside and Now' through System 3 (operational control) charged with stabilizing and optimizing the local Environment making sure the vertical Variety can match the horizontal Variety coming in from all System 1s (implementation). It is connected to the 'Outside and Then' as just described in the previous chapter. Let us now look at how the lower Levels of Recursion take care of their task of matching the Variety coming in from their local environments. To be explicit, a local Environment in the recursive sense is in fact the envelope Environment of the next lower Level of Recursion; therefore it is the System 4's (intelligence) task of that lower Level of Recursion to explore this Environment. Since the System 4 (intelligence) is so weak on all Levels of Recursion, the whole Metasystem collapses into System 3 (operational control), which is fatal to any organization. It also lacks further will and drive (System 5). Beer describes this pathology, the System 3–4–5 collapse, in terms of a decerebrate cat [Beer, 1994a, p. 265]:

'You can take a perfectly good cat, anaesthetize it, and remove the cerebrum. You can pin the decerebrate cat to the table, and keep it fed. It lives on; its viability is ensured by a bogus Environment, and is sustained by artificial sustenance. If you prod its leg, it kicks back. And this is called 'living'. If we think this through in institutional terms, we diagnose a major pathology of our times.' I have to recall that note of a Peer Review Team member: *'They are doing a lot of things, but they are not sure they add up to catastrophic planning'* [U.S. DHS, 2006b, p. 5].

The HHMS System 4 (intelligence) badly needs implementation on all Levels of Recursions instead of only awareness of its need. On Recursion 1, the System 3–4 communication exists, but with a large time lag. The State Civil Defense (SCD), System 3 (operational control), stalls waiting for FEMA, System 4 (intelligence) and 5 (identity), to elaborate the

Concept of Operations (CONOP) for a catastrophic hurricane impacting the State of Hawai'i draft. The Homeland Security Exercise and Evaluation Program (HSEEP) is not fully implemented and, hence, the HHMS's needs are not discovered, since no continuous focus for System 4 (intelligence) activities exists. Currently, the HHMS is not viable in Beer's terms as diagnosed before, also due to this missing interaction. The CONOP was just developed in 2007 and the System 3–4 homeostat emerged, but is not in gear yet.

On Recursion 2, the System in Focus, it is not pre-set how the Area Command Post (ACP) and Unified Command Posts (UCPs) would be set up on O'ahu for the HHMS, a missing System 3 (operational control) task that is impossible to accomplish without System 4 (intelligence). Evacuation, for example, is not planned or coordinated from one location, but by HHMS personnel in the field. This excessive System 1 (implementation) autonomy on Recursion 4 shows a lack of System 3 (operational control) coordination and a search for synergies.

Further, it seems not to be within the capacity of the HHMS personnel's imagination to deal with a catastrophic hurricane event. In the interviews, mostly examples of small scale events were given ignoring the conditions given by the Makani Pahili exercise scenario. One of the challenges for the HHMS organization is to transfer innovations from the staff of System 4 (intelligence) where they originate to the managers who will implement them at System 3 (operational control) [Leonard, 1999]. The HHMS is stuck here.

Pre-staging information on loading time, decision time, unloading time and distribution time, among other factors, must be considered with an assumed temporary 30 ft inundation [Browning, FEMA RISC Conference, 2007]. System 4 (intelligence) needs to provide this critical information to System 3 (operational control) to be able to coordinate and direct the System 1s (implementation) well before a hurricane threat or potential hit to deal with the environmental Variety of every single System 1 (implementation).

One cause of failure is that with 15 different ESFs, five Area Command divisions and three governmental levels, the Metasystem eventually would end up with 15x5x3=225 committees. Calculating Variety this accumulates to 225x224 = 50'400 relationships. If we assume a binary situation of only good or bad relationships, ignoring all the grey shades, this accumulates to a Variety of $2^{50'400}$. System failure is evident.

3.3.4 Variety Engineering – how to balance into chaos

By nature, the inner complexity of an organization is far less than the complexity of its outer Environment. This differential is regulated by the VSM through 'Variety Engineering' (C3 in Figure 39), the art of management. Hence, all Variety imbalances need to be addressed through processes of Variety attenuation and amplification – leverage strategies – to get the complexity of the Environment within the organization's response range, as measured by the organization's inner complexity or Variety. Ultimately, it is complexity that threatens to overwhelm any system.

Measuring Variety is not an exact science. Variety is used to compare relative complexities. Variety Engineering means managing the complexity differential inherent in most relationships. If there is enough regulatory capability in a control function to manage a situation it has 'Requisite Variety' [Leonard, 1999]. The Viable System Model (VSM) addresses the Variety implicit in a management situation from two angles: the horizontal relationship along the Environment and the System 1 (implementation); and on the vertical axis connecting the management of System 1 (implementation) with the Metasystem 3–4–5. Those two should equate as stated in the first Axiom of Management (see Glossary).

The sum of all System 1 (implementation) management Varieties (e.g. on LoR 4: Area Commands) must be consequently equivalent to the Variety disposed by System 3 (operational control) (the EOCs) as stated in the first Axiom of Management (see Glossary). The EOCs are overwhelmed by the AC requests in a catastrophic disaster and it is then the job of the Metasystem of this Recursion to absorb this extra Variety. The EOC needs to deal efficiently with the AC requests while it performs the Metasystemic functions of System 3–4–5, while still being aware of performing System 1 (implementation) tasks looking at a Level of Recursion higher. This way, the VSM is a check if all necessary tasks are fulfilled. If a system fails, it alarms System 3 (operational control) through an Algedonic Alarm [Beer, 1989b] on its relevant Level of Recursion. This means, if the county EOC cannot perform its tasks of System 3–4–5, it alarms as a System 1 (implementation) its System 3 (operational control), which would be in this case the state EOC. In a catastrophic hurricane event, all Levels of Recursion would be on a constant alarm due to the failures discussed so far.

Beer designs a Management Unit that can cope with both Variety generation – amplification – and reduction – attenuation between the System 1 (implementation) management (the lower Recursion Metasystem) and the

System 1 (implementation) operations (entailing the lower Recursion System 1 (implementation) as a whole plus their environments). Overall, a manager has to control a number of activities that are usually depicted on an organizational chart as boxes. Beer explains that these boxes are in most cases not transparent, but clouded if not opaque, translucent at best. How can management know what input to insert into a muddy box to receive an intended output? *The First Regulatory Aphorism* says that 'it is not necessary to enter the Black Box to understand the nature of the function it performs' [Beer, 1994a, p. 59]. If incoming information has too much Variety, a manager has to select aspects that fit his low Variety models. Practically, efficient managers develop skills to select the information they need and ignore the rest while remaining alert to signs of change and incipient instability [Leonard, 1999]. For a manager, ways to destroy Variety are to divisionalize, functionalize, manage by exception or set objectives to ultimately prevent interaction between elements. According to Beer, this can be a dangerous destruction of Variety, since opportunities might be overlooked because they are not in the protocol or in the list of objectives. The problem with managing these muddy boxes arises through wrong assumptions and projections and the limited time a manager has available to study them. So how can this Variety be measured? The *Second Regulatory Aphorism* says 'it is not necessary to enter the Black Box to calculate the Variety that it potentially may generate' [Beer, 1994a, p. 47]. Variety Engineering is best accomplished in small workshops on all Recursion Levels as being practiced, e.g. by Malik Management in Switzerland, and are based on Chart IV of 'Diagnosing the System (see Figure 64) [Beer, 1985].

Chart IV basically demonstrates the Variety Commence on the horizontal level with the three elements of System 1 (implementation): the local Environment, operations and management. The incoming Variety from the local Environment is the highest and has to be attenuated by operations, which still has a higher Variety than management, which in turn has to attenuate the operation's Variety – three steps in total on the horizontal axis. After defining the Variety generating elements for all three (Environment, operations, management), the cybernetician together with the system's stakeholders can determine if that Variety is being attenuated or amplified in reality. This way, the Variety commerce as a status quo can be recognized. As a further step, critical management task can be developed and be divided on all five management functions (System 1–5). Developing workshops based on Chart IV are highly valuable and design an organization as a Viable System in the end. This exercise is outside of this book's capacity

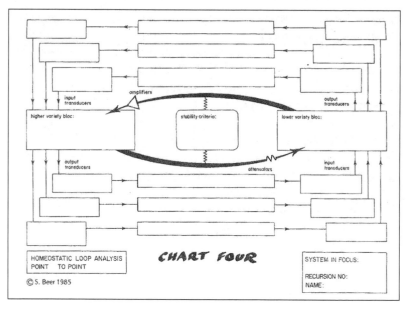

Figure 64: Chart IV

to demonstrate cybernetics. In the following, some examples are given to demonstrate Variety Engineering – amplification and attenuation – for the HHMS. Instabilities are detected through Algedonic Alarms and if a sum of those reaches a certain limit necessary action can be proactively called upon well ahead of any disaster situation.

Now, how can we understand *'amplifying internal Variety to match internal Variety'*? System 3 (operational control) can amplify its Variety on the vertical axis to match the Variety coming in from System 1 (implementation) on the horizontal axis (see Figure 30). It can 'improve communication and interoperability; provide first-responder training and credentialing; improve the ability to collect accurate information, analyze it, and respond accordingly, adapting quickly to changing conditions; take advantage of services the military can provide in emergencies, such as transport expertise and storage facilities; develop collaborative relationships that allow all involved—military, federal, state, local, and nongovernmental organizations—to leverage their assets in a way that minimizes bureaucratic obstacles and complements and strengthens the response; train, equip, stockpile, and stage before disaster strikes – early declarations and mobilization of resources are essential; restructure federal agencies and align federal processes for clearly defined roles and responsibilities; strengthen the Federal Emergency Management Agency (FEMA) by ensuring that it has the resources it needs and by providing direct reporting authority to the President during states of emergency and disaster declarations; amend the Stafford Act to allow local solutions that are cost-effective, safe, and appropriate for the community, and that address long term recovery needs' [ICCMA, 2006, pp. 3]. Public information and education is one way for this Variety commerce to be balanced: The American Red Cross shelter exposition in the Hawai'ian Convention Center during the Makani Pahili exercise 2007 matched internal Variety by inspiring individuals and families to be prepared and proactive, e.g. not running to the store two hours before storm. The public was introduced to long-term shelters and evacuation shelters informing them that nothing will be provided, but that they are a safer place than their home. The Hawai'i Humane Society, the DLNR, the NWS, FEMA, CD and the PDC gave presentations [Richards, 2007c]. Those examples regard different Levels of Recursion and dispersion throughout the HHMS would be the cybernetic goal for System Cohesion. In order to do so, several participants of the respective System 1 (implementation) would have to elaborate the Chart IV with a cybernetician to explore the options of increasing effectiveness and efficiency.

Dealing with external Variety, how can we *amplify internal Variety to match that external Variety* coming from the envelope environment? For example, mitigation measures amplify the Hurricane Hazard Management System's (HHMS) Variety to deal with external Variety. Already in 1993, actions for which statutory authority existed and minimal additional resources were required were identified: enforcement of existing regulations, designation of high hazard areas, review of floodplain maps, definition of shoreline setback, adoption of UBC 1991, implementation of tax credits, monitoring of FEMA grant availability for hazard mitigation, encouragement of private groups and creation of incentive program. 'Actions for which statutory authority existed and additional resources were required: hurricane mitigation advisory board, beach monitoring program, coastal retreat strategy for high hazard areas, funding for training programs on the provisions of the 1991 UBC for County Building Department Officials and Building Contractors, wind hazard program, public information program (risk reduction), hurricane recovery and hazard mitigation plan. Actions for which statutory change and additional resources will be required: income tax credits, low interest loans' [University of Hawai'i at Mānoa , 1993]. Further action to amplify internal Variety to match external Variety is community emergency planning that includes 'animal control experts in disaster planning; identifies alternatives for long-term shelter, such as vacant warehouses, leased space, and hotel facilities; develops aid agreements with hotels so that they know they will get paid to shelter emergency personnel and evacuees; and develops contracts with multi-family apartment owners for long-term shelter is a good strategy to minimize contract management and invoicing overload' [ICCMA, 2006, pp. 8]. Most emergency plans do not consider long-term shelter needs and rely on schools and arenas, which are inappropriate for anything other than immediate shelter. To amplify that internal Variety, for example, the faith-based community could be included as a resource in plans; a plan to manage volunteers and get to know the leaders of key volunteer organizations as part of preparedness work could be evolved; nonprofit organizations can provide training for volunteers and manage their assignments; and a plan for transportation to evacuate the frail and poor could be developed [ICCMA, 2006]. Again, those actions would need further work along Chart IV and should only exemplify part of the Variety commerce.

After Hurricane 'Iniki on Kauai 1992, lack of information was a major problem immediately after the hurricane. All the radio stations were knocked out, and KONG, the designated Civil Defense station, was off the air for two days until someone thought to string a wire between two trees as a temporary antenna, recalls KONG announcer Ron Wiley. Gregg Gardiner, then the publisher of the now defunct weekly Kauai Times, talked the Navy's Pacific Missile Range into flying him to O'ahu, where the Honolulu Star-Bulletin printed his newspaper. The papers were loaded onto the Navy plane and flown back to Kauai to be delivered [Starbulletin, 2002a]. Here, two individuals increased their individual Variety to match the external Variety.

Now, how can we *attenuate internal Variety to match internal Variety*? One of the best ways to resolve multiagency coordination issues that arise during an incident is to ensure that officials with decision-making authority are at the Emergency Operation Center (EOC) at all times. Having all key personnel in one place facilitates discussion and rapid problem-solving as issues arise [Emergency Management Institute, 2007b]. Therefore, Variety attenuation is facilitated through meetings and being in one place. Further, this ensures Transduction and Channel Capacity. The State Civil Defense (SCD) National Incident Management System (NIMS) training officer also reminded Hurricane Hazard Management System (HHMS) personnel not to let themselves become overwhelmed, but to order resources beforehand [Richards, 2007f]. In VSM terms, this System 1 (implementation) autonomy enforcement provides for Variety attenuation. Often, the HHMS challenge is that those orders cannot be fulfilled in time, Homeostasis cannot be established, and the system becomes unstable and ultimately non-viable. System 4 (intelligence) needs to provide a prestaging plan. This is only one example, but in a discussion a much more detailed and realistic Variety attenuating critical management task can be developed.

At the Federal Emergency Management Agency Regional Interagency Steering Committees (FEMA RISC) conference it was stressed that it is not necessary that 'everybody talks to everybody', for example the single firemen to President Bush. The leadership is physically co-located at the Joint Field Office (JFO) with relevant counterparts to make critical decisions and is connected to and talking with their teams in the field. Therefore, Variety is attenuated every time information is summarized and filtered before reported to a higher level [Latham, 2007]. Further, informal communication is of crucial importance and attenuates Variety to a great extend. Those conversations happen in the walkways, during lunch, via email, among other ways. They are enhanced by an appreciation of openness and an atmosphere of trust. Conversely, they are constrained by group-thinking, internal competition, intolerance of failures and high levels of risk aversion [Leonard, 1999]. Variety attenuation through those 'gate-keepers' can be dangerous, since crucial information might be lost.

The last possible of four situations: How can *external Variety to match internal Variety be attenuated*? The public is part of the external Environment the HHMS has to handle. To attenuate the external Variety to match the internal Variety, public education is an efficient tool. The Emergency Management Institute informs that there are three actions the public needs to take at the time of a hurricane approach: keep themselves informed of the progress of the threat; take preparatory actions such as getting ready for an evacuation or stockpiling essential resources; and be ready to take more specific steps if public officials order them [Emergency Management Institute, 2007a]. The public, being part of the envelope Environment is handed information to amplify their Variety to match the Variety explosion of the hurricane impact, also within the envelope Environment. Consequently, external Variety is attenuated for the System 1s (implementation).

Variety can explode at any point in time in the System, so let us look at some sources of *Variety Explosions*. The most obvious one is of course the disaster impact – within the envelope Environment – itself, which will create endless unknown complexity. It holds the potential for huge Variety explosions because the concatenation of events is unpredictable, even after the hurricane event itself. After hurricane 'Iniki 1992, the Kauai Fire Department lost trucks due to flattened tires caused by nails on roads [Witwer, 2007]. Or, a fire problem arose after another hurricane hit due to the dead wood [Witwer, 2007]. Other safety concerns such as downed power lines and less-known obstacles such as the back feeding of generators can also constitute a seemingly small element in the chain of concatenations of events that have to be monitored for cybernetic reasons. But let us look at some examples at lower Levels of Recursions.

A democratic society creates a lot of Variety due to its participatory demands in the social, political and economic planning process performed by the government. What needs to be considered for the Hurricane Hazard Management System (HHMS) is how much Variety this system can handle and prioritize the most urgent needs to have the most effective improvements for the HHMS. For example, the democratic right of the media can create a high Variety proliferation. If the media pick on one of the many governmental issues arousing the public, the government needs to amplify its Variety to deal with the consequence of an upset public. Information on hurricane preparedness, vulnerability and mitigation measures can cause high Variety proliferation. If certain information about high vulnerability issues reach the public and become a concern, the government needs to respond, which might be of advantage for public safety, but might not necessarily be in the interest of politicians.

The pet-friendly sheltering has a social and cultural aspect to it, since a certain percentage of the population will not leave their pets behind in a disaster, will not shelter and put themselves at risk. What should be considered is the percentage of the population affected by that. Due to the highly vulnerable overall situation affecting the population as a whole, specifically the shortage of shelter spaces and lack of effective evacuation planning, the time spent on this topic seemed not in relation to the obvious urgency of unaccomplished basic disaster preparation tasks. In a democratic society all voices want to be heard but in the case of a life-threatening disaster the Variety explosion created by consideration of those factors cannot be handled by the System 1s (implementation) on any Level of Recursion. Prioritization, for example using the Analytical Hierarchy Process (AHP) [Saaty, 2001], and Variety Engineering are needed here.

Due to the HHMS's incapability to efficiently handle a catastrophic hurricane hit on Oʻahu, it seems that the only way Variety explosions are dealt with is through ignorance which is the most lethal Variety attenuator. As Ed Teixeira stated, the consequences of a catastrophic hurricane hitting Oʻahu are so enormous, so hard to imagine, that they were not dealt with on the level of detail necessary [Teixeira, 2007a]. As a consequence planning parameters are set so unrealistically for a hurricane Category 4 or 5 that they can be fulfilled. For example, it was stated that Honolulu International Airport is envisioned to be available, the planning is set to operate this airport. Figure 60 has shown that this is certainly not the case but the planning horizon is set to fix electronics and landing capabilities [Rosenberg, 2007b]. In general, the Makani Pahili exercise concerned with such a catastrophic event in a five day real-time scenario is conducted with all players using routine in-place agency communications systems. A completely unrealistic picture of functionality of the communication system was given. Consequently, the scenario cannot display real-event conditions. The external Variety is displayed lower than it would be in an actual event and feeds a false sense of reality and security. The incapability to match that external Variety is known but ignored, which increases the system's vulnerability and will lead to panic in a real event in case of total system failure. This panic amongst Hurricane Hazard Management System (HHMS) staff will further reduce the internal Variety, since they did not expect those conditions. Instead of running away from that Variety explosions, more scenarios should be played and reality being faced otherwise all Variety balancing capabilities are at risk to be lost.

In sum, the VSM does not offer quick fixes to solve a complex problem. It is a fine-tuning tool that points a manager into direction where to go and what to look for. A detailed hurricane scenario with a complete CONOP application is a first step. The VSM also makes clear the importance of this System 4 (intelligence) task, so that other tasks can be seen in relation to that. A prioritization of tasks to accomplish on the ever-lasting list of 'things to do' could be a major achievement of a VSM application.

3.3.5 Information systems

In a catastrophic hurricane disaster as assumed for the annual state-wide Makani Pahili exercises, the communication system will fail to a great extent due to power and infrastructure failure as described in the vulnerability analysis in chapter 1.4.2. System 4 (intelligence) would be the place for communication capability enhancement. The agreement of Hurricane Hazard Management System (HHMS) departments and agencies on a common plan is the actual obstacles [Fenton, 2007] representing missing System 2 (coordination) and 4 (intelligence) in VSM terms. Some twists and turn should be discussed here to exemplify how cybernetics can improve the HHMS's effectiveness and efficiency.

Information has to be free within the HHMS [Holmberg, 1989] and is prescribed by NIMS in this way as well. But, currently, the HHMS departments and agencies do not even have to share information. As observed in the Makani Pahili exercise 2007, the State Civil Defense (SCD) is aware of the importance of creating trust and good relationships and wants everybody to understand data usage and confidentiality. But due to the lack of System 2 (coordination) implementation this free flow of information is hindered because it is not clear what relevant information is for whom Consequently only data is transferred and the HHMS hangs in a cloud of noise – a good example is that 300 page Emergency Operations Plan that employees feel overwhelmed by. The DEM Emergency Operation Center (EOC) would be the central point to collect and disseminate information. But, the Joint Field Office (JFO) and all other Emergency Operation Centers (EOCs) and Incident Command Posts (ICPs) are very dependent on IT, power and communications. Managerial overlaps and confusion between the Incident Commander at the Unified Command Post (UCP) or Area Command Post (ACP) and the Emergency Support Function (ESF) commanders emerge once communication fails and time lags become abound. The system starts to break down and System Cohesion is lost from the lowest Level of Recursion upward. If communication fails the mission fails and first responders will not be able to fulfill their tasks.

The county Emergency Operations Plan (EOP) a la NIMS prescribes timely information reporting: 'At the onset of the threat or the occurrence of a disaster situation, prompt reporting of information to the City or District Emergency Operation Center (EOC) as frequently as practical by the most expeditious means is critical to official decision making' [City and County of Honolulu, 2007, p. 15]. The system is cybernetically sound in theory, but in practice it is not implementable. Major reasons of concern are the physical capabilities, interoperability of communication systems and lack of NIMS training, System 1 (implementation) and 2 failures in VSM terms. More importantly, once a hurricane approaches it is too late to set Algedonic Alarms or react to them. This is a process that has to be inherited within the system throughout time and in real-time to be effective when a Variety Explosion, in this case imposed through a hurricane, is on its way.

Further, free information flow regarding the public cannot be guaranteed within the HHMS because information management is necessary, specifically not to create panic or regarding issuance of Watches and Warnings. This is a good example though for filtering data into relevant information, without creating noise. How those filters should be set, is an almost ethical question. Specifically in Japan now, after the Fukushima disaster, it is highly questionable how the information filters from the government and TEPCO, the company of the nuclear plants, are set towards the public. One might go as far as asking if certain disaster management information management could be described as a crime. Levels of radiation not dangerous for human health are set higher and higher. The US Seventeenth Fleet moved its ships from its position of 100 miles off-shore from Japan due to low radiation levels as stated in MSN – but obviously enough contamination to be of concern and move the whole fleet [MSNBC, 3/15/2011], but people in Tokyo (180 miles from Fukushima) were not evacuated. The problem here is obvious: it is not feasible to evacuate 35 million people. In the Chernobyl disaster of 1986, the government exposed their population to high levels of radiation due to failure of informing the people in the highly contaminated areas. Political and economic reasons can be assumed to be the source.

In general though, information is a great resource to enhance effectiveness and efficiency even with a great breakdown in structural resource. Beer's work in Chile showed how System 2 (coordination) and 3 (operational control) were able to balance the complexity hitting System 1 (implementation): even though only 30% of Chile's transportation system was available, the information regarding System 1 (implementation) – i.e. the factories – was so thorough and up-to-date that much of the loss of the transportation system could be efficiently dealt with due to real-time information [Walker, 2001]. This shows how much tacit potential lies within a system: even though the structure falls apart to 70%, real-time relevant information can enhance the system's effectiveness substantially even with less resources, may it be money or even the structure itself.

The VSM and its language are useful tools in helping the members of an organization to take a systemic view of their communication processes. 'The modeling tools define an underlying structure for communications in support of viability whilst providing a valuable template for both structural and organizational design and the mapping of strategic IT architecture' [Espejo and Gill, 1997, p. 6]. 'The NIMS identifies the requirement for a standardized framework for communications, information management (collection, analysis, dissemination), and information-sharing at all levels of incident management' [U.S. DHS, 2004a, p. 5]. In theory, those elements are present, but in practice are not implemented. There are several reasons for obstacles, besides the IT compatibility mentioned in chapter 3.3.2. Many organizations serve as transducers trying to provide common understanding (Channel Capacity) of the situation: for example, the Virtual Joint Information Center prescribed by the National Response Plan, the National Weather Service along with Central Pacific Hurricane Center, the Pacific Disaster Center, the Joint Information Center (JIC) and the Center of Excellence in disaster management and humanitarian assistance. But the physical limitations and vulnerabilities have to be resolved in order for the transducers to become viable. The telecom industry (Verizon, Moby, Sprint) have to be open for coordination instead of their independent activities keeping secrets that stymie their cooperation. On the US mainland, consortia are established that ensure coordination [Gilbert, 2007b]. Variety Engineering is distorted. In such a situation, a Syntegration can reveal the common reasons why cooperation is a win-win situation for all stakeholders and is capable of new-directing a seemingly stuck situation (see chapter 3.3.10).

It is important that the information time lag is within limits of viability, which depends on the system and its survival criteria. For the Hurricane Hazard Management System (HHMS), this regards the annual cycle of the hurricane season. In this time frame, the HHMS has to correct systemic instabilities to sustain viability. The documentation keeping track of real-time information needs to be built into the design so it is automatic. This type of information flow is essential along the Accountability Loop, from System 3* (audits) to System 1 (implementation) and between System 3 (operational control) and 1 (implementation) on all Recursion Levels. Further, this information system must be capable to generate appropriate Algedonic Alarms in real-time. Additionally, System 4 (intelligence) needs information regarding the envelope Environment to adapt to environmental change to produce strategies [Walker, 2001]. In this step, techniques should be developed to ensure that a thorough system for up-to-date information is in place. Beer stresses that this is an alternative to authoritarian management. Therefore, appropriate information needs to be measured and feed-back used to modify the way people work. Real-time information systems based on performance indicators using these indicators to send Algedonic Alarms when necessary need to be designed. This will be accomplished in chapter 3.4 along the Homeland Security Exercise and Evaluation Program (HSEEP). If funding is lacking it seems hard to increase a system's capabilities but the soft factors give enough room to improve effectiveness and efficiency.

3.3.6 "Do you understand the words that are coming out of my mouth?" – Channel Capacity and Transduction

"I don't know if I understand the words that are coming out of your mouth!" Or, in other words: Channel Capacity and Transduction (C3 in Figure 39) are critical to ensure that information flows efficiently through the system, otherwise it will be distorted and cause inefficiencies. Problems arise when people do not speak the same 'language' – Channel Capacity is not given – or if information is assumed to be understood, but it is not – Transduction fails – or if translators don't have Requisite Variety as transducers. They might simplify and therefore attenuate Variety and thereby loose important information. A specific problem of the vertical loop – the Metasystem relationship to the System 1s (implementation) – is given when 'the senior manager insists 'But I told him/her!', but the information was not transduced. Closed-loop communication means: I know that you know that I know. Often it is required to 'read between the lines' and certain distinctions are necessary, but Requisite Variety is not met in the Transduction – the person receiving the information was not able to understand it 'right' [Beer, 1994a, p.124].

Situation reports (channels) and committees (transducers) often do not represent Requisite Variety and less formal methods may then (self-consciously) be used so Varieties can be absorbed on both sides. He introduces the concept of a 'gate-keeper' – taken from a social psychological context – where one man can channel the reduced Variety of several hundred people. For example, if people in an organization are geographically dispersed, they will not have time to create the Requisite Variety needed through immersing themselves in the Environment that they need to deal with. Hence, much-attenuated reports are written and sent through the formal channel. They will not have the Requisite Variety to induce any change. A 'gate-keeper' channels information and transduces it in informal ways – through conversations during or after lunch, for example [Beer, 1994a].

For Channel Capacity and Transduction to work properly, a functioning System 2 (coordination) is essential. The Joint Information Center (JIC) and the Joint Information System (JIS), the National Weather Service, the Center of Excellence in disaster management and humanitarian assistance or the Pacific Disaster Center serve as transducers for information and therefore represent information brokers attenuating Variety. The National Incident Management System (NIMS) requires that communications and information systems be interoperable and redundant [Emergency Management Institute, 2007b]. Even though a well designed System 2 (coordination) prescribed by NIMS exists and is cybernetically sound, its implementation on the System 1 (implementation) levels of all Recursion is missing. For example, NIMS prescribes that communication equipment, procedures, and systems must operate across jurisdictions and that developing an integrated voice and data communications system, including equipment, systems, and protocols, must occur prior to an incident. NIMS also prescribes three elements for effective ICS communications: modes – the 'hardware' systems that transfer information; planning – for the use of all available communications resources; and networks – the procedures and processes for transferring information internally and externally [Emergency Management Institute, 2007b]. It describes in detail all envelope environmental Variety that the HHMS could face and prescribes how to amplify internal Variety to match it. But the limitations of information technology implementation and its interoperability in Hawai'i restrict effective System 2 (coordination) implementation [U.S. DHS, 2007a].

The capacities of the Hurricane Hazard Management System (HHMS) are bound on the one hand by technology and on the other hand by learning difficulties. The age of the HHMS personnel plays a role. The unfamiliarity with IT restricts the older generation in regards to knowledge transfer. For example, the younger generation uses creative learning environments that overcome space and time. A professor with a high level of experience and knowledge might be inaccessible due to his location or IT skills. The challenge is to update these resource holders in order to make their knowledge and experience available and keep time-relevant questions up to par. A 25-year-old student that teaches a professor how present 'young people' learn and live could be a starting point – those students are the customers for the professor's knowledge and they are supposed to use and further develop their knowledge pool. Due to their day-by-day activities, there seems to be no time to be up to date with current developments. It is part of the human condition to focus on the daily operations and to be stressed by daily new and challenging learning experiences. Still, sharp learning experiences are needed and the contact with young professionals is essential for the development of the knowledge pool and the continuity of research and development efforts, the System 4 (intelligence). The power to interrelate together at speed is a new challenge.

In general, Channel Capacity and Transduction is not cared for within the HHMS because, according to the National Response Plan (NRP), only agencies receiving FEMA funds have to comply with NIMS. Further, other factors hinder those cybernetic functions such as the hierarchical structure that causes many points of interaction between the governmental levels amplifying Variety. The more information channels, the higher the chances are that Transduction and Channel Capacity do not match. Especially in organizations dealing in information such governments, banks or the insurance industry, Requisite Variety in Channel Capacity – the transmission – and Transduction are crucial, especially in regards to the Environment because of complex overlaps. Beer proposes the Syntegrity process [Beer, 1994b].

Further, Transduction is manipulated in many ways by information management. During the Makani Pahili exercise 2007, it was asked of Hurricane Hazard Management System (HHMS) personnel to 'share what you can share' [Richards, 2007c]. It implied that certain information is not transduced due to a Variety of reasons – from competition between private companies such as within the telecommunication industry to political motivated disclosure of information.

Ignorance and false information also poses major problems for Channel Capacity and Transduction. As stated before, sheer ignorance is the most lethal form of Variety attenuation. If external Variety overwhelms the system, categorization would be another way to attenuate Variety instead of ignoring the facts altogether. Channel Capacity is distorted and Transduction manipulated when information is not flowing free through the system, but is attenuated to the point that important information is unavailable or not understood. There are distinctions: Ignorance and false information within the HHMS and among the public, which will both be treated here. Within the HHMS, Honolulu International Airport is envisioned to be available for planning parameters, which is very unrealistic [Rosenberg, 2007b] (see Figure 60). Planning is concerned about the electronics and landing capabilities [Rosenberg, 2007b]. As the vulnerability analysis showed, the airport area will be under water for the time of the storm's impact with consequential catastrophic destruction. This form of ignorance facing a Category 4–5 hurricane is forced upon the HHMS due to its incapability of solving the anticipated problems. In regards to communication capabilities, the cell phone towers will be affected when sustained wind speed reach 60 mph. Consequently, satellite phones and image radio will be the only resource of communication after a catastrophic hurricane hit. In the Makani Pahili exercise, this was disregarded and many participants were unaware of this situation. Further, this unrealistic picture gives a false sense of functionality of the communication system, which will lead to panic in a real event in case of total system failure [Richards, 2007c]. The ignorance regarding Meteorology, even among people of important rank, such as the spokesman for the Hawai'ian Electric Company, is evidence of lacking Channel Capacity and information cannot be transduced. As an example, he was of the belief that the Big Island's land mass would push the storm towards Kauai and that leeward O'ahu and Kauai are most in danger of a hit [Rosegg, 2007a]. This view has long been discredited [Schroeder, 1993].

Secondly, the public is found to be not properly informed about a potential catastrophic hurricane impact. They also are found to have wrong expectations regarding a possible hurricane response [Tengan, 2007a]. For example, *the Honolulu Advertiser* published a statement saying that when Civil Defense officials plot the recovery phase of a disaster, the counties plan as if no outside help would arrive for up to two days, and the state likewise plans to rely entirely on resources within Hawai'i for two to four days [Honolulu Advertiser, 2005b]. In the Makani Pahili exercise 2007, this information was that it would take a lot longer. If Channel Capacity is not established, information cannot be transduced and the public's perception and capability to respond is distorted.

In the real-life cases and the exercises, officials say, Hawai'i's system worked well, and the state and counties have received high marks from various sources for aspects of their preparedness levels. The plaudits, however, do not reflect the serious gaps that remain in the overall system. For example, O'ahu has a shortage of about 60,000 shelter spaces, and statewide the shortfall is 124,000 [Honolulu Advertiser, 2005b]. That falsely displayed information not only fails to warn the public about these gaps, but also leads to distorted public perception and behavior. Additionally, the shortfall of shelter spaces is underestimated. The shelters are built to withstand winds up to 80mph but a hurricane Category 1 starts at 85mph winds. Roofs will be flying off as known by officials but in their helplessness it was stated that 'well, we did not tell anybody they will stay dry'. Realistically, the statewide shelter shortfall ranges in the several hundred thousands.

The Honolulu Advertiser stated in 2005 that it would likely be three to four days after a hurricane clears Hawai'i before outside supplies, equipment and personnel arrive [Honolulu Advertiser, 2005a]. This disregards the fact that until resources can be distributed over O'ahu due to the debris management requirements, many more days, weeks or months will pass. 'Col. John Kelly, Chief of Staff for U.S. Army Pacific, said military authorities here have almost everything needed to respond to a natural disaster [Honolulu Advertiser, 2005a]. In a report on a major hurricane event, this gives a false sense of security. The military will be required to achieve operability first before being able to help the public. 'We have the forces and can get there quickly,' Kelly said. 'We know what kind of stocks we have. We know there are 150,000 MREs (Meals Ready to Eat) right here. We have water. And all those things can move very quickly by military air both by National Guard and active forces, to any place around the islands' [Honolulu Advertiser, 2005a]. The Federal Emergency Management Agency Regional Interagency Steering Committees (FEMA RISC) conference revealed that the MREs will run out quickly and water availability will be a problem due to power outages and the consequent inoperability of pumps for water distribution. Resource inventories are lacking regarding the sustainment of the population. 'With a single phone call to Schofield Barracks, Kelly said he can marshal 2,500 soldiers and a fleet of trucks and move them across the island in as little as three hours'[Honolulu Advertiser, 2005a]. This information disregards the debris management problem leaving roads and airfield inoperable. 'It is a powerful force when you can do that with one phone call,' said Kelly, who has worked on several hurricane relief efforts while stationed on the East Coast [Honolulu Advertiser, 2005a]. This information disregards that the situation for Hawai'i is different due to its isolation, its confined space, the debris management requirements and the population density with no possibility to evacuate. Not even debris management infrastructure is on-island. Until its arrival, asset distribution will be highly difficult.

Adding to it, the military installations will be heavily impacted. The Federal Emergency Management Agency (FEMA) will back them up first and military has a large resource demand. The public expects military to help, which is impossible in the response phase [Suizo, 2007]. DoD Joint Task Force – Homeland Defense (JTF-HD) cannot provide Support to Civil Authorities unless it restored the capabilities of their own forces, which will be a long lasting process [Suizo, 2007]. As a consequence, the public has wrong expectations.

In *the Honolulu Advertiser*, the public is informed about 145.000 homeless people that would result from a landfall of an 'Iniki-type hurricane on O'ahu, which is not an adequate estimation for a catastrophic storm. 'Using tents, hotel rooms, rental properties, homes of friends and relatives and other facilities, Civil Defense officials project that temporary housing could be found for the majority of those who don't leave the island' [Honolulu Advertiser, 2005b]. A wrong picture of the situation is drawn here, given the assumption that evacuation is realistic and feasible. As learned during the Makani Pahili exercise 2007, evacuation is neither possible nor feasible with the damage assumptions given for a Category 4 hurricane scenario.

But even after exhausting those options, that would still leave some 45,000 people in need of shelter, creating a daunting task of finding suitable sites where they could live possibly for months. Local parks would be an option, Teixeira said [Honolulu Advertiser, 2005b].

It has to be noted, that 'the destruction of coastal structures on Kauai by Hurricane 'Iniki appeared to have done little to discourage property owners from rebuilding in what are clearly hazardous areas' [University of Hawai'i at Mānoa , 1993, p.13]. Overall, this results in high social vulnerability because people rely on these statements, which give a false sense of safety and confirms the assumption that the State and the federal government will take care of everybody. It fails to communicate the need for self-sufficiency. The media does a bad job in communicating essential information, on top of officials who make wrong statements.

Further, the public is not knowledgeable regarding scientific climate information or other sophisticated information, e.g. insurance policies or risk management. For example, Flood Insurance Risk Maps (FIRMs) designating explicitly high hazard areas exist and are used by county governments, but those are little known to or understood by the general public. Interviews revealed that people had been told to get Federal Flood Insurance without knowing that they purchased property or built in high hazard areas [University of Hawai'i at Mānoa , 1993]. Channel Capacity is missing between the System 1s (implementation) of Recursion 1 (the federal government), of Recursion 4 (e.g. the Insurance Industry) and the Environment. Also, the usability of scientific information needs improvement. 'The need to understand usability of scientific information has received much attention from a communications perspective, but little from an organizational perspective' [Pulwarty, 2004].

3.3.7 The 800 pound gorilla – power struggles

How can the VSM give us insights into handling power struggles any better? A great advantage of the Viable System Model (VSM) is the combination of both qualitative and quantitative diagnostic capabilities. Even though the VSM is a functionalist approach, it specifically considers 'soft' issues (C3 in Figure 39) of management: the relationship between people and groups of people. It is able to deal with 'messy' problems. Beer states that 'the heart of the organization is embodied in its own people' [Beer, 1994a, p.560]. It needs to be recognized that all interactions and decisions have subjective character and depend on the individual's personality.

The soft factors influencing the viability of the system and its effectiveness are often not recognized in organizational analyses. Channel Capacity, Transduction and the overall information flow depend on them. Soft factors relate to personal and psychological-related parameters that influence the effective functioning of the HHMS, e.g. trust and skills. Sometimes it seems that a coworker is saving fish from drowning and his behavior remains unclear or is even offensive to others. These factors are elaborated in this chapter and will be included as measurement variables in the next chapter 3.4. It is an important task of System 4 (intelligence) to explore how networking, keeping good relationships and trust can be established. This was motivated during the Makani Pahili exercise 2007 [Richards, 2007f]. It was also concluded that the difference of National Incident Management System (NIMS) functioning in different states, e.g. Florida and Louisiana, are due to those soft factors, specifically competence, trust, solidarity, familiarity with the situation and their coworkers or leadership skills. System 2 (coordination) as a whole depends highly on those soft factors. If people do not pull on the same string, power is lost. In disaster management, that has a clear goal, power struggles and conflicts should not exist.

Every institution – from a firm in the private sector, a government agency, an industry in the public sector or a department of government itself – has to 'make an investment into its own viability in terms of money, time, talent, care, attention, etc.' [Beer, 1994a, p. 251]. The power struggle arises when System 4 (intelligence) taking care of the 'Outside and Then' only gets the resources left over by System 3 (operational control), and providing funding for System 4 (intelligence) is less important than it should; or, when System 4 (intelligence) spends all the money System 3 (operational control) makes. Practically, this is a 'resource constraint needing balance between operational and strategic planning, between present needs and emerging future needs with changing modes of response' [Beer, 1994a, p. 251]. For example, if quick fixes are the main disaster management technique and mitigation measures are hardly considered, there is an imbalance between System 3 and 4. Algedonic Alarms would sound throughout the system because of this deficiency, which can be resolved if disaster management personnel understand their contribution to the whole and the reasons for that way of resource allocation. This holistic, synoptic view changes their perspectives and smoothes collaboration in a great way. Being part of a Syntegration process is key to such developments (see chapter 3.3.10).

Consequently, the System 3–4 loop needs to be monitored and balanced. Therefore System 5 (identity) is invented. For the System 3–4 interaction

Beer suggests 'a Management Center that replaces the common Board-room, the Executive Suite and committee rooms, also called the Operations Room' [Beer, 1994a, p. 251]. For the HHMS, this should be accomplished by FEMA on Level of Recursion 1. But throughout the year, only the low-est Level of Recursion is active and the Recursions in between cannot be monitored. Their System 3s (operational control) and 4s (intelligence) lack monitoring by a System 5 (identity). The single HHMS departments and agencies are present all year, but do not practice the system. It is required to comply with NIMS to receive funding, but the lacking System 3* (audits), as diagnosed before, does not ensure its functioning.

Political issues play a major role in the Hurricane Hazard Manage-ment System (HHMS) [Breakout Session Infrastructure, 2007]. Politics determines who gets the contracts, but also introduces time lags while the political criteria are settled first and that ultimately determines the pace of the planning and response. Those factors greatly impede Transduction and introduce time lags. If different System 3 (operational control) decision makers have different priorities, central direction will lack and synergy is not conceivable. Problems occur when power and authority are exercised without information and consequently Requisite Variety. Communica-tion and free information flow are distorted and Transduction cannot be guaranteed. Stakeholders will not communicate in an effective way, since they use different jargon, their decisions are based on different interests and they are equipped with different power. In the HHMS, it was stated that a '800 lb gorilla' – meaning a person with high seniority causing conflict also due to personality issues – can ultimately be circumvented by special legal authority in effect during a catastrophic disaster [Richards and Tengan, 2007]. System 5 (identity) is strong and in place and allows non-compliant elements to be rendered void. The overarching priorities on the top Level of Recursion are clearly set by System 5 (identity) through System 2 (coordina-tion) – in short saving lives and protect property. But on the lower Levels of Recursion, priority conflicts emerge. The different HHMS departments and agencies have their own lists of priorities and blending is necessary. For example, the Hawai'ian Electric Company (HECO) is a full-profit pri-vate organization and consequently has different customers and different priorities than a governmental department or agency, for example one is determined within a free market and one underlies political aspects. Also, Emergency Support Function (ESF) 1, 3 and 12 have different priority lists and need to be blended. It was unclear if the personnel responsible were aware of that problem [Breakout Session Infrastructure, 2007]. Time needs to be invested to establish a clear System 2 (coordination) on the lower Recursions. System 5 (identity) serves as Variety attenuator. The squiggly lines need to become alive. According to Beer, a system's overall purpose is survival. Therefore, two options exist when conflict arises: (1) to persuade the organization to change or modify its purposes or (2) to destroy the organization physically, pick up the pieces and start over again, which equals war [Beer, 1994a]. Option (1) will be supported by the articulation of the Metasystem to deal with more psycho-social related conflicts regarding individual personality or caused by political aspects as prescribed see chapter 3.3.10. A Syntegration as introduced later can solve those challenges in a short amount of time before a disaster approaches. Personal skills and assets are revealed and evaluated in the most effective and efficient manner because competence, knowledge base is defined and abilities as much as an individual character shows through attitudes, interests and personal preferences. The psychological aspects cannot be underestimated in this process. Its power also lies in its effects on the attitude, self initiative and self interest of system employees. Several personal characteristics can influence Hurricane Hazard Management System's (HHMS) effectiveness. The attitude towards learning, change, cooperation and other important factors for an effective functioning of the HHMS, as well as the tendency of self initiative and self-interest in the HHMS activities varies greatly from individual to individual. Those are hard to measure and yield to subjective parameters. Other personal characteristics critical to the VSM are reliability and solidarity, which matter to System Cohesion as concepts of System 5 (identity). All of those factors are tuned through a Syntegration.

An important factor is the competence of people working in the Incident Command System (ICS), which involves 'switching hats' from one day-to-day routine task to a non-routine task in the case of a disaster. Ideally, training and drill lets these non-routine events become routine for the HHMS personnel. Ideally, most appointments in the ICS (job positions) are long-term, so people can develop the trust and reliability needed for extreme events. A combination of those factors will eventually lead to a more effective disaster management through the ICS. Further it has to be noted that it is problematic that 'managers hold a job due to technical competence, not social competence' [Holmberg, 1989, p. 271]. A Syntegration takes care of the right Human Resource development as well.

Under the NIMS principle of resolving issues at the lowest practical level, the JFO Coordination Group 'provides strategic guidance and resolution of any conflicts in priorities for the allocation of critical federal resources.

If policy issue resolution cannot be achieved between JFO Coordination Group members, the PFO may raise the issue through the National Operations Center – National Response Coordination Center (NOC-NRCC) to the Incident Advisory Council (IAC). Either concurrent with action in the IAC, or for issues not resolved by the IAC, the Secretary of Homeland Security or any other federal department or agency head may take an issue of concern directly to the President, the Assistant to the President for Homeland Security and Counterterrorism, the Assistant to the President for National Security Affairs, the Counterterrorism Security Group, or the Domestic Readiness Group, depending on the type of incident' [U.S. DHS, 2006a, p. 23]. This hierarchical flow of information to resolve power struggles is cybernetically pathologic and inefficient.

For example, on Kauai after Hurricane 'Iniki in 1992, the first thing needed in the police and fire departments' responses was spare tires because the debris on the road flattened the trucks' tires [Starbulletin, 2002b]. It would be a System 4 (intelligence) task to be aware and self initiative is needed in an unexpected situation to proceed effectively. This attitude also showed when people took chainsaws to shelters without being asked to reopen roads after the storm [Starbulletin, 2002b]. When the public shows this proactive initiative and becomes part of the HHMS it greatly attenuates external Variety. Additionally, in Hawai'i, the 'Aloha Spirit' flows through the HHMS. In disaster situations such as the earthquake in October 2006, emergency crews proved to be dedicated employees and most people came to work without being asked [Rosegg, 2007a]. In Japan, the trusting attitude of the masses in governance is outstanding and directing the masses was successfully mastered. Wrong information could have led to mass panic resulting in unnecessary deaths.

Different personalities of individuals play a significant role in the effective functioning of the Hurricane Hazard Management System (HHMS). Higher up in the hierarchical chain of command stronger personalities are persistent [Richards and Tengan, 2007]. That can be positive, e.g. personnel with leadership skills contribute to Variety attenuation, and consequently enhancing effectiveness. But, certain personalities can have negative effects. Problems arise from personality traits, e.g. when a person acting autonomously in this position has a tendency to use their power. It was stated that many local level personnel are 'weak' and have no knowledge of correct problems or cannot multi-task. This is also due to a lack of opportunity to learn and they do not take the initiative to look for it. They do not learn from exercises, are not capable of functioning in a different Environment and are easily overwhelmed. They lack psychological capability, have no vision or power to see a solution in a difficult situation [Richards and Tengan, 2007]. Giving then the right outlook on their contribution to the whole can make them change perspectives, which is the way forward. People do not necessarily resist change, but being changed. Also, problems can arise due to cultural issues. In Hawai'i, the respect for the Hawai'ian culture and authenticity is of high value. Complying with those values or not is a big turning point and constitutes part of Hawai'i's social capital.

The social capital was improved greatly by the Federal Emergency Management Agency Regional Interagency Steering Committees (FEMA RISC) conference held during the Makani Pahili exercise 2007. Specifically building relationships by meeting face to face, putting faces to names, networking and establishing trust were facilitated on top of the factual information exchange at the FEMA RISC conference in, 2007. Given the lack of resources because of funding deficiencies and the fact that it is impossible to have all resources on the island, the social capital within the HHMS personnel is of high value. It enhances Channel Capacity and Transduction. The implementation of System 2 (coordination), e.g. through education and training, can strongly enhance social capital value. The greatest attribute in this equation is the prevalent long history of and long-term personal relationships in Hawai'i due to its geographic isolation, which varies from the US mainland. They are essential for teamwork and team-building within the Hurricane Hazard Management System (HHMS). For example, the Department of Transportation's administration trusts in their bus drivers who voluntarily report infrastructure damage to the police and are known for their Aloha Spirit, e.g. to take care of the public by informing them, taking care and being very flexible [Romaine, 2007]. On Kauai, some personnel involved in the 'Iniki response 1992 stated that they grew up with most of the people they worked with, which enhanced efficient decision making. It decreases efficiency when representatives are not present for exercises or meetings, or when every time a different representative attends. Conversations with the State Civil Defense in Hawai'i revealed that the effectiveness and efficiency in Mississippi after Hurricane Katrina in 2005 compared to Louisiana came from the fact that teams worked together before in the Pacific [Richards, 2007f]. The comfort level with each other is important, which is a personal issue and subjective [Richards, 2007f]. After Hurricane Katrina in Mississippi 2005, it became clear that personal relationships are the core of the Unified Command (UC). It was stated that personality compatibility is one problem and that the state level personnel did not trust each other, which impaired the system's effectiveness. It was concluded that the system will not work unless those relationships are fixed [Latham, 2007]. Patience, respect and an understanding where the other person is coming from are crucial and missing professional politeness hinders effectiveness, since they influence Channel Capacity and Transduction. Communication through body language is also influential [Richards, 2007f]. A Syntegration can reveal this value greatly and induce the much desired change here.

The physical presence of the HHMS personnel should not be underestimated, even without long-term relationships. For example, the National Incident Management System (NIMS) online training as a tool produces its results, but will never replace the effectiveness of exercises where people are physically collocated in one room. The combined effect of building personal relationships and learning efforts and effects enhance effectiveness greatly [Latham, 2007]. It was stated that the Hawai'ian Electric Company (HECO) has a close community and that some personnel are present for 30 to 40 years. Consequently, personnel are well-trained, committed, have a good attitude and are trusted that in a disaster situation, once their own home is secured, they would come to work [Rosegg, 2007a]. These soft factors effect great Variety attenuation to match internal and external Variety.

In one of Beer's case studies, the problem of Transduction was based on the fact that the system actors did not trust the VSM's capabilities. They stated 'one day it will be possible', 'clever tricks, but I have to get back to the office' [Beer, 1994a, pp. 256]. They understood his concepts only momentarily when the model was explained, and hence Requisite Variety was established for that time. But ultimately they mistrusted his suggestions and Requisite Variety was not established. But, trust is key.

Leadership has a strong Variety attenuating effect enhancing effectiveness and efficiency: After Hurricane 'Iniki on Kauai 1992, Lt. Toy, a Hawai'i National Guard officer working with U.S. Army Pacific arrived with Guard personnel as chief of operations right after the hurricane and stayed for several months, since his presence alone set the civilian population's mind at ease [Honolulu Advertiser, 2005a]. His leadership and the trust people gave him greatly attenuated Variety, e.g. by making the public cooperative. The respect that personnel with leadership skills are given attenuates internal Variety, since they are trusted. To take on leadership in a situation is also a System 4 (intelligence) task. For example, if the SCD identifies mitigation needs for repairing a dam, but it involves City and county property, the SCD cannot interfere due to the City and county's autonomy. But the SCD took on responsibilities and leadership and performed damage assessments to inform the City and county of the shortfalls, and consequently the mitigation measures were accomplished [Richards and Tengan, 2007]. This proactive interest is a high System 5 (identity) value.

3.3.8 Hurricane psychology

A significant percentage of O'ahu's population has not experienced a hurricane, a high-impact-low-probability event. 'The probability of a direct hit from a hurricane of 'Iniki's strength is very small and the potential costs are astronomical. The probability of a Hurricane 'Iwa scenario is much higher. The potential costs would be much lower, but the costs of asset damage alone could conceivably be higher than the annual state budget' [University of Hawai'i at Mānoa , 1993, p. 26]. 'Insurance rates would increase, a range of new risks and equity issues would emerge and would carry political costs. Some areas might experience an increase in insurance rate for seemingly – for the lay eye – unknown reasons. Why should federal tax payers support disaster relief to people, who choose to live in hazardous areas' [University of Hawai'i at Mānoa , 1993, p. 27]? Since a catastrophic disaster has not happened to most of the public in the State of Hawai'i, they do not perceive the risk. Sometimes, this leads to a false sense of trust, but, since Hurricane Katrina, more awareness exists. Those psychological factors hinder Channel Capacity and Transduction since ignorance and unrealistic expectation distort information. Ultimately, ignorance is a common way to deal with such a complex catastrophic disaster, as elaborated in 3.3.4 'Variety Engineering'.

'Experience on Kauai in 1992 showed that most people felt they were in such great danger that they were giddy and giggling when the storm passed. In the first week or two, everyone was euphoric' [Starbulletin, 2002a]. Sandy Ritz, of O'ahu, wrote her dissertation for her doctorate in public health on the humor used by disaster victims, based on her interviews with people on Kauai, stating that this is called the Honeymoon Period. Since they have survived, they do not realize the losses yet [Starbulletin, 2002a]:

'Lavish block parties began all over the island as residents, stores and restaurants gave away the food from their now useless freezers. …Several food stores tried to give away canned goods, but Kauai residents insisted on paying for them.'

Cybernetically, this leads to Variety attenuation for the HHMS originating from the local Environment, which the public is part of from a HHMS perspective. On the other hand, negative psychological aspects such as stress and frustration have a major influence disaster management's effectiveness and efficiency. In a catastrophic hurricane disaster, those will be plentiful and need special attention. For the public, the American Red Cross has specific counseling personnel available, but Hurricane Hazard Management System (HHMS) personnel are highly in need of those services. During the disaster response, this is mostly not a priority and has effects on the effective functioning of the HHMS. A firm system has to be set up ahead of time because in crisis 'nobody has time to think' [Suizo, 2007]. Once the system becomes unstable, the stress the HHMS personnel are exposed to reduces the potential to amplify internal Variety. Amplifying internal Variety could be learning and understanding innovative processes, which is to be researched by System 4 (intelligence) ahead of time. Under stress, this potential cannot be utilized at all or only with difficulty and time lags causing inefficiencies. Further, it was stated that experience showed that people under stress are more likely to act in unethical or illegal manner [Fenton, 2007] – disintegrating System 5 (identity) principles manifested in System 2 (coordination). The psychological aspect if the family of the HHMS personnel is impacted is significant and affected HHMS personnel might not be available for their tasks, choosing to stay with their family instead [Suizo, 2007]. Some of the HHMS personnel stated that frustration was high, since disaster management is an underappreciated job and affected people are often unthankful [Richards and Tengan, 2007]. This attenuates internal Variety and complicates matching external Variety proliferation.

National Incident Management System (NIMS) prescribes that the HHMS personnel and equipment respond only when requested or when dispatched by an appropriate authority [Emergency Management Institute, 2007b]. During the response to Hurricane Katrina in Louisiana in 2005, it occurred that a helicopter standing next to drowning people was utilized to save lives without being ordered and dispatched, which ethically is justifiable. As a consequence though, this resource might not be available for dispatch to another place when ordered [Breakout Session Infrastructure, 2007]. System 2 (coordination) falls apart and System Cohesion is lost. System 2 (coordination) disintegrates under the extreme stress people are exposed to in a catastrophic disaster situation and coordination becomes impossible. Those factors need to be accounted for in designing a Viable System and would show in Variety Engineering exercises in their relevant importance to get a cybernetic grip and indirect control mechanisms set up for a seemingly uncontrollable disaster situation. In the real-time event itself, one will be better prepared with a much higher resource effectiveness and efficiency.

3.3.9 Hawai'i is different

Hawai'i's geographical isolation and history led to a high cultural diversity. In a cultural melting pot, one could assume that problems in the HHMS implementation can arise due to a variety of soft factor differences and diverse ideas about ethics, gender-related issues, and power relations, among others. In the interviews, the contrary showed evidence because Hawai'i has gained a sense of community through its geographical isolation. Hawai'i created a culture of its own [Richards and Tengan, 2007][Rosegg, 2007a]. For example, in safety issues, barriers do not exist due to a mutual understanding of safety concerns, which ultimately aim at protecting life and property, a firmly established System 5 (identity) element intended to be implemented by System 2 (coordination). Problems arise rather from personality issues, not due to cultural issues [Richards and Tengan, 2007].

Still, the special characteristics of the State of Hawaii need to be considered, which will be investigated in the following.

Hawai'i's isolation requires a different treatment of disaster management parameters. For example, the typical training applied on the mainland US is not applicable to Hawai'i due to major differences, such as the lack of a transportation network, the inaccessibility of airports and the necessity of transporting most resources via ship and truck. The main reason for a plan not being in place until May 2007 is the difficulty of planning and feasibility issues [Rosenberg, 2007b]. The vulnerability analysis in chapter 1.4.2 illustrates the shortfalls, which are so massive that a very coordinated and all-encompassing approach is needed, which is outlined in the FEMA CONOP [FEMA, 2007], but not yet elaborated in a comprehensive manner. Further, a HECO representative stated that decisions are based on an awareness of Hawai'i's isolation. For example, if one critical turbine is turned on too early and breaks, it takes a long time to replace it. Consequently, in an emergency decision-making favors the protection of basic infrastructure because the loss would have long-term consequences [Rosegg, 2007a].

Due to Hawai'i's isolation, a different awareness rose within the public and the Hurricane Hazard Management System (HHMS) personnel. It aims for self-containment, since it has no neighbor support as on the US mainland. The time factor has to be considered, e.g. a budget plan for x days of self-support and a higher urgency in preparation measures is prevalent. On the mainland, the focus lies on one-day-operations because if overwhelmed, neighbor support applies through the contract EMAC (Emergency Management Assistance Compact). Overall, the difference lies in the level of urgency, the scale and the necessity. Hawai'i's isolation is an advantage regarding training and exercises, since it represents a micro-cosmos. It is consequently more effective than the US mainland because of the awareness of urgency and because they have to cooperate. On the US mainland, in the case of disagreement in support requests, another department or agency can be a cooperating partner [Richards and Tengan, 2007]. Consequently, disaster management operations in Hawai'i differ from the US mainland. In Hawai'i, all counted, measured and gauged assets are definite in the sense that support from elsewhere cannot be counted on. To be aware of the status quo of these assets is therefore more of an urgency as well as to calculate the planning horizon, e.g. that policemen burn out in three weeks. For those reasons, mainland personnel are not prepared to work in Hawai'i unless they consider those special circumstances [Richards and Tengan, 2007].

Further, due to Hawai'i's isolation, the population's mentality is that the government has to take care of its people when in actual fact the government is not capable of it [Gilbert, 2007a]. For example, after the earthquake on O'ahu in October 2006, the Hawai'ian Electric Company (HECO) employees were working overtime, but there were numerous complaints about the 18-hour blackout for parts of the island. In comparison, in Buffalo, NY, on the US mainland, 100,000 people were without power for four days, which caused much less criticism. The expectations of the public in Hawai'i are higher due to their isolation [Rosegg, 2007a]. The public expects that the military will offer support because there is such a large military presence on the island. Even though O'ahu has military as support from army, navy and air forces, the military has its own priorities, specifically when needs arise in their community. Their own needs have priority before they can support the public [Richards and Tengan, 2007].

On the other hand, the area on O'ahu where followers of the Mormon Church reside has the best prepared individuals. They take preparedness very serious and are self-sustaining for over one month [Gilbert, 2007a]. Their cultural and religious identity and isolation enhance their effectiveness in disaster management.

The more complex the organization, the more challenging and vital is communications, especially because cultural and social factors define people's common understanding of each other's meanings. In VSM terms, this regards the Channel Capacity and Transduction and a firm System 2 (coordination) establishment. For example, the American Red Cross shelter exercise handout 'Shelter Resident Information' [American Red Cross, 2005] includes valuable information for a situation where the cultural Variety present on O'ahu are confined to rules of behavior. It states information regarding: welcome, registration, smoking, personal belongings, pets, children, medical problems or injuries, alcohol, drugs and weapons, volunteering to help, telephones, housekeeping, quiet hours, news media, special requirements, problems and complaints. This is highly Variety attenuating.

The Aloha Spirit of Hawai'i was mentioned throughout this book and a constant recognition of the soft factors involved explains the glue of System Cohesion [Beer, 1994a] in the Hawai'ian case. It was stated that a situation in Louisiana reported as looting and involving other criminal activities would not occur in Hawai'i due to a different mentality [Gilbert, 2007a]. The Aloha Spirit also showed in certain federally declared disasters where disaster management personnel voluntarily worked overtime while Federal Emergency Management Agency (FEMA) personnel did not. The solidarity with their own population is higher than on the US mainland, since it has a stronger cultural identity [Richards and Tengan, 2007].

Local knowledge is also highly valued. A catastrophic hurricane needs to be managed on the federal level, but with absolute autonomy of the local level. The VSM stipulates this requirement in asking for System 1 (implementation) autonomy under the aspect of Cohesion. The cohesive glue and the identity of the System are just as important as keeping the System 1 (implementation) autonomous enough to react to a fast changing Environment. A State Civil Defense (SCD) representative postulated that it would bring much improvement to listen more to local people [Richards, 2007f]. The SCD can be understood as a mediator between the federal and the local level.

3.3.10 Resolving human conflicts – the syntegrative healing process

Beer states that the psycho-political issues dissolve with the establishment of an Operations Room or a Management Center, which one is to be designed depends on the cultural settings and the management style. For the HHMS, the EOCs on all governmental levels represent this on Recursion 1 and 2, which are not in place in Metasystemic Calm throughout the year. Those institutions hibernate and only exist after a hurricane threat or hit.

This is a major deficiency in the HHMS: the higher Levels of Recursions are hibernating and lack presence in non-disaster times. The Makani Pahili exercise is not sufficient in keeping those Recursions alive. This System 3 (operational control) dominated place cannot just consist of System 1 (implementation) management heads and meet annually. Its interconnectivity, which has an emotive background, and knowing what System 1 (implementation) constitutes must be taken care of on a continuous basis [Beer, 1994a]. Therefore, the Metasystem must articulate itself.

The Metasystem is the HHMS's nervous system and its sensors disseminate 'through time and organizational space' [Beer, 1994a, pp. 379]. The articulation of the Metasystem depends on the managerial style, where human and cultural terms reveal themselves [Beer, 1994a], shown in Figure 65 [Beer, 1994a, p. 391] as perceptual filter and psychological space.

For the HHMS, the Federal Emergency Management Agency (FEMA) articulates the Metasystem on the highest Level of Recursion through its principles contained in National Incident Management System (NIMS). FEMA represents the self-consciousness of the HHMS in awareness of the infinite Recursion – the NIMS is to be applied throughout the United States as a whole. But, to be more effective and efficient, FEMA should classify situations and decisions according to the tripartite model shown in Figure 66 [Beer, 1994a, p. 393] to understand its Calm and Alarm ambience in a cybernetic sense. This guide can be useful for all Metasystems on all Levels of Recursion.

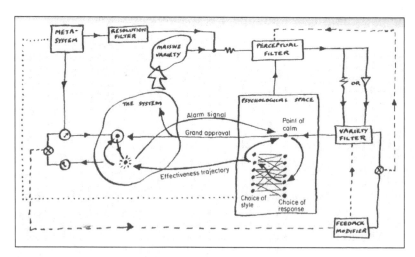

Figure 65: 'Handling incipient stability'

HOW TO CLASSIFY MANAGERIAL SITUATIONS AND TO DECIDE

Criterion of Effectiveness:

A representative point of the system, becoming incipiently unstable, must be returned to stability (within acknowledged physiological limits) within a time-scale that does not allow immanent disaster to become actual.

This satisfactory conclusion is to be recognized by the return of the representative point in the manager's psychological space to its POINT OF CALM.

Procedure:

Consider the range of alternative actions that are addressed to the problem.

Eliminate those possible actions that cannot meet the criterion of effectiveness within the time-scale available: leaves *n* alternatives.

Estimate the relaxation time for each of these *n* alternatives, and match each to a stylistic mode that would most meet the criterion.

Eliminate those possible actions for which the **effective** style is not available or is implausible.

If more than one solution remains, choose between the stress of adopting an unnatural style (given the psychology of the manager and the culture of the situation) and the speed of the effective response (given the degree of threat imposed by the incipient instability).

In Case of Failure:

Recast situation.
Look especially for new alternatives, not hitherto considered.
Entertain new styles, not hitherto envisaged.
Contemplate new relaxation times, which means changing metabolic rates.
If all this fails, it is necessary to resign.
Therefore consider under what terms (fundamentally changing available alternatives, plausible styles, and conceivable relaxation times) it might be possible to continue.
Propose such changes.
ACT.

In Case of Failure:

RESIGN. (And do not fail to do so.)

Figure 66: 'The procedure for using the model of handling incipient instability'

Then, the Metasystem – FEMA on Level of Recursion 1, for example – can 'bring closure to the system and embody the infinite Recursion as a living process' [Beer, 1994a, p. 394]. Reiterating the loops an infinite number of times until the state is 100 % changed, can change the situation, so Beer [1994a]. In this way, the goal generates itself and the infinite Recursion generates self-representation. This represents exactly what was meant earlier with 'mathematical Buddhism': everything is a process with no beginning and no end. In HHMS terms, this means that System 5 (identity) is dispersed through everything like god. The problem for the HHMS lies in the dispersion of Metasystemic articulation through all Levels of Recursion since self-consciousness 'is reached by a system that has developed the power to recognize itself at the infinite Recursion' [Beer, 1994a, p. 373]. This concerns setting climates of opinion.

In sum, the specific identity and culture of Hawai'i is not considered by FEMA and local issues are too often attempted to be handled on the federal level, which ignore local circumstances that can render a system ineffective that is well-designed on paper but neglecting those human-cultural factors. In that context, Beer points that 'no finite model is possible, because we do not have Requisite Variety to make it; and all we can do is to contemplate the *process* whereby such models are endlessly capable of generation. And that is to define the infinite Recursion; and that is to explode into self-consciousness' [Beer, 1994a, p. 374]. For the HHMS, this translates to the need of FEMA to recognize and incorporate the local specificities.

To resolve soft factor issue, it is highly important that the information system is properly designed to recognize incipient instabilities and Requisite Metasystemic Variety is shared between comradeships in the EOCs on all governmental levels. Management information systems are massive Variety attenuators. This way, the Metasystem, e.g. FEMA on Level of Recursion 1, can become aware and self-conscious. Unfortunately, all Emergency Operation Centers (EOCs) are only established under a hurricane threat or potential hit and throughout the year, those cybernetically essential Management Centers are missing, which hinders a cybernetically sound process to help to resolve soft factor issues. But, the Metasystem, e.g. FEMA, must be alert to not let the whole system fall asleep and sink into a coma, which eventually leads to the death of the system. Therefore, the Algedonic Alarms have to be set right by effective design [Beer, 1994a] and would in this case alarm FEMA to create a Management Center to keep the HHMS alive. This will be elaborated in chapter 3.4.

Further, the articulation of the Metasystem is a negotiation process and a continuous struggle for power, which Beer denounces as the human constraint in a Viable System. In this context, Beer refers to 'comradeship', which is negotiated by the Metasystem, System 3–4–5, and is perceived as 'leadership' by System 3–2–1. Beer points out the importance of informal relationships in this process, which play a great role in Hawai'i and the HHMS and distinguish it from mainland practices: through its isolation, Hawai'i profits from long-term and trustful relationships. In practice, this 'comradeship' is a balance of interpersonal Variety – a power struggle of qualitative means – instead of a balance of managerial Variety equations concerning only quantitative issues. Often, a consultant is engaged in the balancing of these interpersonal Variety equations. This dilemma mostly leads to a reorganization of the organization that usually fails, since it lacks recognition of the real problem – the system's qualitative issues are ignored. 'If the objective is to solve the equations of managerial Variety without disturbing the continuously adjusting solutions to the equations of interpersonal Variety, then we are explicitly seeking an articulation of the Metasystem that is self-conscious with respect to its cybernetic, as well as to its psycho-social adequacy' [Beer, 1994a, p. 373]. For the Hurricane Hazard Management System (HHMS), the articulation of the Metasystem is founded on psycho-social factors such as the ethical and moral commitment to save lives and property, Hawai'i's cultural identity, including the 'Aloha Spirit, the solidarity between HHMS personnel and the public and the aspects of its isolation. Ultimately, on this basis, Metasystemic Calm needs to be designed.

The syntegrative healing process is the best tool cybernetics provides for this design. Most Variety is absorbed by intelligent behavior of System 1s (implementation). The remaining residual Variety is left for the Metasystem to be handled. Consequently, the Metasystem needs enough Variety to provide Cohesion. The Syntegration as intelligence enhancer is capable to generate big change here. As in an ant colony, the collective intelligence is accessed through the Syntegration: neither the single ant – nor even the ant queen on the very top of the hierarchy – has the knowledge or synoptic view that the ant colony as a whole has. This tacit knowledge is an unused resource and has to be accessed to deal with the proliferating Variety. Realistically, the demanded services in a catastrophic disaster on O'ahu cannot be met by the service providers and demand varies by type, timing, place and urgency. Those systems are easily overwhelmed when Variety explodes within the envelope Environment, the Environment en-

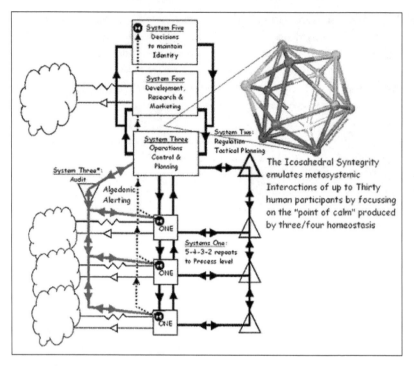

Figure 67: Beer's Team Syntegrity within the VSM

capsulating all local environments, when a catastrophic hurricane hits. But the best use of resources regarding time, assets, financial demand can be set up by integrating the most important stakeholders in a Syntegration. The knowledge of over 40 people and multiples thereof can be accessed and increase the effectiveness of disaster management manifold using their collective knowledge in the intelligence-enhancing, brain-interlinking architecture of the Syntegration.

The Syntegration is a revolutionary highly innovative tool based on over 30 years of research tradition in cybernetic management. This method is an extremely effective and efficient problem-solving tool with groundbreaking superlative results to deal with high complexity and solve the biggest challenges and the most pressing decisions of the top management level. In its advanced version, the Malik Super Syntegration, it has three parts: (1) an innovative cybernetic communication process for knowledge and intelligence enhancement (2) the application of holistic management systems for effective and efficient functioning of organizations and (3) a menu of simultaneously implemented cybernetic instruments to control complexity. The decision process is speed up 100-fold and the people effectiveness is enhanced 80-fold: It accomplishes goals in a 3,5 day process where organization usually take about one year – 3,5 times 100 equals about one year (350 days); and it deals with 40 people simultaneously – its Variety would be 40x39 assuming that a relationship can only be good or bad totaling 1560 possible states of a system. A usual workshop of five people has the Variety of 5x4=20, hence its effectiveness is about 80-fold. It is holistic and integrates 4 dimensions: technical, cultural, management/control and time level [Malik, 2011].

The process draws upon geometry, graph theory, neurophysiology and communications theory to attain more than 90 percent sharing of information among participants. A Syntegration utilizes the three dimensional figure of the icosahedrons to organize discussions. The twelve topics are represented by the vertices; and the thirty people by the edges. This provides a non-hierarchical discussion structure in which everyone plays an equivalent role Leonard [1999]. The Syntegration process is a huge Variety attenuator and Figure 67 shows its function as interaction and facilitation of information exchange between System 3 (operational control) and 4 (intelligence) [Beer, 1994b].

Right after a catastrophic event, as seen during Katrina and in Haiti, resources poor in and much efficiency and effectiveness is lost in the beginning due to coordination and information failures. This unique tool comes to solutions with enormous speed and implementation power to coordinate organizational networks. The Syntegration has proven successfully in over 500 applications without failures, in the business and non-business sector. I am proposing to use this tool as a setup to coordinate disaster management efforts and enhance resource (time, money, manpower) efficiency by a great deal to help victims more quickly [Reissberg, 2011].

3.3.11 Summary

At first sight, the Hurricane Hazard Management System (HHMS) shows cybernetic principles at work producing effective outcomes. As we have seen, there are several Levels of Recursion involved in a VSM analysis, each consisting of five systems and numerous cybernetic linkages making it obscure to understand what the main problems of the HHMS currently are. In chapter 3.3 the processes inbetween the structure elaborated in chapter

3.2 were discussed. In a catastrophic hurricane disaster, the Environment flushes the system with an amount of Variety on a short time scale so that System 1 (implementation) and 3 (operational control) get overwhelmed for some time. This concerns first the lower Level of Recursion 4 on the vertical and horizontal axis and then develops up to Level of Recursion 1. Several tasks remain unsolved so far. System 3 (operational control) is overloaded by Variety from System 1 (implementation) in form of resource requests on any Level of Recursion. Regarding Relaxation Time, the HHMS would jump viability boundaries since it would take ten years to reach Homeostasis, but one year is required to be viable by definition. Consequently, the HHMS is not viable and a redesign of structures and processes would be cybernetically desirable.

Overall, it was concluded that some elements of the Hurricane Hazard Management System (HHMS) have too excessive autonomy, specifically the System 1 (implementation) elements on the lowest Levels of Recursion 4, namely the single HHMS departments and agencies. Those are then organized on Level of Recursion 3 as Emergency Support Functions (ESFs) that, in contrast, are hierarchical, a cybernetic mistake, and where the System 1s (implementation) have too little autonomy, especially regarding the Preliminary Damage Assessments (PDAs) and Rapid Need Assessments (RNAs).

Another major failure within the local Environment is the System 3* (audits) channel that runs between the System 1s (implementation) operations and 3 (operational control). Independent evaluation of progress in disaster management tasks are ineffective, as elaborated in detail, because System 3 (operational control) lacks adequate real-time information. The only System 3* (audits) check on the HHMS happens on Recursion 3, the federal level HSEEP that implements the annual Makani Pahili exercise. Consequently, System 3 (operational control) does not know how fit System 1 (implementation), the disaster management departments and agencies, is to deal with external Variety. Good and right disaster management means to deal with the situation once it arises, being aware it will be overwhelmed to the point of losing total System Control and Cohesion, as stated in the conferences. During Katrina, lack of resources slowed the process. But even with enough resources, System 3 (operational control) would not have been capable to deal with the requests (Variety) coming from System 1 (implementation) disaster managers, further hindered by a lack of System 2 (coordination) implementation. Those failures were investigated in detail, such as legal issues preventing efficiency, the lack of clear roles and responsibilities, lack of training, system incompatibilities, misleading geographical differentiation and wrong assumptions leading to a distorted information system. Those failures further lead to ineffective resource allocation and distribution. The missing System 2 (coordination) implementation can only be resolved through more National Incident Management System (NIMS) training plus more frequent activation of the Recursion 3 through joint exercises. Unfortunately, falsely understanding that Variety has been attenuated under 'established practice' and assuming those squiggly lines are vivid, leads to ineffectiveness. Closed-loop communication is missing. The Accountability Loop needs to be strengthened through an appropriate System 3* (audits) function.

In addition, the difficulties to balance the Hawai'ian disaster management system with the envelope Environment and the importance of the communication channels with the public were pronounced. The Variety Engineering workshops as being practiced and implemented by Malik Management were suggested to improve the ability to deal with such external disturbances in the future on O'ahu, cybernetically the Variety on the horizontal level, and the Advanced Syntegration recommended to solve the Metasystem's problem to deal with the Variety sent up from the System 1s (implementation) on the vertical level. Ignorance was identified as a major Variety attenuator when facing a catastrophic hurricane disaster on O'ahu: therefore, planning for a high-impact-low-probability event like Hurricane Katrina on O'ahu has not much evolved 'because it was unthinkable and too hard to think about' [Teixeira, 2007b]. The importance and urgent need of a compatible real-time information system on O'ahu was emphasized and its influences on Channel Capacity and Transduction, the glue within a cybernetically sound information system, were highlighted. Finally, the role of soft factors was analyzed with suggestions of the VSM given with the articulation of the Metasystem, System 3–4–5, to solve those problems. Hawai'i's isolation and cultural identity play a major role in the processes investigated. The Advanced Syntegration, as suggested by Malik [2011] is capable of taking care of those systemic interferences through a bionic communication structure that uses the swarm intelligence of all involved in as short as three days. From there, those soft issues dissolve within a one-year long action plan elaborated by a team of about 40 people, or multiples thereof.

Generally, the cybernetic language and VSM application are very abstract and do not necessarily translate into common language and understanding that easily. A good analogy to the HHMS is that of a soccer team, which is used to explain some of the major obstacles to effective hurricane hazard management in Hawaii.

The soccer team analogy entails that the hurricane hit compares to the tournament with an unknown Variety explosion within the system, as mentioned before. If the HHMS would be viable, a hurricane hit would not matter, and it would have Requisite Variety to counterbalance such environmental disturbance. Most obviously, this 'sleeping system' keeps from falling into a coma through regular exercises and stays competitive this way. But since the players are lazy, they are often too uncoordinated to win a game. The single players constitute the System 1s (implementation), which have to keep fit themselves: eat healthy, avoid injuries, have certain character traits (e.g. being organized to be in time for exercises and games), and so on. The single players regard one Level of Recursion lower than the System in Focus 'soccer team'. Hence, the System 1s (implementation) need to be viable by themselves to contribute to a Viable System as a whole. For the HHMS, this is questionable, because the System 1s (implementation), the single HHMS departments and agencies, are not viable by themselves in HHMS terms for the most part.

The major obstacle is the infrequency of exercises, a missing System 2 (coordination) part, and therefore, the System 1s (implementation) do not speak the same language. The soccer team ideally learns the 'soccer team language' to ensure Channel Capacity and Transduction in regular and frequent training sessions. If one player does not understand the concept of 'Abseits' – the Channel Capacity – he has no chance of transducing this information and understand it 'right'. The HHMS constitutes a 'soccer team' with eleven team players that don't know their names, do not speak the same language and everybody has their own rules of the game. Then someone shouts: PLAY! It is just chaos. Further, the CONOP for Hawaii, the specific System 2 (coordination) for that Level of Recursion, a geographically specific plan, was not in place at the time of writing, a missing System 4 (intelligence) accomplishment. Due to the cybernetically unsound hierarchical structure of the HHMS, this is a structural failure of the highest Level of Recursion, which involves FEMA. It compares to a national soccer team trainer who prescribes the game strategy for all teams nationwide. But, they would need to be flexible, in cybernetic language 'autonomous' enough to decide their strategy by themselves and in the moment it happens. This shows the importance of real-time data the VSM prescribes. The plan, System 1 (implementation), needs to comply with the System 5 (identity) 'identity' that flows through all systemic parts. System 5 (identity) of the soccer association are for example 'fair play' or 'to win the game'. Of course the trainer cannot plan to play a game in a country, where the teams would be unwelcome or unfamiliar with soccer – he would risk System Cohesion.

The trainer compares to System 3 (coordination) of the VSM. In a soccer team, it is important to evaluate the team players. Specifically, this should not happen on a constant basis – the player might feel intimidated and it would cost the trainer too much time and effort to focus on one single player. The trainer checks on each player sporadically and monitors and influences the team spirit – in cybernetic terms he coordinates the System 1 (implementation) synergies (the squiggly lines). The sporadic evaluation, the System 3* (audits), is faulty for the HHMS. There are sporadic checks, the After Action Reports after each annual exercise, but those results remain unchecked and are not evaluated by 'the trainer', the State Civil Defense (SCD) in the case of the HHMS. The missing System 3* (audits) makes the exercise less valuable and costs effectiveness. On a good note, the SCD looks for synergies and promotes collaboration, but it is voluntary and not bound to funding or other incentives and more control is needed here. The HHMS would need a constant monitoring of processes in real time and the sporadic spotting of bad news has to run on the Alarm Channel throughout the system. That alarm would lead System 5 (policy) to wake up from its Metasystemic Calm and go into action to establish again Homeostasis, e.g. change certain parameters within the system.

Unfortunately, there is no significant work in systems analysis on such 'periodic' systems, which should be investigated further in the field of management cybernetics. Overall, the lack of exercises and lack of resources are both important and obvious, but the VSM analysis highlights the deeper reasons behind it and investigates the quality of the system's functionality. Of course, if you have a structure and no resources to plug in, the system does not exist. The VSM's contribution is to more precisely emphasize the non-resource factors that make sports teams and disaster management departments and agencies viable, despite the fact that they very infrequently actually play the game. It suggests that with given resources a system can increase its effectiveness by eliminating wrong assumptions and misunderstandings. Information has more influence than hierarchical power. The VSM increases the quality of a system immensely without simplifying: 'without resources, the system is dead' – the HHMS is not a dead system, but an unpracticed system that can highly profit from cybernetic 'fine-tuning' through VSM Variety Engineering or the Syntegration.

In the following, the design of certain parameters to fulfill the HHMS's viability requirements should exemplify how the VSM works in detail. Beer states that cybernetic principles assert themselves, since it is the way of nature. If we wait for nature to assert these laws, it will be ineffective. Then, viability is purchased at enormous cost. Hence, a Viable System should be designed under cybernetic principles. To design a Viable System effectively means to examine all loops under the *Three Principles of Organization*, the three principles of Variety Engineering [Beer, 1994a](see 'Principles' in the Glossary). The *Fourth Principle* deals with time. That means that the two loops between local management, operations and Environment need to be designed by cybernetically sound Variety amplifiers and attenuators. The VSM offers a system design with both functional decentralization and Cohesion of the whole.

The cybernetic analysis accomplished here lacks possible interaction with key personnel in disaster management and more interaction with the system would have been needed to get a more detailed picture on how to cybernetically help the disaster management community. Those tasks are hard to fulfill for a PhD student and in a consulting contract the availability and willingness to accomplish a cybernetic analysis would be assured. As a consequence, this work does not claim completeness and detailed enough information on cybernetic ways to improve the effectiveness and efficiency of disaster management. But, in any case, it demonstrates the ability and capabilities of the cybernetic approach to fulfill this task.

3.4 The HHMS's viability requirements

After having evaluated the structures and processes within the HHMS, C4 in Figure 39 leads us to the 'Diagnosis and redesign of Hurricane Hazard Management System's (HHMS) viability requirements'.

The purpose of a VSM diagnosis and design is to point out ways to achieve effective governmental and private sector preparedness for prompt, fully coordinated, flexible response and assistance for a catastrophic hurricane striking the City and County of Honolulu. This achievement needs coordinated efforts of the city, state and federal agencies, supporting private-sector organizations and volunteer groups.

The problem of design in general is that it represents the selection of one configuration out of many. It is an annihilation of alternatives. Variety Engineering, as practiced by Malik Management Switzerland in a series of workshops, is a determined and sound way to achieve Requisite Variety. Along those outcomes are, for example, detailed job descriptions and critical management tasks that are necessary and sufficient to contribute to Viability of the system as a whole. If the System is 'OK' or 'not OK', which sets of the Algedonic Alarms within the Hawaiʻian disaster management system, have to be set beforehand and are bound to an appropriate timeframe, which needs to be defined to set criteria of viability measures. For this purpose the Homeland Security Exercise and Evaluation Program (HSEEP) should serve as an example to demonstrate the VSM's capability to enhance the effectiveness of the system.

3.4.1 Relaxation Time for viability

The Relaxation Time is defined as the time it takes after incipient instability has emerged to return to stability. If a new shock comes in before stability is reached again, disaster is imminent and no learning, no adaptation or evolution happens [Beer, 1994a]. For the Hurricane Hazard Management System (HHMS) that seems imminent in case of a catastrophic hurricane on Oʻahu, currently.

Since the hurricane occurrence in Hawaiʻi lies within an annual cycle – from June to November – the annual cycle seems appropriate. On Level of Recursion 1, FEMA provides the Homeland Security Exercise and Evaluation Program (HSEEP) process to States to evaluate their disaster management capabilities. This process should serve as an exemplified VSM measurement application. This could also be exerted on the Incident Action Plan (IAP).

3.4.2 The Homeland Security Exercise & Evaluation Program (HSEEP) Improvement Process

According to the HSEEP shown in Figure 68 (C4 'HSEEP' in Figure 39) [U.S. DHS, 2007b], After Action Reports (AAR) are sent to the Department of Homeland Security (DHS) annually and as a consequence legislation is passed to meet resource requirements. It represents the Resource Bargain and the Accountability Loop on Level of Recursion 1. The State Civil Defense (SCD) is required to follow HSEEP which runs on an annual cycle serves the verification that the National Incident Management System (NIMS) is implemented, training standards fulfilled and is a requirement for the HHMS departments and agencies to access funding.

Recursion 1, the HSEEP is accomplished once a year as well as the Makani Pahili exercise on Recursion 2. It has to be noted, that HSEEP is only partially fulfilled for the State of Hawai'i and that the EOCs are activated in this exercise, but the Joint Field Office (JFO) is not established and exercised, so parts of Recursions 1 and 2 are missing. Hence it is not sufficiently established and the exercise conditions are not realistic. Recursion 3, the Emergency Support Function (ESF) establishment is not accomplished during the exercise, and Recursion 4 concerning the single the HHMS departments and agencies are exercising once a year, but due to the lack of exercising the Recursion 2 and 3 activation major elements of the exercise goals cannot be achieved. Further, on the lower Levels of Recursion, a more frequent training is necessary.

In the State of Hawai'i, the annual Makani Pahili exercises promoted by the State Civil Defense (SCD) serve to coordinate hurricane hazard management along the Homeland Security Exercise and Evaluation Program (HSEEP), but not the whole HSEEP process is accomplished yet. The first three – out of six – steps 'Exercise', 'Hot Wash after Action' and 'After Action Analysis and Report' are executed, but the other three steps 'Improvement Plan', 'Improvement Tracking and Implementation' and 'Plan Exercise to validate' are not accomplished even though funding is available for those activities [Richards, 2007a]. Cybernetically, this inefficient open loop is incapable of being efficient and needs closure.

The HSEEP in theory is a self-sustaining exercise program, a continuous improvement process and a tool for planning. Three preparatory conferences preceded the actual Makani Pahili exercise to exchange information on resource inventories, exercise planning status, needs and to find synergies – System 3 (operational control) activity to find synergies between the System 1s (implementation) on Recursion 2. It is a forum to solve problems beforehand and to surface tacit knowledge that does not exist on paper necessarily yet [Richards and Tengan, 2007]. The exercise itself then bridges Levels of Recursion 2, 3 and 4 making the HHMS departments and agencies understand how SCD works and vice versa. The exercise itself needs eight months of planning within the annual HSEEP process [Gilbert, 2007b] but ultimately renders itself inefficient due to its incomplete System 3* (audits) lacking the implementation of all six steps as mentioned above.

The Makani Pahili exercise underlies certain unrealistic assumptions and cannot display a real-time event scenario because it is a highly accelerated play, which does not represent realistic conditions in regards to time. Damage assumptions, such as a functioning Honolulu International Airport after a catastrophic hurricane, which is highly unrealistic [Rosenberg, 2007b], render this exercise not efficient, since System 2 (coordination) cannot function. Post-landfall exercise activities were only partially accomplished and were based on enough damage to do some training, but not enough damage to stress the system [Rosenberg, 2007b], which does not provide an exercise for catastrophic conditions. The DEM EOC communication software E-team was not used in the exercise, since it would have been difficult to keep it real-time – the storm moved 100nm within one hour [Gilbert, 2007b]. Further, landlines were used for the exercise, which certainly will not work after a catastrophic hurricane made landfall on Oʻahu. The exercise gives a false sense of security and ignores the shortfalls of the HHMS. The opportunities for improvement of the HHMS that the Makani Pahili exercise could provide are ignored and the disinterest due to a System 3* (audits) failure on Recursion 2 is accepted without further consequences. The system falls into a coma instead of being in Metasystemic Calm.

Exemplified, certain measurement parameters should be calculated in the following to lead the reader through the cybernetic measurement process. In practice, the Senior Management, the Metasystem, subjectively chooses those parameters.

On Recursion 1 and 2, annual measurement cycles are appropriate. On Recursion 3 and 4, a more frequent measurement timeframe is necessary. Ideally, a bi-monthly cycle serves as the measurement cycle, since the ESF structure, Recursion 3, and the HHMS departments and agencies, Recursion 4, are the basis for the HHMS functioning and need to be alive to wake up the higher Levels of Recursion 1 and 2 in case of incipient instability.

3.4.3 Design of information flows and criteria of stability

The VSM requires thorough and up-to-date information systems. Ideally, the information system measures everything it needs to know continuously, but the Metasystem only needs to become aware if something changes through signals called Algedonic Alarms. Information needs to be filtered. As long as the business runs as usual, nothing has to be done. The design of those Algedonics is the alternative to authority. Those Algedonics are completely missing in the Hurricane Hazard Management System (HHMS) and need to be designed. Literally, there are no pain sensors in that disaster management body to cry out for help.

Figure 68: The Homeland Security Exercise & Evaluation Program (HSEEP)

Senior Management must know itself, listen to itself and set the criteria of stability [Beer, 1994a]. Measurements need to be designed to ensure the Resource Bargain and the Accountability Loop, among others. Algedonics need to be set and the time-lag for the system to realize something went bad need to be defined. System 4 (intelligence) needs this thorough, up-to-date information to design those parameters to adapt to environmental change and to produce strategies. Moreover, it needs an appropriate model of the capabilities of the 'Inside and Now' so it knows what tools it has at its disposal. If this is not well definable, daily measurements can be appropriate in the beginning phase. The HHMS is equipped with HSEEP, an annual process, and therefore the Metasystems on any Level of Recursion have only historical data and lack a complete model of their System 1 (implementation) – it basically is not informed on the status quo.

Practically, computers have the ability to make many correlations, generate an abundance of data and consequently people are not selecting among them and ensuring they are useful. This leads to a Variety imbalance, and information overload, because the irrelevant data produced overwhelm the Metasystem. Managers mostly have more problems with too much data rather than too little. The data flow needs to be well designed for consistency and coherence and to make sure that filters are in place to let the basic important measures and the anomalies through and to hold routine information until or unless someone needs to access them – a System 3* (audits) role – for special examination [Beer, 1994a].

HSEEP represents the HHMS's viability measurement. The HHMS's viability is defined, as mentioned before, along the annual hurricane cycle. Hurricane season lasts from June to November and the HHMS can correct instabilities within the one-year cycle and stay viable unless the number of instabilities, or red flags, cause the system to become unviable and unable to respond effectively. But, as long as instabilities are responded to throughout the year effectively, which is measured subjectively as explained in this chapter, the HHMS could become viable.

The dynamic reporting system

Planning is a continuous process for any Viable System embedded in another Viable System providing the cohesive glue [Beer, 1994a]. It starts arbitrarily, since a continuous process is a 'total loop with organizational closure with no inferiority or superiority' [Beer, 1994a, p. 339]. The Hawai'ian disaster management system is analogously not running on epochs, but is a dynamic process without end or starting point. Starting at System 1 (implementation), the central axis of information supplies System 3 (operational control) with the continuous message 'I am OK' along the Resource Bargain and Accountability Loop, in theory. But to invent System 1's (implementation) future and accommodating incipient change in its local Environment, System 3 (operational control) wants to know System 1 (implementation) intentions. Overall, the collected data that is shaped or filtered into information has different purposes depending on the Level of Recursion – a lower Level of Recursion is lacking the synoptic view.

The problem is that the HSEEP process is not continuously reporting data and filtering information. On O'ahu, the Joint Field Office (JFO) in a disaster situation has to receive filtered information from the Emergency Support Functions (ESFs) lying on one Level of Recursion lower. This information must be aggregated in such a way, that the JFO can deal with its Variety. The Incident Action Plan (IAP) is structured for that purpose, but the Hawai'ian disaster management system's data collection and analysis involves several Levels of Recursions simultaneously – e.g. the PDAs and RNAs –, which cybernetically problematic: departments and agencies of several Levels of Recursion, such as FEMA, the State Civil Defense, County Civil Defense and the American Red Cross, collect data (PDAs, RNAs) simultaneously and filter it in a different way with different informational outcomes – Variety explodes here. The VSM points out the importance to fix this problem and its destructive systemic consequences.

For example, if System 3 (operational control) gives 'rubrics' for the Resource Bargain, such as the IAP, Variety will proliferate, since it does not necessarily match System 1's (implementation) necessities and intentions. He suggests instead turning the classification or categorization into a process between those two systems [Beer, 1994a] – it has to be a fluent process of input and output, not a firm, hard-to-change information process. On O'ahu, a check of the IAP's functionality could reveal deficiencies that hinder efficiency of those processes. Cybernetically, the 'I am OK'-message would from that Black Box would turn into 'I am not OK' and an Algedonic Alarm would sound. A filter would determine when to call the Metasystem, the senior management, into action and make changes to the information process – continuously. Senior management would perceive the reality of the situation in real-time, much like a pilot sees his instruments in front of him all the time.

It has to be underscored that the concept of causality has to be abandoned, which is hard to grasp in the management world of today. The search for the unique cause of systemic failure does not lead to the desired outcome or to the measurements relevant to a system's viability or effectiveness [Beer, 1994a]. One Algedonic Alarm would not matter to the overall viability of the system, but many small ones will. Consequently, it is the system's stability that should be monitored and measured, not parameters of muddy boxes.

Designing performance indicators, filtration and Algedonics

The design of measurement variables is a System 4 (intelligence) function. Thereby, quantitative as well as qualitative measures are of equal importance. Beer reminds to let System 4 (intelligence) only act on its Level of Recursion. The quantitative measurement indicators prescribed by FEMA are given by the Homeland Security Exercise and Evaluation Program (HSEEP) and define the Hurricane Hazard Management System's (HHMS) information flow. The qualitative aspect is not measured or indicated by FEMA, but plays a major role and will be included for the design. Specifically, the Levels of Recursions need to be kept separate; otherwise the too many links cause Variety overloads.

First of all, performance indicators have to be designed individually and evaluated under the aspect of Relaxation Time. The measurement indicators should emerge from negotiations between System 1 (implementation) and 3 (operational control) personnel along the Resource Bargain and the Accountability Loop [Walker, 2001]. Then, statistical filtration needs to be applied to extract relevant information and to automatically generate Algedonics in real-time to inform the Metasystem to wake up from its Metasystemic Calm. As a consequence of an Algedonic Alarm the affected System 1 (implementation) loses its autonomy, which should be designed with a complete analysis of the problem and the appointment of trouble-shooter, for example.

Performance measures of Actuality, Capability and Potentiality

The System 1s (implementation) are responsible for measurement and documentation. System 1 (implementation) only reports the operations to the Metasystem that are fundamental to viability. The After Action Reports produced annually for the Makani Pahili exercise are the crucial indicators and the audit System 3* (audits) needs to do to stay informed. As mentioned, an effective Accountability Loop is needed for that, which is not the case for the HHMS. Within the Accountability Loop System 1 (implementation) activities are measured and the accurate information is sent to System 3 (operational control). Again, the HHMS's data is historical, since it is measured annually, which is not frequent enough to keep the HHMS alive and viable.

Relevant information needs to flow through the system, but as long as everything goes as usual, no reports are needed. The Viable System Model (VSM) information system is fundamentally different in that it is based upon performance indicators, which measure whatever is important within each System 1 (implementation), not just financial information and that it is based upon measurements in real-time [Walker, 2001].

Realistically, there would be a constant error sound in the case of the HHMS, since the System 1 (implementation) resource requests will currently overwhelm the Metasystem. But if the variables regarding what is to be called unstable are set low and would be increased over time, at least a current model of System 1 (implementation) could be achieved and increased efficiency could be reached over time. As a first step, if the information system is properly designed to recognize incipient instabilities and if there is a Management Center in which requisite Metasystemic Variety is shared between comradeship, the senior management can become aware of what it is really doing' [Beer, 1979, p. 396] and reach self-consciousness. Self-recognition through self-confrontation is the first step towards improvement of the situation. A comprehensive monitoring system can enhance System 1 (implementation) autonomy, since intervention only occurs if agreed limits are reached. In a timely manner, deficiencies can be absorbed and will not cause Algedonic Alarms, enhancing System 1s (implementation) autonomy.

The meter of effectiveness indicators

A meter needs to be designed to do so. Certain performance indicators could, for example, be measured bi-monthly and be displayed in meeting rooms to complement the model of System 1 (implementation) operations accumulated during work and discussions. The meter measures the 'I am OK'-message on a continuous basis. Figure 38 shows the Metasystem and its Black Box, the System 1s (implementation) into which the Metasystem does not dive. The setup is taken from control engineering and functions like a thermostat.

The 'I am OK'-message implies three indicators of effectiveness: Actuality, Capability and Potentiality. The measure of Actuality relates to the Metasystem stating 'we normally produce X', the status quo, and the System 1 (implementation) – the muddy box – responding to it that x % of that value is accomplished. For example, it states 'Actuality is (not) accomplished by 25 %'. The meter measures the ratio between the declaration and the response of each of the three criteria. ONE would mean for Actuality that the situation remains stable [Beer, 1994a].

The measure of Capability relates to the Metasystem stating 'we plan to produce X', the intention, and the System 1 (implementation) – the muddy box – responding to it that x % of that value is accomplished. For example, it states 'Capability is (not) accomplished by 25 %'. ONE would mean for Capability that the stability of the plan is assured [Beer, 1994a].

The measure of Potentiality relates to the Metasystem stating 'we wish we could produce X', the will to advance, and the System 1 (implementation) – the muddy box – responding to it that x % of that value is accomplished. ONE would mean for Potentiality that the normative expectation is stable [Beer, 1994a, p. 293]. Overall, System 4 (intelligence) monitors the Environment to raise System 1s (implementation) Capability and Potentiality and System 3 (operational control) monitors the Environment to raise System 1 (implementation) Actuality. Qualitative and quantitative measurement variables that ensure the Accountability Loop and the Resource Bargain are to be designed.

The design of quantitative measurement variables

Within HSEEP, the Corrective Action Program (CAP) is used to track the exercise status and to evaluate effectiveness through an evaluation plan and tools. Its Exercise Evaluation Guides (EEG) evaluate 37 target capabilities (Table 11).

The Mass Care EEG is exemplified to diagnose the HHMS's reporting system and to create performance measures that might be missing for the HHMS's viability requirements [U.S. DHS, 2007a]. Overall, the 37 target capabilities might be sufficient to evaluate the HHMS's viability and to monitor its status, which ultimately has to be evaluated by the HHMS personnel themselves and is not the cybernetician's task. The VSM only invokes missing links to fulfill a system's viability requirements.

For example, the Mass Care EEG evaluates a status asking to 'designate sites to serve as mass care facilities to include shelters, feeding sites, reception centers, food preparation sites, distribution points, etc.'. Under 'Time of observation/ Task Completion' it evaluates the time and the task completed as 'fully', 'partially', 'not' and 'N/A', four categories. It also states a target time. Consequently, HSEEP relates time to the tasks, making an evaluation of Relaxation Time possible and tracks the status of tasks fulfilled – not in percentage as proposed by the VSM, but as four categories.

The Department of Homeland Security (DHS) as another example also gives four categories as shown in Table 12.

The main problem with the HHMS's reporting system on its viability, is that annual reports cannot reflect the System 1 (implementation) model the Metasystem needs to monitor, on any Level of Recursion. This historical data monitoring system needs to be turned into more frequent data collection and analysis system, a dynamic reporting system that measures viability continuously. For example, the evaluations of the EEGs should be accomplished more frequently – again, how frequent would be the choice of the HHMS personnel. What is important is that the HHMS personnel are capable of fulfilling their tasks and consequently their training status should also be measured. Further, Algedonic Alarms need to be designed. Certain

Common Capabilities	• Planning • Communications • Community Preparedness and Participation • Risk Management
Prevent Mission Capabilities	• Information Gathering and Recognition of • Indicators and Warning • Intelligence Analysis and Production • Information Sharing and Dissemination • Law Enforcement Investigation and Operations • CBRNE Detection
Protect Mission Capabilities	• Critical Infrastructure Protection • Food and Agriculture Safety and Defense • Epidemiological Surveillance and Investigation • Public Health Laboratory Testing
Response Mission Capabilities	• Onsite Incident Management • Emergency Operations Center Management • Critical Resource Logistics and Distribution • Volunteer Management and Donations • Responder Safety and Health • Public Safety and Security • Animal Health Emergency Support • Environmental Health • Explosive Device Response Operations • Firefighting Operations/Support • WMD/ Hazardous Materials Response and • Decontamination • Citizen Protection: Evacuation and/or In-Place Protection • Isolation and Quarantine • Urban Search and Rescue • Emergency Public Information and Warning • Triage and Pre-Hospital Treatment • Medical Surge • Medical Supplies Management and Distribution • Mass Prophylaxis • Mass Care (Sheltering, Feeding and Related Services) • Fatality Management
Recover Mission Capabilities	• Structural Damage and Mitigation Assessment • Restoration of Lifelines • Economic and Community Recovery

Table 11: Target Capabilities List

Ranking	Cumulative Score	Description	Detailed Description
4	1.51 – 2.00	very effective	All essential questions are rated as "Meets" or higher, and all non-essential questions are rated as "Partially Meets" or higher.
3	1.01 – 1.50	effective	At least 75% of essnetial questions are rated as „Meets" or higher and non-essential questions are rated as "Does not Meet".
2	0.51 – 1.00	partially effective	No more than 50% of the essential questions are rated as „Partially Meets", and less than 25% of the non-essential questions are rated as "Does not Meet".
1	0.00 – 0.50	marginally effective	More than 50% of the essential questions are rated as "Does not Meet".

Definitions

Essential: A negative response suggests that executing the evaluation is at serious risk of failure.

Non-Essential: A negative response suggests that executing the evaluation may be impaired or degraded but will not result in failure itself.

Table 12: Question ranking used in the Department of Transportation assessment by the Department of Homeland Security

cybernetic requirements are fulfilled, but not to its full extent. What is further missing are measurements that consider the human factor, the human condition. That VSM insight besides its structural commentaries is crucial. This includes the training status as well as soft factors such as motivation, skills or knowledge base. As two examples, the variables 'resource status' and 'change or roll-over of employees' should be elaborated here.

Analogously, the variable 'resource status' can be measured in terms of Actuality, Capability and Potentiality. The National Incident Management System (NIMS) provides a credentialing system for resource tracking, resource typing and personnel, which is not fully accomplished yet. This national credentialing system can document minimum professional qualifications, certifications, training and education requirements that define baseline criteria expected of emergency response professionals and volunteers for deployment as mutual aid to disasters [National Integration Center, 2008].

For example, for the variable 'training status' of Hurricane Hazard Management System (HHMS) personnel the measure of Actuality relates to the Metasystem stating 'we normally have 50 % of our personnel trained to NIMS standards', the status quo, and the System 1 (implementation) – the muddy box – responding to it that 20 % of that value (Actuality) is accomplished. The meter measures the ratio between the declaration and the response of each of the three criteria. The measure of Capability relates to the Metasystem stating 'we plan to have 80 % of our personnel trained to NIMS standards', the intention, and the System 1 (implementation) – the muddy box – responding to it that 12,5 % of that value is accomplished. The measure of Potentiality relates to the Metasystem stating 'we wish we could have 90 % of our personnel trained to NIMS standards', the will to advance, and the System 1 (implementation) – the muddy box – responding to it that 11 % of that value is accomplished.

It would give a constant error sign in the case of the HHMS. The training status could be measured as the 'number of disaster workers of a department or agency', Recursion 4. The measurement scale could run from 1 to 10 representing 'the training days accomplished'. This data could be collected weekly and be sent to its System 3 (operational control), in this case the Emergency Support Function (ESF) federal agency coordinator it belongs to, Recursion 4.

Secondly, the variable 'change or roll-over of employees' is interesting and valuable to monitor, since it tracks both quantitative and qualitative parameters. The change of Hurricane Hazard Management System (HHMS) personnel is first of all a quantitative issue, but only appears in a change of measurement when the numbers of employees change. With a credentialing system as proposed by NIMS the human capital can be tracked as well. Still, the soft factors that are severely impacted by such change are forgotten. The importance of long-term personal relationships, of team-building and trust established, influence the effectiveness of a system.

Ultimately, also the subjectivity of quantitative indicators has to be recognized. For example, RNAs or PDAs require consistency and objectivity, but ultimately those assessments are subjective assessments of needs and damages and vary to some degree [Richards, 2007f]. To demonstrate the importance of those soft factors and to find the right measurement parameters, they will be investigated for the HHMS in the following section.

The design of qualitative measurement variables

Analogously, Actuality, Capability and Potentiality can be measured for the HHMS's qualitative factors, which should be accomplished by the HHMS personnel in negotiation with each other and written on notice boards, for example. All the HHMS personnel should send in weekly indices as a vital sign. Variables could include happiness, morale (attendance of training or absenteeism), skill availability, motivation, autonomy, mood of optimism, feeling to have made a real impact on society, solidarity, safety, tidiness, leadership or vision. For example, within the HHMS, the attendance at meetings is dwindling and no incentives are available, which is known, but not recognized or dealt with at the higher Levels of Recursions. As two examples, the variables 'morale' and 'knowledge' should be mentioned. Morale could be an index combining several variables such as the subjective happiness rating including the difference between morning rating and evening, the motivation and the rating about the work Environment (enjoyable vs. frustrating).

The value of an individual's knowledge and intellectual capital is difficult to measure because it is usually time- and context-specific. Some long-term efforts may not be effective on the short run, such as taking a degree. Regarding the HHMS, the status of the NIMS training level could be measured subjectively from 1 to 10. It also depends on personal interests (in disasters e.g.), personality, intellectual capability, life situation (stress, mobility), job requirements etc. There would be a great deal of Variety attenuation if the individual would rate him- or herself on that scale. The problem hereby is the level of truth that can be acquired. It has to be assumed that the statement by the individual is honest. The cybernetic self-organizing effect is important here: If (s)he rates him(her-)self too high, no training will be provided, which will damage that person on the long run professionally, because there will be others who will succeed. Self-organization is induced since that person will avoid self-damaging behavior.

Further, some knowledge is not of measurable external value, like knowing how to keep emotionally and physically fit, but those factors make the individual's action more effective. Individuals should assume conscious management of their personal intellectual assets. Tacit knowledge can be rendered explicit when documented in the process of preparing training courses or qualifying for a certification [Leonard, 1999]. Overall, the organization's knowledge and intellectual capital could be measured this way, or at least estimated. The Cohesive Glue also consists of informal factors.

For example, the HHMS personnel over time learn to know what their boss stands for and what suggestions or comments regarding the HHMS are desirable or not. This tacit knowledge also influences the systems effectiveness.

Ultimately, System 1 (implementation) generates the data for System 3 (operational control) representing Actuality, Capability and Potentiality for all Levels of Recursion, since System 1 (implementation) on Recursion 1 is the Metasystem of Recursion 2. In the next step, relevant information will be filtered from that data.

Statistical filtration to extract relevant information and
to break the time barrier

As mentioned before, the Metasystem is not supposed to dive into the muddy box but to operate outside the muddy box. In theory, 'it is possible to clear the muddiness through special inquiries, but in managerial reality, Variety proliferates too far and too fast' [Beer, 1994a, p. 58]. Hence, there are time lags between the manager's input and the Variety proliferation he is trying to control. To smooth these, a manager needs to design Feedback Adjustors to compensate the time lag in the measurement system.

In detail, one intended output state should be selected from all possible output states by the System 1 (implementation) management that it seeks to hold constant, e.g. a specified percentage of upgraded shelters to withstand Category 4 hurricane wind forces, for example 80 %. The vulnerability analysis in chapter 1.4.2 shows the quantitative and qualitative shortfalls regarding shelter spaces. Comparators are then set up to compare the actual output with that constant, from moment to moment. The resulting error signal – the deviation of the output measurement from this constant – can then be used to modify the input. For example, if repairs turn out to be less costly in some shelters than in others or upgrading is accomplished faster, resources for repairs can be redirected to where it is needed. This measurement technique would get the HHMS close to be acting 'real-time'. But, since this error-controlled negative feedback is a dynamic process, the time lag is still problematic leading to explosive behavior: after a correction is correctly measured, time passes for it to be signaled and to become effective. By that time the muddy box has changed its outputs, which leads to over-corrections – the whole system explodes and is unstable. Control engineering suggests installing a Feedback Adjuster to make adjustments for the time lag in the measurement system. Beer exemplifies that the steersman treats the boat as a Black Box and manipulates the input-output relationship by adjusting the rudder. He does not 'dive into the sea and try to understand it analytically' [Beer, 1994a, p.76] and deals in likelihoods. How this art could work for the HHMS is elaborated in the next paragraphs.

The data that the meter produces needs to be filtered to extract the relevant information by the Black Box, shown in Figure 38, and performance measures are developed from those measurements. The ratio of Actuality to Capability is called Productivity, Capability to Potentiality is called Latency and Actuality to Potentiality is called Performance [Beer, 1994a]. Those three performance measures express the likelihood that something goes wrong. Beer says that there is no unique reason for that to happen, but it is due to pressures within the total system that modify the behavior of the subsystem, abandoning the concept of causality. Theory of probability uses statistical filtration to report on the likelihood of incipient change, which is an immense Variety attenuation. Statistical Quality Control (SQC) has been used for decades on the shop floor, but not for the management information system in any boardroom, which represents Beer's invention.

First of all, a precise rule set needs to be set into the Black Box, which in fact makes it transparent [Beer, 1994a]. Naturally, those measures will not have the value 1.0, so it will be, for example, that the Productivity for this loop in this subsystem will run at 0.75 instead of 1.0. 'Usually, management urges the employees to work harder and introduces incentive schemes, for example, whereby the criteria are chosen mysteriously' [Beer, 1994a, p. 294]. Beer requires those measures to be designed. The Metasystem now needs to decide on what is to count as a destabilizing mixture of Productivity, Latency and Performance. Systems enquiries are prescribed to solve the problem in a personal setting [Beer, 1994a], which were not practical for this dissertation.

An example for the HHMS should be elaborated here. The intended output state to be constant in the example given before was that 80 % (0.8) of the shelters should be upgraded to withstand Category 4 hurricane wind forces, which represents Potentiality. If currently, only 30 % of the shelters are upgraded to withstand Category 4 hurricane wind forces, Actuality is 0.3. If the HHMS is capable to upgrade 45 % of the shelters with available resources, Capability is 0.45. Consequently, Productivity is said to be 0.67. If Potentiality is 0.8, then Latency is said to be 0.56 and Performance 0.38. Those three performance measures (Productivity, Latency and Performance) express the likelihood that something goes wrong and the Metasystem now needs to decide on what is to count as a destabilizing mixture, e.g. Performance must run at 50 % (0.5). If Performance runs better than expected in other areas of risk reduction, for example regarding putting utility lines underground, resources can be redirected and this action is based on real-time occurrences, not based on historical data. This technique is a Feedback Adjuster, where a high-Variety box is managed by manipulations of the input patterns in terms of the reading taken from the output pattern.

The following insights are gained through the VSM: Our ordinary notions of measurement are historical, equally for the HHMS. It has to be emphasized though that the VSM serves by anticipating events, not predicting the future. Those messages about stability are meta-messages. The guesses of managers are replaced by those ratios produced by computers. 'A probability-plus-computer monitoring system can detect a change (= information) in the movement of a performance index long before a human being can detect that change by eye in a graphical time series' [Beer, 1994a, p. 295]. Beer used a computer program called Cyberfilter to extract important information from a system of indices.

Secondly, it needs to be accepted that the Black Box is black, but it is a filter that learns. 'This filter sets its own parameters by experiment. The experiments are automatically provided by experience, which can be regarded as a succession of unplanned experiments' [Beer, 1994a, p. 296]. The difference to control engineering is that in management, the system and its Environment are not given, but subjective issues, and so are its purpose, its nature and boundaries. Consequently, the Feedback Adjustors cannot be found analytically. In control engineering, this problem is solved by moving outside the box for self-regulation. For management purposes, we need to operate outside of the whole system, and induce self-organization. The manager takes on the role of an Adjuster Organizer that oversees the whole system that the Feedback Adjusters are trying to cope with and then he modifies its design based on experience. The Adjustor Organizer is that learning device.

Practically, 'the muddy box is able to generate massive Variety, especially under environmental disturbance, and therefore, this Adjuster Organizer is needed' [Beer, 1994a, pp. 64]. At times, the Feedback Adjustor, the regulator, might break down under the weight of proliferating Variety. This problem has to be solved by self-organization, by the Adjuster Organizer who monitors and modifies the design of this regulator to accommodate higher Variety induced by environmental disturbances. For the HHMS, an Adjuster Organizer could not be identified and has to be designed. Therefore, the manager of a System 1 (implementation), for example the head of emergency sheltering, needs input from the Metasystem, which is perceptually and logically on a higher level. 'This input operates not as a set of commands, but as the derivation of an organizational landscape. This will precondition, though not determine, the work of the Adjuster Organizer in continuously monitoring the design of the Feedback Adjusters' [Beer, 1994a, p. 69]. Operating continuously all year long, an Adjuster Organizer takes care of setting those regulative measurement devices and monitors them constantly. Realistically, there would be a constant Alarm signal sounding from the emergency sheltering part of the Viable System. The main problem was found to be lack of funding [Tengan, 2007b]. The insights the VSM delivers originate from the real-time data collection informing the management how to redirect resources and use existing assets more effectively to reduce vulnerability.

In terms of Variety Engineering, the Feedback Adjuster reduces operational Variety in the representation of reality that constitutes the muddy box and the Adjustor Organizer adds operational Variety to that regulatory process by being able to respond to a more complex world [Beer, 1994a]. The statistical filtration elaborate here makes the System 1s (implementation) responsible for their own development and their information is an immediate representation of their status quo. This is real-time regulation that uses cybernetic filtration of information in order to generate Algedonics.

Real-time Algedonic Alarms

'Why is it important to measure instabilities in terms of Algedonic Alarms? Both exceptions and trends are departures from a norm. They could just be statistical freaks and should not be reacted upon. But this is only a static statement about a dynamic equilibrium between bits of the system – hence we are to measure instabilities' [Beer, 1994a, p. 303].

Several different time-lines and signals or alarms need to be differentiated. A hurricane watch or warning causing sirens to warn the public are a Hurricane Hazard Management System (HHMS) signal in reaction to a threat or risk. In VSM terms, this does not mean that the system has already become unstable. An Algedonic Alarm signals the system's instability, which could be caused by the storm's impact, or even during evacuation procedures before the actual storm hits, when the shelter capacities are overwhelmed. Further, in VSM terms the Algedonic Alarm is also set to give warnings about incipient instabilities during the year without a hurricane threat, for example when the training status of the HHMS personnel falls behind the set conditions of viability. Overall, the HHMS's warning system regards only the actual threat of a hurricane in the disaster cycle's preparation time whereas the Algedonic Alarms of the VSM can signal instabilities at any time unrelated to an actual risk. The hurricane warning signal for Honolulu is not the Algedonic Signal for Recursion 2 or lower, but for Recursion 1, it signals the point of time when the Federal Emergency Management Agency (FEMA) resources start to deploy to Hawai'i. Consequently, Algedonic Signals exist for the HHMS on different Levels of Recursion, but the actual consequent actions need to be planned and implemented. This process of System 4 (intelligence) activity was observed to be weak and not coordinated well. This activity is proactive and progressive in VSM terms, since actual instability did not occur yet, but in the face of potential Variety explosion the HHMS takes preventative steps to be able to cope with the Variety proliferation. The alarm for this to happen occurs when the National Weather Service (NWS) reports a hurricane to cross 140 degree West longitude. As mentioned before, the HHMS mostly likely is in a constant alarm, since the desirable state is far from being reached in many places, as described in the vulnerability analysis.

It will take some time to recognize what an Algedonic Alarm is. What percentage of variation in indicator x means 'not OK' and on what timeline? Some suggestions on the timeline were made for the different Levels of Recursions. The responsiveness of the program (e.g. Cyberfilter) needs to be established so it does not send out an Algedonic Alarm if 'someone sneezes' and the pathological severity of the situation is far too small to alert the system as a whole. For example, the postponement of a couple of shelter exercises from December to February can be handled as non-alarming, considering other more pressing issues such as the fact that only 30 % of the shelters are upgraded to withstand a Category 4 hurricane.

The computer program Cyberfilter mentioned before is a computer program to produce performance indicators and Algedonics. The data is put in daily or weekly at the end of the day, depending on the data generation designed by the Metasystem. The history of the indicator shows as a graph and if something unexpected happens, it generates an Algedonic, e.g. when equipment breaks, a change in personnel parameters occurs (indicators slip, training was insufficient, learning happened). This feedback is needed for the whole system to adapt and learn, but is only useful with up-to-date information, not with data. This way, the viability of a system can be held in check.

3.4.4 Summary

This chapter set out to show how an Algedonic Alarm system could be designed for the Hurricane Hazard Management System (HHMS) giving some examples of measurement variables. In order to achieve this, a dynamic real-time information or reporting system must be designed. Further, performance indicators, set by the manager, who is part of System 3 (operational control) of the respective Level of Recursion, need to be set, as well as filtration. This way, Algedonic Alarms can sound when the system starts to be instable in a proactive way. Quantitative as well as qualitative measurement variables can both be designed, a special feature of the Viable System Model (VSM). Ultimately, statistical filtration can be designed to extract relevant information in real-time.

The final chapter should now give an overview of this dissertation and summarize the conclusions drawn from this VSM application. The applicability and usefulness of the VSM to disaster management will be evaluated and its merits both for geography and the field of hazard management will be highlighted.

3.5 VSM application Summary

First, the HHMS's measurement system of viability was clarified. The timeline of the measurement system is the annual cycle of the hurricane season and the federal 'measurement' system is constituted by the Homeland Security Exercise and Evaluation Program (HSEEP). In Hawai'i, the State Civil Defense (SCD) executes the annual hurricane exercise called 'Makani Pahili'.

The Cybernetic measurement system involves the indicators of effectiveness and performance measures. Those express the likelihood that something goes wrong and are taken constantly. The VSM designs this measurement system with parameters subjectively chosen by actors within the HHMS. Variables to measure are e.g. the resource status, the change of employees, morale or knowledge. If certain pre-set values are exceeded, a red flag will alarm the system and induce action to proactively prevent the failure of the disaster management system as a whole. Overall, one red flag would not matter to the system, but many small ones can. Those red flags are called 'Algedonic Alarms' because one needs to be aware that those alarms are not used in everyday language and are not caused by an approaching hurricane or some related threat. These Algedonic Alarms sound due to ineffective or dysfunctional elements within the HHMS and are preemptive signals about dysfunctions. They have to be in real-time because managers must be alert to instability in real-time. For example, the testing of the emergency generators, usually lasting for half an hour, does not proof that the system it supports will run for the necessary amount of time in a disaster. Ultimately, the requirement for viability is that the Algedonic Alarms have to be fixed within the Relaxation Time for the HHMS to remain viable. For example, the Relaxation Time for Level of Recursion 1 is the annual cycle along the mentioned exercises, for Level of Recursion 3 could be the training status, measured monthly and set subjectively. For the HHMS, a constant alarm signal would sound and would be loud. The HHMS in its current status is certainly not viable, due to its many deficiencies.

Overall, the VSM leads you to choose a System in Focus and then investigate one or two Levels of Recursion up or down from there. The System in Focus was chosen to be the Joint Field Office (JFO) and its organizational structure, the Incident Command System (ICS). As shown in Table 8, the Level of Recursion 1 regarded the NIMS framework including all Emergency Operation Centers (EOC) and Incident Command Posts (ICPs). Level of Recursion 3 was constituted by the Emergency Support Functions (ESFs) and Level of Recursion 4 involved all departments and agencies filling the ESFs.

3.5.1 Diagnosing the structure – the static HHMS

First, the static Hurricane Hazard Management System (HHMS) was investigated along its structure, followed by the diagnosis of the HHMS processes. A major structural drawback was evident because the VSM requires a non-hierarchical structure, but the NIMS elements are hierarchical. There's a managerial hierarchy in an organization, but the higher levels are characterized by its order of perception and language in logic, not by its capacity to command. In disaster response, when quick action is necessary, waiting for authorizations to be approved can be costly in terms of damage to both victims and the reputation of the responders. The hierarchical setup is cybernetically wrong. In sum, the VSM revealed that all system elements are in place, but the balance, quality and importance of some need adjustments. This can be exemplified on Level of Recursion 3 (see Table 8). In Figure 69, the deficiencies on Level of Recursion 3 are shown, with the ESFs as the System 1 (implementation).

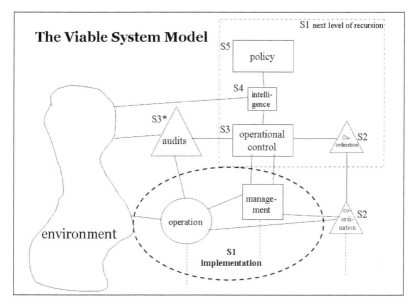

Figure 69: Deficiencies on Level of Recursion 3

If the VSM is applied to the HHMS, the Federal Emergency Management Agency (FEMA) represents System 5 (identity), the State Civil Defense (SCD) and the county Department of Emergency Management (DEM) represents System 3 (operational control) and 4 (intelligence). System 2 (coordination) is defined by the National Incident Management System (NIMS) and the National Response Plan (NRP). The Emergency Support Functions (ESFs) represent all System 1s (implementation)(see Figure 70).

System 1 (implementation) has 15 ESFs instead of a maximum of 8 elements prescribed by the VSM. Stafford's recommendation of six to eight System 1s (implementation) was based on G.A. Miller's famous 1956 paper 'the magic number 7 + or – 2' [Miller, 1956]. If high redundancy between the System 1s (implementation) exists, the number of nine might be exceeded, but the ESFs are very heterogeneous. The number 7 + or – 2 represents the level of differentiation the human brain can easily accommodate without additional patterns. The paper summarizes research on light levels (visual), sound levels (auditory), sweetness, sourness, taste, among others and is the basis for the choice of seven digits for phone numbers. In that case, the VSM suggests inserting another Level of Recursion to summarize those activities (ESFs). Another major deficiency is evident because System 2 (co-

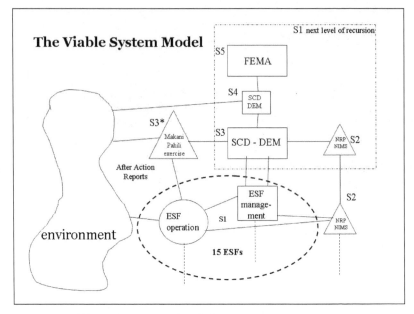

Figure 70: VSM application on Level of Recursion 3

ordination) exists only on paper, but is not implemented. As a consequence, HHMS personnel think that they have a system to use in an emergency, but its application is not exercised or even planned for. Therefore, HHMS personnel have a false sense of security, and in catastrophic event, they do not know their roles and responsibilities. A major deficiency is further that no ICS application for a catastrophic event is elaborated on the local level and that decisions would be made on a case-by-case basis, a major System 2 (coordination) and System 4 (intelligence) deficiency.

The misjudgment regarding Honolulu International Airport (see Figure 60) [US Army Corps of Engineers, 2007] were mentioned in chapter "Interaction based on System 2 (coordination)(Channel 6)" where the operability of Honolulu International airport was assumed at a major preparation conference (FEMA RISC 2007), but the US Army Corps of Engineers showed an airport scenario from before and after the landfall of a catastrophic hurricane at the Debris Management Seminar, which made clear that its usage would be impossible. Effective planning is out of reach if it does not even have the same planning assumption regarding such major critical infrastructure. Such Variety explosions greatly influence all processes in the HHMS and are cybernetic deficiencies in structure as much as in processes.

Another problematic issue is the geographic differentiation of O'ahu. The DEM divides O'ahu into six districts, FEMA divides O'ahu into eight districts, based on census districts, and for debris management O'ahu showed four divisions as discussed in chapter

Interaction based on System 2 (coordination)(Channel 6).

Effective planning is made impossible, which consequently is evident for all Levels of Recursion. Another System 2 issue highly affecting Channel Capacity and Transduction is the inconsistency regarding damage assessments, where different organizations involved – SCD, DEM, ARC – use different assessment tools and language. Overall, the VSM shows that effective disaster management is not necessarily a problem of resource constraints, e.g. funding, and that there is room to improve efficiency in different ways.

Furthermore, System 4 (intelligence) has too little emphasis. More long-term planning would be necessary that involves all ESFs while being aware of their capabilities to create synergies between them. Regarding System 3* (audits), a major deficiency shown by the VSM is that the After Action Reports after the Makani Pahili exercise are accomplished internally, and that there is no external evaluation. This is not sufficient in terms of quantitative or qualitative audit needs because in this situation, only the 'positive' side is highlighted. It is the HHMS department's or agency's decision what to report, what conclusions are drawn, what actions are necessary and implemented. No control mechanism exists from FEMA, SCD, DEM to ensure that those reports are accurate and therefore effective. That also means that System 1 (implementation) autonomy is too high and system Cohesion is lost. The VSM pronounces the importance of those factors for the overall system efficiency. Otherwise, these 'minor' problems might not be fixed or its heavy systemic impact underestimated.

3.5.2 Diagnosing processes – dynamics of the HHMS

The main concepts of system processes are the Resource Bargain, the Accountability Loop, Channel Capacity and Transduction. As an overview, each concept will be treated here shortly.

Looking at the Resource Bargain, the System 3–1 interaction, a known problem is the underfunding of the Hurricane Hazard Management System's (HHMS) departments and agencies. In terms of Variety, that means that System 3 (operational control) is overwhelmed by System 1 (implementation) resource requests. For example, if animal shelters are taken into account, environmental Variety is amplified, but one needs to ask what can be done with given resources. Ashby's lay says that a governor can only control with what he has available and that the Variety of a governor is limited. And further, System 5's (identity) identity must be pursued by System 3 (operational control), which will constrain System 1 (implementation) autonomy regarding their wishes and needs, for example if they go greedy. Of course, even with a perfect cybernetic structure, without resources to plug into this structure the system will fail. The State Civil Defense (SCD) cannot help the Honolulu Police Department if it does not exist, as happened in New Orleans. We know, resource constraints exist, but there are other constraints regarding resource allocation and logistics that could alleviate the problem of lack of resources. In the United States, there are enough resources, but it is a matter of system effectiveness rather than resource constraints if resources are in place when and where they are needed.

Regarding the Accountability Loop, no evaluation or check if the resources are used efficiently or no coherent reports exist, a System 3* (audits) failure. Inefficiency persists due to excessive System 1 (implementation) autonomy and a lack of System 2 (coordination) implementation. Channel Capacity, the measure of the amount of information transmitted in time X, is insufficient due to the System 2 (coordination) failure: information cannot flow where language or concepts are not understood. This problem exists on all channels. Transduction, the mechanism for information crossing boundaries from one component to another (e.g. military-government) and for accepting input in one language or realm of reference, and send it on in another, suffers also from the missing System 2 (coordination) implementation. It shows up, for example, regarding the interoperability of communication systems, the language differences between the military and the government, and also regarding the command-and-control versus the democratic structure. Further, it is Transduction where soft factors come into play: power, conflict, personal skills and assets, the cultural identity in Hawai'i or stress and frustration. The VSM recognizes their importance and influence regarding the viability of the system and its effectiveness. Ultimately, the information flow depends on them. Ultimately, in a situation of a catastrophic hurricane on O'ahu, we have a Variety explosion within the Environment. For the HHMS, that means it has to counterbalance that Variety. In general, disasters generate a sudden data overload for those who want to manage in them. Finding out how the actors in the system are coping with that overload is a way to understand their way of Variety Engineering. Many examples were given throughout this dissertation.

4. Is the Viable System Model worth the effort?

On the positive side, the VSM is a bonified methodology, but it is a craft, that requires practice. Beer used the VSM in consultancies for four decades and demonstrated increases in efficiency of between 30 % to 60 % [Walker, 2001]. It is not only explanatory as a diagnostic tool, but sets up a real-time measurement system and therefore is proactive. In sum, the VSM does not offer a quick fix or promises to solve specific problems, but it shows why things go wrong and it deals with messes. It is a fine-tuning tool that can point out the improvement potentials of a system. Instead of prescribing drastic actions to be instantly taken, which would destabilize the system, the VSM suggests a continuous cybernetic process to promote viability. It needs to be accepted that the implementation of the cybernetic process to evolve to a viable system takes time. The VSM seeks true coping ability and demands to be proactive and prepared. In addition, it is expandable with other models (see chapter 5).

The VSM is unique because it shows how to increase efficiency with given resource constraints, as was shown regarding the System 2 (coordination)-related inconsistencies. It shows that a well-designed information system can be used as an alternative to authoritarian control. The VSM highlights the balance between autonomy and control, managing present and future activities, and makes clear distinctions between different management functions, so that people in organizations can be conscious of what the context of their decision making is. For example, the VSM can clarify if it is an issue about (S5) identity or values; or about (S4) potential actions or preparations; about (S3) the 'here and now' necessary choices; about (S3*) detailed investigation of a specific area of operations; or about (S1) decisions about interactions with the Environment.

Further, the VSM distinguishes seven different channels of communication. It highlights the importance of certain functions and processes that otherwise would not get much attention, e.g. the missing external check on After Action Reports or the missing checks on ICS implementation and it highlights the need for real-time data, a factor which is often disregarded. The VSM makes gaps in information flow visible: A lot of knowledge is available locally, but there is no requirement or incentive to share this information. The VSM is comprehensive because it is very abstract using a cybernetic Meta-language, but therefore it can entail many other approaches.

The VSM enables us to make diagnoses and distinctions more effectively by carving out a particular operational domain from the 'messiness' that is reality, and to look at that carved-out bit according to certain explicit rules and conventions. For example, one FEMA representative stated that emergency management in the USA is a system of sequential failure. After each level of government fails, the next level steps in from the county level to the State level to the Federal level. Instead of sequential failure, the VSM would call for proactive action that is necessary to enhance systemic effectiveness, e.g. FEMA resources should be in the field earlier, before failure occurs [Fenton, 2007]. To achieve this proactive perspective, the VSM argues that a system failure does not stem from cause-and-effect relations, but from the pathology of the system as a whole. A cybernetic approach aims at designing an effective system beforehand.

The VSM is, therefore, an integrative tool based on the natural laws and hard science underpinning control engineering, while simultaneously accommodating soft factors. The fact that it is rooted in the functionalist paradigm yet exhibits flexibility toward the interpretative realm is one of its great merits. It thus overcomes a major deficiency marking many purported 'systems approaches', in particular the Incident Command System (ICS). Even though a system might have all the necessary elements from a functionalist perspective, this might not be sufficient for the system to run efficiently and effectively from an interpretative standpoint. Ultimately, social elements determine how the system is executed. For example, social factors such as trust, leadership, authority and credentials challenge any functionalist approach. Taking these factors into account constitutes the essence of VSM, as Beer says, 'the heart of an organization is its people' [Beer, 1994a, p. 576].

Another VSM advantage is in being reality-based, flexible, and robust. The VSM is reality-based in that it highlights the need for real-time data, a factor which is often disregarded. The need for real-time data leads to the important point that management is a continuing, infinite process. VSM's flexibility allows for inserting elements into a particular Level or Recursion without making dramatic changes to surrounding structures. Its robustness is achieved through a:

'Long-term focus rooted in the identity of the organization, and integrated structures evolve over time instead of radical discontinuous change. In many organizations, radical change through 'restructuring' processes, for example, causes oscillations and damages longer term effectiveness as structures, systems and human relationships are disregarded' [Espejo and Gill, 1997, p. 6].

Overall, the VSM is certainly useful for diagnosing problems in and prescribing solutions for system improvement. It is also capable of dealing adequately with the discontinuous temporal character of a 'hibernating' system such as a disaster organization. On the other hand, it is impractical in a Variety of ways and the drawback to VSM application is discussed next.

First of all, its language is too specialized to be learned easily, its concepts too abstract to be easily adopted, and, most important, it is not intuitive in situations where politics is 90 % of the game and expertise 10 %, where the real decision-makers have other priorities and interests, for example, getting re-elected. Further, it takes several years to apply the VSM to a super-organization such as a HHMS. During that process, the turn-over of staff will itself become a problem [Beer, 1989b]. Those are major drawbacks to VSM application.

Paradoxically, one of the greatest strengths and weaknesses of Beer's VSM is that it does not provide clear prescriptions, but rather explains why things do not work – a critical but not necessarily constructive outlook. The 'prescription' the VSM delivers is the abstract model of the Viable System itself, and the elaboration of this abstract model is subjective. For, Beer as a research philosopher states that scientific neutrality is impossible [Beer, 1981]. Consequently, there is no normative model of the Hurricane Hazard Management System (HHMS) or of any other system to be diagnosed from a VSM perspective. And, the quality of the diagnosis depends completely on the capabilities of the cybernetician who is dependent on the system's actors – on their subjective understanding, their willingness and Capability to communicate their understanding of the system to the cybernetician. But, if the VSM offers no prescription in the traditional sense, it is an explanatory or diagnostic tool. Beer emphasizes all through his research that VSM does not solve specific problems, but is a fine-tuning tool par excellence that can point out the improvement potentials of a system in focus.

The metaphorical, or paradoxical, quality of VSM is seen particularly in that the free information flow within the HHMS is not realizable. In part, this is due to competition between the private companies involved, e.g. telecom companies, and disaster managers. In part, and more important, some aspects of the human condition are just not computable, which greatly frustrates real-time data collection. For example, within the HHMS, it is assumed that its personnel are honest at all times, which is quite unrealistic. Other incomputable factors are the number of absent days of employees, or the quality of their relationships. Both factors lead to an incomplete real-time information system within the HHMS. But a complete real-time information system with free information flow is required in the VSM. Paradoxically then, the VSM explicitly limits the scope of its claims about the quality of humanity and human individuality. The VSM acknowledges that human Variety always remains a Black Box and is in some way or another ineffable. 'The basic element from a systemic point of view is a system of relations between people knowing each other and dealing with each other in interdependent activities and creating their meaning out of the interaction between the work they do and their relations' [Harnden, 2006]. Again, paradoxically, because it is basically a metaphor, the VSM has no ability to address the complexity of human behavior in practice, e.g. personnel fluctuation within the VSM, or people having their own self-interests and the human mess cannot be considered fully by the VSM because it is too dynamic. But this is not what the VSM is trying to achieve. It is exactly that 'redundant untidiness of the human condition that leads to the ability of a complex system to be viable' [Beer, 1994a, p. 326]. A system's stability is reached exactly because of this unseizable complexity. Therefore, the VSM is both paradoxical and an excellent metaphor.

Ultimately, Beer believes strongly that 'it is both silly and agonizing to reach successful organizational outcomes by trial and error, if the rules of the game are already known' [Beer, 1989b, p. 212]. Beer believed that mathematics, and by extension models based on them, are either tautological or wrong. The VSM is a pragmatic explanation and is not right or wrong, or tautological or consequential, but more or less useful – parallel to Wilson's definition of a model that requires above all its usefulness [Wilson, 1990].

Beer emphasizes that manager and cybernetician need to work hand in hand [Beer, 1989b]. What is crucial in consulting is the model-user relationship. The VSM is perfect and tautologous by itself, but the capability of the user to apply the model causes the problems. Consequently, the focus should be on the user, on the individual, who is the ultimate Recursion of the system. Therefore, Beer called himself a Guide, Philosopher and Friend pronouncing the importance of personal relationships in this consulting process of VSM application, as he said, 'there had to be long and detailed discussions about the mode and its diagnoses' [Beer, 1989b, p. 248]. The

VSM application requires from the HHMS people their willingness, intellectual capability and a profound understanding on top of fulfilling their regular job.

An overall question is if the VSM is practical. This research came to the conclusion that after the big effort in the beginning shortens with more experience, the insights are highly useful. In sum, the VSM can be seen as a treasure map: You can run around an island and find the treasure by chance. This way, one can know about the treasure, but take forever to find it. The VSM, in contrary, leads you right to it. The insights could maybe be found out without the VSM, but it would take a longer time to reach those insights. Plus, one would need a Variety of other approaches to do so and therefore need a Variety of experts that speak the same meta-language. This is the great advantage of a VSM application: it can integrate different fields of knowledge and therefore fits into the field of Geography. Therefore, the cybernetic meta-language is necessary, highly useful and worth learning. Overall, the VSM is a check that all issues are covered.

4.1 System Science – its important role in the field of Geography

The field of Geography is very fragmented and involves a wide range of fields in both the physical and social sciences. That these fields do not necessarily communicate fruitfully with each other is well known. The VSM emphasizes the validity of both. The VSM is an integrative tool because it is based on natural laws and hard science that underpins control engineering, but it also accommodates soft factors. One of its great merits is that it is rooted in the functionalist paradigm but exhibits flexibility toward the interpretative realm. Therefore, it has the capability to integrate the soft and hard sciences.

Specifically because the field of Geography is so fragmented, natural hazard and disaster research today has no separate identity. The problems concern – besides the fragmentation of the field – the disciplinary boundaries and over-specialization, which lead to a slowdown in progress. Lack of power, lack of funds and the fear of identity loss of involved fields worsen the situation for both Geography and hazard research. The debate about scientific truth, the validity and reliability of terminologies keep many research efforts and successes in further distance, unfortunately. The VSM could be one model that shows how those fields can work together and be integrated in a most useful and synergetic way. Its foundation in the hard sciences can advance the acceptance of the integration of the soft sciences. Further, the VSM's holistic concept can handle the complexity of the field of Geography and hazard management research, which other approaches do not accomplish. But, the VSM can be enriched by other approaches, some of which are briefly discussed in the chapter 4.

Advancing both fields, one of the VSM's merits is to provide a 'framework for viability to inject cybernetic language into discussions that usually involve conflict of personalities and apportioning of personal power' [Beer, 1989a, p. 235], factors that the rational actor paradigm does not deal with adequately. Conflict stems from differences in values, knowledge, *Weltanschauungen* and personalities. The VSM recognizes that power relations need to be considered, as well as trust, solidarity, stakeholder involvement and participation. In general, these subjective social concerns are often underrepresented in disaster management decisions, since short-term thinking governs politics and long-term disaster mitigation measures fall behind popular policy measures.

Geographers and social scientists have studied natural hazards from a Variety of perspectives. Over the last century there has been a shift of focus from the impact of the Environment on humans to the impact of humans on the Environment. The recognition of the human as dominant factor was a huge step and opened the door to more integrative studies. The VSM supports research that focuses on the human factor and on social relationships within a system, aside from the physical factors. Beer invented Syntegrity for the purposes of free information flow within a complex social system that is highly interconnected within and to an outside Environment [Beer, 1994b].

In 1983, Hewitt's revolutionary book "Interpretations of Calamity" was a push towards the integration of social and physical sciences that the VSM promotes as well. He argued that it is social organization that causes disasters. The VSM can be used to investigate exactly those complex interrelations and entails all aspects of vulnerability. The term vulnerability has been misused by being used very broadly. Blaikie's [2004] states that vulnerability does not simply mean poor environmental conditions in a deterministic way, but that it must be investigated how social, economic and political factors lead to very specific vulnerabilities [Blaikie, 2004].These complex interdependencies can be investigated using the VSM. In cybernetic terms, vulnerability is the potential or the risk for a system to become unstable.

How this risk is perceived, rated and the actions to avert it highly depend on the System 5's (policy) identity and its management style. In sum, the VSM represents the stance Blaikie, et al. [1994] follow. The problem solving style of this paradigm is collegial, and done with creativity, imagination, and pressure, if necessary. It involves a bottom up approach and community involvement aiming at decentralization. The philosophy is egalitarian using holistic methods and aiming to live with nature. Overall, there are many approaches in the field of Geography that explain why things go wrong. It is rare, and the VSM takes that extra step, that a model not only diagnoses the shortcomings but aims to improve a system in focus.

4.2 Insights for the field of hazard management research

This dissertation introduced a cybernetic approach stemming from systems thinking to the field of natural hazard research, a realm that Geographers dealt with intensely. Geography's contributions to natural hazard research derive from its multi-disciplinarity, its broad theoretical and methodological diversity, multi-facetted technical sophistication and a history of well-received pragmatic research. The interaction of people and Environment has always been at the core of Geography, especially how human and engineered systems react to stressors and how humans transform their natural Environment. The Viable System Model (VSM) has the capability to incorporate all those elements and systems.

Additionally, the difference between the VSM and conventional management models is its foundation in holism. Instead of examining cause and effect in a linear manner, the VSM specifically looks at the links that hold the system together in a holistic manner and therefore takes a system's full complexity into account. It is in tune with other whole-systems ideas like acupuncture, the Gaia hypothesis, most of modern physics and many aspects of Eastern religions, instead of the perspectives set by the worldview of Newton and Descartes [Walker, 2001]. For these reasons, cybernetic management should be incorporated into the field of Geography and social sciences in general and natural hazard research in particular and its benefits should be claimed.

Watts [1983] evaluated natural hazard research from the standpoint that our knowledge is critically shaped by our preoccupations and that interpretation of the world happens within the limits of our conditioned imagination, and hence our theories and concepts. He critiques that in geography, attributes of social life are misrepresented and the deterministic view reduces humans to objects without history or social relationships. Criticism regarding empirical studies pointed out that the data gathered under 'normal, average' social conditions from governments and centralized institutions were standardized and hence not average or normal for different groups of people. Beer sets up a personal relationship to the system's actors and focuses on their subjective perceptions, which are cybernetically expressed in the Transduction and Channel Capacity, and overcomes this critique.

More recently, in the hazard management literature, authors such as Mileti (1999) and Blaikie et al. (1994) emphasize underlying economic and environmental factors and concentrate on social vulnerability and building resilient communities. The focus lies on man-made influences on susceptibility of risks and human vulnerability to natural disasters. A holistic view of disaster emerged that natural hazards are conditioned by the social, cultural, political and historical context. Political ecology provides a framework for understanding and integrating the social construction of vulnerability and climatic risk. It reflects the confluence of political economy and human ecology and refers to ways in which vulnerability is rooted in people, values, institutions, and the Environment [Pulwarty, 1997]. The local and envelope Environment of the VSM can house all those factors and can get to the level of detail required by a thorough analysis using different Level of Recursions. Therefore, the VSM is an all-encompassing approach that highly suits the field of hazard management.

As indicated above, this development was a shift from the beginning of the century, where a deterministic view dominated the field of natural hazards, to the risk reduction and vulnerability focused research of today that dwells on anthropogenic causes. The VSM is a progression of this research and can incorporate and relate to such concepts used widely within Geography, e.g. the concept of resilience. The VSM relates to resilience through its central concept of viability. If a system is viable, it is resilient. But, a non-viable systems can also be resilient. That means that viability entails more than resilience. Overall, resilience is less subjective than viability. The concept of optimization can be put in relation as well. There is no optimization of viability, because no system is ever stable. No system is ever what it strives to be or should be. With such approaches new viewpoints or critiques can be added to a Variety of geographical concepts and induce new ways of thinking.

Cutter (2003) pointed out that current hazard research trends are too focused on local social dynamics or identification of physical exposures and too broad in their applications and models. These examine only individual risks, not multi-hazard or multiple risks and she suggests integrated approaches that incorporate social, natural and engineered systems. Further, different scales need to be addressed. Management cybernetics could fill in those gaps as a holistic approach to complex problem solving. As this research showed, the VSM can incorporate multiple risks and incorporate systems varying from social, environmental to economic types. Attempts were made, amongst others, by the United Nations, the South Pacific Applied Geosciences Commission (SOPAC) and other institutions to develop indices to measure vulnerability. The flaws in regards to averaging and leveling out important information make the effort compared to the outcome not feasible. Generalized statements as a result have limited use and the validity is questionable. The cybernetic management approach a la Beer offers those measurements of effectiveness.

Overall, the focus of disaster management shifted from the response to events after the occurrence to a proactive approach emphasizing the importance of preparedness, adaptation and resilience. The VSM promotes exactly such a proactive approach by setting up an Algedonic Alarm system that informs the manager of any incipient instability within the system he manages.

The VSM could be further enriched by Blaikie's, et al. [1994] view of the political economy of disasters and their Access Model and their Pressure and Release Model. In the Access Model, they elucidate how political and economic systems on the national and international level influence social processes, in which social variables (welfare, class, caste, occupation, ethnicity, health status, immigration status, race, gender, age, etc.) lead to unequal access to opportunities (work, resources, etc.) and exposure to natural hazards (risks). These factors all lead to the instability of the whole system as they disrupt the well-functioning of the units and could serve as measurement variables on different time scales in a VSM application. The natural Environment is spatially varied, parallel to the VSM's local environments, and provides an unequal distribution of opportunities and hazards, but the access to those are determined by the social, economic and political factors mentioned above. The opportunities tie in with the livelihood of people that can render them vulnerable or resilient depending on the access to income, knowledge, training, resources, etc. as explained in the Access Model [Blaikie, 1994]. A specific definition of viability can be set for a VSM application along such variables. In sum, the Access Model shows how a disaster impacts people and how stresses reverberate through livelihoods and have negative impacts on the ability to cope with and recover from future shocks and stresses. The VSM takes one step more than this model and aims at improving the situation as a fine-tuning tool that evolves over time.

Further, Blaikie, et al. [1994] emphasize that vulnerabilities are embedded in the daily routines of everyday life. In cybernetic terms, that would have to be researched on the lowest Level of Recursion, the single human being. They link root causes on the global level to dynamic pressures and unsafe conditions on the local level and demonstrates the social progression of disasters in the Pressure and Release Model that shows how do disaster happen, which is complemented with the Access model demonstrating how people are impacted. Both models can greatly enhance the VSM's capability to be usefully applied to a disaster management situation and improve that system's effectiveness.

In general, differences in research emphases regarding the impacts and management of natural hazards have, for the most part, resulted from two fundamentally different views of environment-society relationships. In one view, a self-correcting, *homeostatic process* operates, in which society and environmental hazards are inexorably adjusted, toward some acceptable equilibrium. This view infers that people and institutions are committed to removing known risks from life and fail to do so only where the risk is highly uncertain. Proponents of a second view argue that vulnerability is constructed from an *open-ended* development process that determines the ways in which a hazard is likely to constitute a disaster [Pulwarty, 1997]. This Variety proliferating second viewpoint is certainly that would fit into the VSM application to the Hurricane Hazard Management System (HHMS). The VSM can live up to a highly complex viewpoint of disaster management because it embraces life in general as never-ending process. This problem is solved in cybernetics through the concept of recursive structures. Further, Alexander argues that no single disaster theory exists, but every disaster has its own theory [Alexander, 2000] because disasters are a complex compound and a concatenation of facts and events. An application of the VSM enables the cybernetician to include all potential aspects of a disaster. Mileti [1999] argues that without humans in a certain location, there would be no disasters. For example, a major storm over the open ocean is no disaster per se. Mileti [1999] argues that in the ideal case, the individual units would simply not move themselves into harm's way. Hence, if there is no vulnerability, there is no disaster. Though, this approach disregards a Variety of human factors such as ignorance, the blaming of others, the transferring of risks by buying insurance, insufficient knowledge, among others. Those factors are recognized within the VSM and its goal is to measure them and alarm the manager of incipient instability, in the ideal case. If vulnerability is not recognized or transferred, and hence for the observer non-existent, a disaster might still occur. Ultimately, Mileti wants disaster resilient communities evolving, which are independent from (non-)governmental relief aid and can withstand a natural hazard. Since resilience is incorporated within the cybernetic concept of viability, the VSM would be an extension of Mileti's ideas and research aim.

The systems approach is valuable since it pronounces the connectivity within. It postulates that the whole is more than the sum of its parts – as opposed to reductionism, which argues that the whole is the sum of its parts. Even if a single or several units suffer a total breakdown, the system as a whole can still be stable and fix the units under stress. Management cybernetics respects those mentioned viewpoints since it depends on the choice of the system in focus by the cybernetician and ultimately on the identity of the system, which is subjectively chosen by System 5 (identity).

In sum, the VSM grasps the full complexity of the field of disaster management, including hibernating systems. It is flexible because it is capable to entail any Level of Recursion, any organization, any disaster type, size of disaster, on any timeline. It emphasizes a proactive stance to reduce vulnerabilities – and therefore fits in today's paradigm. It points out vulnerabilities in all realms: economic, environmental, social and cultural. It promotes a non-hierarchical approach and therefore a participatory approach, which is often aimed for in disaster management today. Further, it highlights the non-resource factors instead of arguing that all shortcomings are founded in lack of funding, for example. The VSM could serve as a framework for improved disaster management efforts, if you put in the time and effort to learn VSM. As Allenna Leonard, Beer's life partner and cybernetician, stated: the VSM finds many interpretations, but only few get its value. The VSM is a vision – if you follow its concepts, the System will improve.

A more interlinked world needs more effective organizations. Cybernetic tools entail completely different, innovative and creative solutions for the business and non-business sector that the methods used today cannot provide. Unnatural, or man-made disasters can be avoided if the human-induced causes are cut out. Ultimately, the question is how flexible human management systems will be to adjust to increasingly complex system changes in both nature and society. Watson reminds us of being aware of the whole and reconnecting with nature's intelligence, which (bio)cybernetics empowers us to do: 'I measure intelligence by the ability to live in harmony with the natural world [Watson, 2008]. And as a whale sanctuary protector he added: ,By that criterion whales are far more intelligent than we are' [Watson, 2008].

Cybernetics, the science of control and communication in the animal and the machine [Wiener, 1948], teaches us how to live viably and offers a useful tool for investigations of those systems through the Viable System Model. This way, Metasystemic Calm, or inner stillness, can be established. In Hawai'ian, inner stillness means 'maluhia' containing the words 'malu' (protection) and 'hia' (desire), the 'desire for protection'. Being protected, a system can rest at calm.

5. Appendix: Other potential approaches inspiring future research

5.1 Potential redesign of the HHMS using Human Activity Systems (HAS)

To enhance the HHMS's viability capabilities over time, the Levels of Recursion cannot be allowed to fall into a coma. As a first step, one way to let the VSM lead to a new design of the HHMS would be to insert a Level of Recursion between Level 2 and 3 and make it viable all year round. This could happen along the Human Activity Systems (HAS) [Checkland, 1999] and the System 1s (implementation) would constitute Mitigation, Preparation, Response, Recovery and Reconstruction. The ESFs would be grouped under those activities. The mitigation and recovery stage of the HHMS would be alive and active continuously throughout the year. Currently, the ESF structure is established after a hurricane hit, when a JFO is established. The squiggly lines between those ESF on the next lower Level of Recursion 4 (after Recursion 3 is inserted) between the HHMS's departments and agencies would be alive. Practically and under a new VSM design they would work together during the year under the ESF structure. Level of Recursion 2, the JFO structure, also should be alive continuously throughout the year and be exercised as such more frequently. All HHMS senior staff should be involved and meetings held to become familiar with the ESF structure under a JFO so when disaster strikes the system can function in an effective manner and the HHMS be viable as a whole. The HAS could proof as a good add-on to the VSM.

5.2 Ackoff's Idealized Design

Usually, management only reacts to stimuli in the Environment. A HILP event is not highly likely to be reacted on. Beer emphasizes the difference between creative ideas and a real internal creative urge. That means that 'System 4 (intelligence) is involved in containing and *generating* environmental Variety' [Beer, 1994a, p. 238]. There must be an initiative originating at the System 4 (intelligence) level for innovation. Ultimately, the System 4 (intelligence) model of itself is an innovation generator. The core concept in the emerging model of System 4 (intelligence) is that it handles double amplification of Variety, which reveals itself as the initiative to invent the future, as well as double attenuation, which distinguishes between two designs of input returned. Dealing with both types of Environment causes double interactions: the envelope and the local ones. Addressing the Environment, the existing arrangements of Variety amplifications, Channel Capacity and Transduction can be used. But those arrangements regarding the answers coming from the Environment, System 4 (intelligence) cannot rely on the existing arrangements, or it cannot receive information about an unknown future since those channels and Transductions are designed to filter out these novelties. Consequently, new attenuating filters and new transducers need to be designed.

The first step is to become aware of System 4 (intelligence) and recognize its revolutionary concept of finding possibilities beyond present perceptions and mobilizing latent creativity by investment in people's time. To design a proper System 4 (intelligence), Ackoff's Idealized Design could be implemented.

Ackoff's approach is interpretative and focuses on adapting and learning. His aim is assisting to design a desirable future where the improvement is based on the client's criteria and to remove conflict. The idealized design is taken from his Interactive Planning Concept that follows three principles: participation, continuity (plans need constant revision) and holism. It entails five phases, which can be applied in any order and where none is ever completed. (1) The 'mess is formulated, (2) the planning goals and objectives defined, (3) the means of that planning determined, (4) resource planning accomplished and (5) the plan implemented. The idealized design stems from phase (2), where a mission statement is formulated, a list of desired properties elaborated and then in the idealized design maximum creativity is required of all participants. It is envisioned that the system would be destroyed last night and only three constraints are admissible. It must be technologically feasible, operationally viable and the design must be capable of continuous improvement. Then, a list of aspects to be covered is elaborated as well as the formulation of closest approximation to design. The gaps between ideal in real is identified and in the next steps the realization of this idealized design while closing gaps is accomplished [Jackson, 2003].

5.3 The Analytical Hierarchy Process by Saaty

The question of how Beer addresses resource allocation was discussed earlier. Another answer might emerge from Steenge's paper about the combination of the AHP and the VSM and other combined applications of the VSM and various systems approaches [Steenge, 1990]. The State of Hawai'i FCO stated that setting operational priorities and pre-scripting a game plan, a set of priorities for the JFO, is needed [Rosenberg, 2007b].

The Analytical Hierarchy Process [Saaty, 2001] is a postmodern approach:. it involves a maximum number of stakeholders (community groups, public hearings, etc.) and includes also affected people. The AHP can deal with problems of complexity, uncertainty and measurement such as incommensurability and intangibility. It shows trade-offs and complements Cost-Benefit Analyses. For example, in search of alternatives of mitigation options for an incoming storm the AHP serves as a decision support tool – but does not make the decision – and can give insight into the problem situation. Marginalized voices can be included and consensus is not necessary. Diversity in developing influence diagrams and cognitive mapping to explore the problem situation is enhanced. After structuring a functional hierarchy through the collection of objectives, impact dimensions, obstacles and consequential actions the eigenvector method, which means comparing two elements against a third, is implemented in a verbal or numerical way. This is a pair wise comparison. Satisfying solutions and decision accomplished to serve constraints are accepted and optimization and absolute conflict resolution is not necessary. In addition, creativity, pluralism and diversity make this method a postmodern way of problem solution.

5.4 Designing a cybernetically sound infrastructure system – Critical Path Analysis

A Critical Path Analysis can be used to elaborate a timeline of activation of resources, incl. pre-staging, which the State of Hawai'i is still in need of [Rosenberg, 2007b] and could complement a VSM project.

Looking at the full spectrum of every catastrophic event, the difficulty in the response, besides the massive loss of life, is the loss of infrastructure. Infrastructure systems in large urban areas are homeostatic, self-balancing systems based on population, demands for goods and economic factors. In a catastrophic event, you lose Homeostasis because the resources to support that population are not available. The distribution network is not in place including the power, communications and transportation networks. The state is short of supplies in addition to a higher demand in emergency services, which results obviously in an overwhelmed system.

One way to prioritize action and to find an optimal approach in disaster management is the Critical Path Analysis. The *first* critical path is fuel to run the power system. Main problems to be considered are the potential contamination and a possible shortage of fuel supply. Even with a stated 30 day fuel supply [Rosegg, 2007a] the problem of a dysfunctional distribution system poses a major obstacle. Further, the gasoline usage must be calculated because bunk fuel is not usable for all needs. Moreover, without power gasoline cannot be pumped, though some small trucks have self-pumping systems. The *second* critical path is transportation with an emphasis on fuel usage of airplanes, the support for emergency transportation and the need for generators at hospitals and shelters. The *third* critical path is communications, which is again dependent on power and fuel. The distribution of public information as well as information exchange of first responders for damage assessments, for example is of high urgency [Rosenberg, 2007b].

Overall it is an engineering problem to figure out the valid numbers and the needed assumptions to execute the planning including time availability considering the un-loading and refueling of airplanes for turnaround, for example. Micro-cosmos research and consultant work is needed in collaboration with teams of the ESF structure. It is estimated that a three to four month research timeframe is needed for this type of plan.

It is important to establish supply chains in a remote location so supplies can be accessed if the community's food, water, materials, and equipment are destroyed. The business model of a "just-in-time inventory" fails in a disaster in the absence of a sophisticated logistics plan (like Wal-Mart's) to deliver quickly in an emergency. Even the Red Cross became overwhelmed when confronted with the magnitude of Hurricane Katrina; it faced the same capacity challenges as the local governments and the EMAC [ICCMA, 2006, pp. 8]. In VSM terms, this is a System 4 (intelligence) task.

5.5 Further research potential

5.5.1 Progress through stability research

It is a valuable task to investigate the impacted systems, such as the population of Oʻahu or the infrastructure system, in terms of stability. *Stability* represents the restoration of the infrastructure system to the initial state. *Resilience* will reflect the time (in days) needed for the infrastructure system to be restored. *Persistence* could be defined as the time (in days) the infrastructure lasts during a storm before it needs to be replaced. This could also be formulated in terms of wind force instead of time. *Resistance* will define the degree of impact from a Category 4–5 hurricane. Regarding complexity, *richness* is defined as the number of elements of an infrastructure system and *connectance* as the number of actual interspecific interactions divided by the number of possible interspecific interactions [Pimm, 1984].

5.5.2 Vulnerability studies

State Civil Defense officials assume that Oʻahu would lose 80 % of its infrastructure and state that the Federal Emergency Management Agency should be prepared to bring in 80 % of the needed infrastructure 10–14 days after the hurricane passed [Richards and Tengan, 2007]. Social pressures would be enormous if public would be informed about Oʻahu's vulnerability: the potential damage and the little preparedness in place currently.

Consequently, vulnerability studies on the local level should be enhanced asking especially how and why certain vulnerabilities emerge. A challenge hereby is to anticipate surprise and develop flexible and sustainable management approaches to adapt to a rapidly changing Environment. It is important to further devote research efforts on equity issues, enhance participation, involve communities in larger research projects, acknowledge local knowledge, research how such knowledge is lost and how it can be regained, improve use of hybrid knowledge of experts and indigenous people and be sensitive to social variables of gender, race, class ethnicity and other minorities. The media needs to be educated and informed about the effects of their biased reports and gender sensitivity should be enhanced.

5.5.3 Lazlo's paper on steering social systems

Laszlo [1979, pp. 252] suggests the indirect steering of systems through the impact of the steerable systems, some of which need to be designed specifically for that purpose. He defines steerable systems (organizations) 'as those of which the members act in a public, social or professional capacity, and are compensated for their actions by the allocation of values (e.g. monies, prestige, or some other desired commodity)' and non-steerable systems (communities) as 'those in which the members act in a nonprofessional or private capacity, and are not specifically remunerated for their actions [Laszlo, 1979, p. 252]. Those two defined systems are exclusive to each other.

Communities are only indirectly steerable because they tend to be too indeterminate to permit adequate cybernetic modeling. Models would become too complex and fuzzy and be practically useless. Further, communities tend not to respond to model-generated policies, especially if they are counter-intuitive. Cybernetic analysis requires that system-related information and specifically decision centers be clearly identified. For communities by contrast make this a difficult endeavor also due to the fuzziness and complexity of data [Laszlo, 1979, p. 253]. 'Cybernetic modeling requires sufficient order in the observed phenomena to justify (on epistemological grounds) the postulation of sensors, effectors, regulators, controllers, comparators, monitors and memory-stores, with determinate information and energy-flows. In the absence of such order, cybernetic modeling loses its validity on epistemological, and its warrant on methodological grounds (the resulting models become largely unoperationalizable) ... A cybernetic model with innumerable loops, points of randomness and low levels of probability fails to provide grounds for operational control' [Laszlo, 1979, pp. 253].

Social systems are suprasystems formed by organizations and communities in interrelation and are cybernetically overcomplex and underdetermined phenomena [Laszlo, 1979, p. 255].

Cybernetics develops models that seem counter-intuitive to members of communities. Those models can only be accepted – and Beer's VSM requires these assumptions – 'if the system's members are willing to (a) follow policies despite a conflict with their own common sense; (b) suspend their common-sense judgments in favor of the model-generated policies' [Laszlo, 1979, p. 255]. Otherwise, communities remain unsteerable and policies evolved through theoretical models remain ineffective. Organizations, on the other hand, are steerable since incentives and prestige create a climate of acceptance even for counter-intuitive policy-decisions [Laszlo, 1979, p. 255].

Consequently, communities can be steered through organizations. For the HHMS this would equal the American Red Cross, educational programs, specific requirements or other incentives.

The HHMS includes Laszlo's 'organizations' and 'communities'. Further it has to be recognized that communities exist within organizations, which makes the application of cybernetic models problematic. On the other hand, Laszlo's definitions of social factors within organizations are disputable.

Laszlo's argument points out possibilities to reduce social vulnerability by public education or other measures. His suggested 'strategy involves using existing adaptive organizations to initiate a consensus-building information flow that, in a subsequent phase, serves as the support for the creation and effective operation of a supranational functional actor entrusted with the task of steering the decisive aspects of the world system ... existing organizations could be adapted to produce a flow of information on the difference between the desirable and the current trends in the world system' [Laszlo, 1979, p. 257]. Social steering should start with the systems most accessible to control and evolve into less accessible systems. Cybernetic modeling is not an end in itself, but can serve as an instrument to design a functional organization to correct social imbalances.

5.5.4 Efforts towards better forecast communication

Climate science as the provider of climate information needs to recognize the needs of climate information users. This requires a better understanding of climate science and the social sciences. Despite the fact that science should be done, some argue, without purpose, the reality is that funding projects conducting science projects serve certain goals, i.e. effective, user-friendly climate information (forecasts), which are essential in improving society (saving lives, property, assets). Ultimately, science is pursued to advance knowledge, but this idealism is unrealistic in the face of limited financial and other resources and constraints.

5.5.5 Other models and ideas adding to the VSM

Multi-objective decision analysis could be added to a VSM application, specifically using optimization models regarding the resource allocation. Further, the GAP analysis could also be of substantial use. Insights from

Weick's paper about the Mann Gulch disaster can bring insights regarding the collapse of Sensemaking in Organizations [1993].

In Decision and Control, Stafford discusses the attractive and repulsive forces of plasma as part of the character of self-organization [1966, pp. 359]. In this context he refers to the coherence produced by Freud's "endopsychic censor", presumably referring to the ethical super-ego. The autonomic System 1–2–3 might be seen as "Das Es", the it. The (algedonodically produced) Metasystem of 4 and 5 can be seen as ego ("Das Ich"- the I) and super-ego ("Das Ueber-Ich"). This seems a compelling analogy. Further, Stafford could be seen as suggesting entropy will produce ethics. Along with Pask, Bateson and Whitehead, is he taking up the panpsychic position?

List of Abbreviations

AC(P)	Area Command (Post)
ARC	American Red Cross
CONOP	Federal Support Concept of Operations for a catastrophic hurricane impacting the State of Hawaii
DEM	Department of Emergency Management
EOC	Emergency Operations Center: The physical location at which the coordination of information and resources to support local or State incident management activities normally takes place.
EOP	Emergency Operations Plan
ESF	Emergency Support Function: A grouping of government and certain private-sector capabilities into an organizational structure to provide the support, resources, program implementation, and services for disaster management activities.
FEMA	Federal Emergency Management Agency
HSEEP	Homeland Security Exercise and Evaluation Program
IC(S)	Incident Command (System)
JFO	Joint Field Office: temporary Federal facility established to coordinate operational Federal assistance activities to the affected jurisdiction(s) during Incidents of National Significance.
NIMS	National Incident Management System
NRP	National Response Plan
RISC	Regional Interagency Steering Committees
SCD	State Civil Defense
UC(P)	Unified Command (Post)
USACE	US Army Corps of Engineers

References

Ackoff, R.L. (1981). Creating the Corporate Future. John Willey and Sons, New York.

Applied Research Associates (2001). Hazard Mitigation Study for the Hawaiʻi Hurricane Relief Fund. Prepared for the Hawaiʻi Hurricane Relief Fund. December 7, 2001.

Argyris, C., Schoen, D.A. (1978). Organizational Learning: A theory of action perspective. Addison-Wesley, Reading, MA.

Ashby, W.R. (1956). An Introduction to Cybernetics. Methuen, London.

Beer, S. (1966). Decision and Control. John Wiley, London and New York.

Beer, S. (1979). The Heart of Enterprise. John Wiley, London and New York.

Beer, S. (1981). Brain of the firm. 2nd edition. John Wiley, London and New York.

Beer, S. (1985). Diagnosing the System for Organizations. John Wiley, New York.

Beer, S. (1986). *Recursions of Power.* Keynote Address to the Seventh European Meeting on Cybernetics and Systems Research. April, 1984. In: Power, Autonomy and Utopia. Trappl, R. ed., Plenum Press, New York.

Beer, S. (1989a). *The Viable System Model: its provenance, development, methodology and pathology.* In: The Viable Systems Model: Interpretations and Applications of Stafford Beer's VSM. R. Espejo and R. Harnden, eds., John Wiley, New York.

Beer, S. (1989b). *The evolution of a management cybernetics process.* In: The Viable Systems Model: Interpretations and Applications of Stafford Beer's VSM. R. Espejo and R. Harnden, eds., John Wiley, New York.

Beer, S. (1994a). The Heart of Enterprise. John Wiley, London and New York.

Beer, S. (1994b). Beyond Dispute: The Invention of Team Syntegrity. John Wiley, Chichester.

Bigelow, J. et al. (1943). "Behavior, Purpose and Teleology". *Philosophy of Science 10*, 1:18–24.

Blaikie, P., et al. (2004). At Risk: Natural Hazards, People's Vulnerability and Disasters. Second edition. Routledge, London.

Burton, I., Kates, R.W., White, G.F. (1993). The Environment as a hazard. Second Edition. Guilford Press, New York, London.

Capra, F. (1996). The web of life: A new scientific understanding of living systems. Anchor books, New York.

Checkland, P.B., Scholes, P. (1999). Systems Thinking, Systems Practice. John Wiley, Chichester.

City and County of Honolulu (2006*). Departmental and agency reports of the City and County of Honolulu for fiscal year July 1, 2005 to June 30, 2006.* http://www. honolulu.gov/csd/budget/index1.htm

City and County of Honolulu (2007). *Emergency Operations Plan. January 2007.* Department of Emergency Management. Honolulu.

Comfort, L. et al. (1999). "Reframing disaster policy: the global evolution of vulnerable communities". *Environmental Hazards.* 1:39–44.

Conant, R., Ashby, R. (1970). "Every good regulator of a system must be a model of that system". *International Journal of Systems Science.* 1(2):89–97.

Department of Geography (1998). Atlas of Hawai'i. Third Edition. S. Juvik and J.O. Juvik, eds., University of Hawai'i, Honolulu.

Department of Land and Natural Resources (1996). *Hawai'i Flood Insurance Plan.* State of Hawai'i.Honolulu. July 1996.

Department of Planning and Permitting (2007). *Hurricanes and Tropical Storms.* Standard Operation Procedures. Folder on File at the Department of Emergency Management. Honolulu.

Disability and Communication Access Board (2007). *2007 Interagency Action Plan for the emergency preparedness of people with disabilities and special health needs.* State of Hawai'i, February 2007. Working group. Department of Health. State of Hawai'i, Honolulu. http://Hawai'i.gov/health/dcab/interagencyplan/index.htm

Dynes, R.R., Quarantelli. 1968. "Group behavior under stress". *Society and Social Research.* 52:416–29.

Emergency Management Institute (2007a). *Course IS-1 – The Emergency Manager.* Independent Study Program. http://training.fema.gov/emiweb/is/is1.asp

Emergency Management Institute (2007b). *Course IS-100 – The Incident Command System (ICS).* Independent Study Program. http://training.fema.gov/emiweb/is/is100.asp

Emergency Management Institute (2007c). *Course: IS-800 – NRP Introduction.* Independent Study Program. http://training.fema.gov/emiweb/is/is800.asp

Emergency Management Institute (2008). *Course IS-120.A – An introduction to exercises.* Independent Study Program. http://training.fema.gov/EMIWeb/IS/IS120A.asp

Espejo, R. et al. (1996). Organizational Transformation and Learning: A cybernetic approach to management. John Wiley, New York.

Espejo, R., Gill, A. (1997). The Viable System Model as a Framework for Understanding Organizations. Phrontis Limited and Syncho Limited.

Federal Emergency Management Agency (2006). Tribal Government And Local Jurisdiction Compliance Activities:Federal Fiscal Year 2006 (October 1, 2005-September 30, 2006). Washington, D.C.

Federal Emergency Management Agency (2007). Federal Support CONOP for a catastrophic hurricane impacting the State of Hawai'i. Draft.

Fletcher, C., Grossman, E., Richmond, B. (2000). Atlas of Natural Hazards in the Hawai'ian Coastal Zone. University of Hawai'i. Honolulu.

Gregg, C. et al. (2007). "Tsunami Warnings: Understanding in Hawai'i". *Natural Hazards*, 40(1):71–87(17).

Guard, C., Lander, M.A. (1999). The Saffir-Simpson tropical cyclone scale for the tropical pacific *adapted from the Saffir-Simpson Hurricane Scale Used in the Atlantic Basin. Water and Energy Research Institute. Guam.*

Hawai'i State Civil Defense (2007a). Debris Management Seminar. Participant Handbook, Honolulu.

Hewitt, K. (1983). Interpretations of calamity. Edited by K. Hewitt. Allen and Unin, Boston.

Holling, C.S. (1977). *The Curious Behavior of Complex Systems: Lessons from Ecology.* In: Linstone, H.A., Simmons, W.H.C. (eds.): Futures Research: New Directions. Addison-Wesley, 114–129.

Holmberg, B.A. (1989). *Developing organizational competence in a business.* In: The Viable Systems Model: Interpretations and Applications of Stafford Beer's VSM. Espejo, and R. Harnden, eds., John Wiley, New York.

International City and County Management Association (ICCMA)(2006). *A networked approach to improvements in emergency management*, Washington D.C.

Intergovernmental Panel on Climate Change (IPCC)(2007). The physical basis of climate change. Working Group I. Cambridge University Press, New York.

Jackson, M. (2003). Systems Thinking: Creative Holism for Managers. John Willey, New York.

Jones, J. (2006). *NIMS. Incident Command System Field Guide.* First Edition. Jeff Jones, Division Chief. Compliments of State Civil Defense, Oregon.

Laszlo, E. (1979). *Uses and limitations of the cybernetic modeling of social systems.* In: Communication and control in society. K. Krippendorff, eds., Gordon and Breach, New York, 249–260.

Leonard, A. (1993). "Modeling response to catastrophe using Beer's VSM: Viability for effective action". *Kybernetes*, 22(6):79–90.

Leonard, A. (1999). "A Viable System Model: Consideration of Knowledge Management". Journal of Knowledge Management Practice, August 1999.

Mackenzie, F. (2003). Our changing planet. Third edition. Pearson Education, New Jersey.

Malik, F. (2011). Strategie: Navigieren in der Komplexität der Neuen Welt. Edition Malik. Campus Verlag, Frankfurt a.M.

Meadows, D.H., Meadows, D (1972). Limits to growth: A report for the Club of Rome's project of the predicament of mankind. Universe Books, New York.

Mileti, D. S. (1999). Disasters by Design. Joseph Henry Press, Washington.

Miller, G.A. (1956). 'The Magical Number Seven, Plus or Minus Two: Some Limits on Our Capacity for Processing Information'. *The Psychological Review, Vol. 63, pp. 81–97*

Munich Re Group (2004). "Natural Catastrophes 2003. Annual Review". *Topics geo2003.* NatCatSERVICE-Info, Munich.

Munich Re Group (2006). *Hurrikane –stärker, häufiger, teurer.* Assekuranz im Änderungsrisiko. Edition Wissen, Munich.

Pacific Disaster Center (n.d.). Solutions for fostering disaster-resilient communities. Kihei, Maui.

Pimm, S.L. (1984). "The Complexity and Stability of Ecosystems". *Nature*, 307(5949):321–326.

Pulwarty, R.S., Broad, K., Finan, T. (2004). *El Niño events, forecasts and decision-making*. In: Mapping Vulnerability: Disasters, Development and People. G. Bankoff, G. Frerks and T. Hilhorst, eds., Earthscan, London, 83–98.

Rabenold, C. (ed.)(2006). "U.S. Billion-Dollar Weather and Climate Disasters". *Natural Hazards Observer*. 30(4), March 2006. The Natural Hazards Center. Boulder, Colorado.

Reissberg, A.C. (2011). "The Advanced Syntegration as the most effective and efficient tool for large-scale disaster response coordination". *Systems Research and Behavioral Science*. 28:455–464. John Wiley & Sons.

Rosenhead, J. (ed.)(1989). Rational Analysis for a Problematic World. Problem Structuring Methods for Complexity, Uncertainty, and Conflict. NY: Wiley

Saaty, T.L. (2001). Decision making for leaders. The Analytic Hierarchy Process Series, Vol. 2. RWS Publications, Pittsburgh.

Sandburg, C. (1954). Abraham Lincoln. The prairie years and the war years. Library of Congress Cataloging-in-Publication Data, United States.

Schroeder, T. (1993). Hawai'ian Hurricanes: Their history, causes and the future. University of Hawai'i, Honolulu.

Senge, P.M. (1990). The fifth discipline: The art and practice of the learning organization. Doubleday, New York.

Shaw, S. L. (1981). A History of Tropical Cyclones in the Central North Pacific Ocean and the Hawai'ian Islands 1832–1979. National Oceanic and Atmospheric Administration.

Sorensen, R.M. (1997). *Basic Coastal Engineering*. Chapman and Hall, New York.

State of Hawai'i (2003). *Emergency Alert System (EAS) Plan*. June 12, 2003.

State Civil Defense (2005). *Report of Recommended Statewide Public Hurricane Shelter Criteria*. Hurricane Shelter Criteria Committee.

Steenge, A.E. et al. (1990). "The decentralization of a sales support department in a medium-large company: a quantitative assessment based on ideas of Thomas L. Saaty and Stafford Beer". *European Journal of Operational Research*, 48:120–7.

Taleb, N. (2007). The Black Swan. Random House, New York.

The White House (2003a). Homeland Security Presidential Directive/HSPD-5. Subject: Management of Domestic Incidents. Office of the Press Secretary. February 28, 2003.

The White House (2003b). Homeland Security Presidential Directive/HSPD-8. Subject: National Preparedness. Office of the Press Secretary. December 17, 2003.

The White House (2006). *The Federal Response to Hurricane Katrina; Lessons Learned*. Washington DC. http://www.whitehouse.gov/reports/katrina-lessons-learned.pdf

The World Meteorological Organization (1997). *Global Perspectives on Tropical Cyclones*. Tropical Cyclone Program. Report TCP-38. Elsberry, R.L. (ed.). Geneva, Switzerland.

Torry, W.I. (1978). "Natural disasters, social structure and change in traditional societies". *J. Asian Afr. Studies*. 13:167–83.

U.S. Department of Commerce, National Oceanic and Atmospheric Administration, National Weather Service (2006). *Hurricanes – unleashing nature's fury*. A preparedness guide.

U.S. Department of Homeland Defense (2007a). *Mass Care*. Final Published Version 1.1. The Exercise Evaluation Guides (EEGs). Homeland Security Exercise and Evaluation Program (HSEEP), Washington D.C.

U.S. Department of Homeland Defense (2007b). Homeland Security Exercise and Evaluation Program (HSEEP), Washington D.C.

U.S. Department of Homeland Security (DHS)(2004a). *National Incident Management System*. March 1, 2004, Washington D.C.

U.S. Department of Homeland Security (DHS)(2004b). *National Response Plan. December 2004*, Washington D.C.

U.S. Department of Homeland Security (DHS)(2005a). *National Preparedness Goal*. Homeland Security Presidential Directive 8: National Preparedness. March 31, 2005, Washington D.C.

U.S. Department of Homeland Security (DHS)(2005b). *Target Capabilities List*. Draft. Washington D.C.

U.S. Department of Homeland Security (DHS)(2006a). *Quick Reference Guide for the National Response Plan*. Washington D.C.

U.S. Department of Homeland Security (DHS)(2006b). *Nationwide Plan Review*. Phase 2 Report. U.S. Department of Homeland Security in cooperation with the U.S. Department of Transportation. June 16, 2006.

U.S. Department of Homeland Security (DHS)(2007a). *Tactical Interoperable Communications Scorecards*. Summary Report and Findings, Washington D.C.

U.S. Department of Homeland Security (DHS)(2007b). *Robert T. Stafford Disaster Relief and Emergency Assistance Act*, as amended, and Related Authorities. FEMA 592, June 2007.

University of Hawai'i at Mānoa (1993). Hawai'i coastal hazard mitigation planning project: findings, recommendations, and technical documents. Prepared by the Center for Development Studies, Social Science Research Institute, the University of Hawai'i at Mānoa , Honolulu.

University of Hawai'i at Mānoa (1996). Hawai'i coastal hazard mitigation planning project, Phase II: findings, recommendations, and technical documents. Prepared by the Center for Development Studies, Social Science Research Institute, the University of Hawai'i at Mānoa , Honolulu.

Umpleby, S. A., Dent, E. B. (1999). "The origins and purposes of several traditions in systems theory and cybernetics". *Cybernetics and Systems: An international journal*, Taylor and Francis, 30:79–103.

Van Bertalanffy, L. (1969). General system theory: foundations, development, applications. George Braziller, New York.

Walker, Jon (2001). *The Viable Systems Model – a guide for co-operatives and federations*. SMSE Strategic Management in the Social Economy training programme. ICOM, CRU, CAG and Jon Walker. Eds., Directorate General XXIII of the Commission of the European Communities.

Watts, M. (1983). *On the poverty of theory: natural hazard research in context*. In: Interpretations of calamity. K. Hewitt, ed., Allen and Urwin, Boston.

Watzlawick, P. (ed.)(1984): The invented reality: How do we know what we believe we know?: Contributions to constructivism. Norton, New York.

Weick, K.E. (1993). "The Collapse of Sensemaking in Organizations: The Mann Gulch Disaster". *Administrative Science Quarterly*. 38:628–652.

Wiener, N. (1948). Cybernetics; or, Control and communication in the animal and the machine. John Wiley, New York.

Wiener, N. (1950). The human use of human beings: Cybernetics and society. Houghton Mifflin, Boston, MA.

White, G.F. (ed.)(1974). Natural hazards: local, national, global. Oxford University Press, Oxford.

Wilson, B. (1990). Concepts, methodologies, and applications. John Wiley, New York.

Zeleny, M., ed. (1981): Autopoesis, a theory of living organization. North-Holland, New York.

Internet sites

Annan, Kofi A. (1999, September 10th). An increasing vulnerability to natural disasters. The International Herald Tribune. http://www.un.org/News/ossg/sg/stories/ annan_press.html; accessed 3/28/2006.

American Red Cross (n.d.). 3 day Emergency Preparedness Kit Checklist. http:// www.scd.Hawai'i.gov/documents/red_cross_kit_checklist.pdf; accessed 2/26/ 2008

Bureau of Meteorology (2008). ENSO Wrap-Up. A regular commentary on the El Nino-Southern Oscillation. Australian Government. http://www.bom.gov.au/ climate/enso/; accessed 2/27/2008.

Businger, S. (1998). Hurricanes in Hawai'i. September 25, 1998. Department of Meteorology, University of Hawai'i. http://www.soest.Hawai'i.edu/MET/Faculty/ businger/poster/hurricane; accessed 9/5/2007.

City and County of Honolulu (n.d.a). O'ahu Civil Defense Agency: Hurricanes in Hawai'i. http://www.honolulu.gov/ocda/hurrl.htm; accessed on 3/15/2006

City and County of Honolulu (n.d.b). Section Two: Hawai'ian hurricanes: Their history, causes and future. http://www.mothernature-Hawai'i.com/county_honolulu/ hurricane_section2-O'ahu.htm; accessed 2/25/2008.

Department of Business, Economic Development and Tourism (2006). City and County of Honolulu. http://Hawai'i.gov/dbedt/info/economic/library/facts/honolulu-county; accessed 2/26/2008.

Department of Homeland Security (n.d.). National Response Framework, Resource Center, Glossary. www.fema.gov/emergency/nrf/glossary.htm#1; accessed 5/9/2008.

Enterprise Honolulu (2008). Business Parks, Incubators and Technology Parks. http://www.enterprisehonolulu.com/hmtl/display.cfm?sid=29; accessed 2/26/2008

Hawai'i State Civil Defense (2007b). ITEP – The Homeland Security Information Technology Evaluation Program. http://www.scd.Hawai'i.gov/ITEP; accessed 4/26/2007

Hawai'i State Civil Defense (2007c). Hawai'i Homeland Security Common Information System H2S CIS. http://www.scd.Hawai'i.gov/ITEP/h2scis.html; accessed 4/26/2007

Heylighen, C. et al. (1999). What are Cybernetics and Systems Science? Principia Cybernetica Web. http://pespmc1.vub.ac.be/CYBSWHAT.html; accessed 3/20/2006.

Hurricane Relief Fund (n.d.). Where have the most wind-related insurance claims been for O'ahu? http://www.mothernature-Hawai'i.com/county_honolulu/hurricane_what_are-O'ahu.htm; accessed 2/28/2008.

McKinley Community School for Adults (n.d.). Contact us. http://mcsa.k12.hi.us/contact.html; accessed 2/28/2008.

MSNBC (2011): Japan PM: Radiation leaking from damaged plant. 3/15/2011. http://www.msnbc.msn.com/id/42066534/ns/world_news-asia_pacific/t/japan-pm-radiation-leadking-damaged-plant/#.T12GvfF5mSM; accessed 3/11/2012.

National Integration Center (2008). Incident Management Systems Division. Frequently Asked Questions. Resource Credentialing. http://www.fema.gov/emergency/nims/faq/rm.shtm#1; accessed 6/13/2008.

Pacific Regional Environment Program (2003). The natural resources of the Pacific Region: http://www.sprep. org.ws/topic/NatRes.htm; accessed 4/11/2006.

Pan American Health Organization (2006). The disaster cycle. Powerpoint presentation 'Introduction to Mass Management System'. http://www.disaster-info.net/carib/INTRODUCTION%20to%20MCM/sld003.htm; accessed 4/10/2006.

Stanford Encyclopedia of Philosophy (2004). Existentialism: http://plato.stanford.edu/entries/existentialism; accessed 2/6/2008.

The National Weather Service (2007). National Hurricane Center, The Saffir-Simpson Hurricane Scale: http://www.nhc.noaa.gov/aboutsshs.shtml; accessed 7/18/2007.

The National Weather Service (2008). Central Pacific Hurricane Center, Glossary. http://www.prh.noaa.gov/cphc/pages/glossary.php; accessed 2/15/2008.

U.S. Census Bureau (1990). State and County Quick Facts. Honolulu CDP, Hawai'i: http://quickfacts.census.gov/qfd/states/15/1517000.html; accessed 2/9/2008.

U.S. Census Bureau (2000a). State and County Quick Facts. Hawai'i. http://quickfacts.census.gov/qfd/states/15000.html; accessed 2/29/2008.

U.S. Census Bureau (2000b). State and County Quick Facts. Honolulu CDP, Hawai'i: http://quickfacts.census.gov/qfd/states/15/1517000.html; accessed 3/9/2006.

U.S. House of Representatives (2006). A Failure of Initiative; Final Report of the Select Bipartisan Committee to Investigate the Preparation for and Response to Hurricane Katrina. U.S. Government Printing Office. Washington DC. http://www.gpoacess.gov/congress/index.html; accessed 3/18/2007.

UNISYS Weather (2006). Hurricane: http://weather.unisys.com/hurricane/index.html; accessed 3/15/2006.

Watson, Paul (2008). "Needle in a haystack". Whale Wars, Season 1, Episode 1:. http://www.tv-links.eu/_gate_way.html?data=MjM4MzBfODEyMjFfNDM0OTTAx; accessed 3/11/2012.

Presentations and interviews

Browning, W. (2007a). State Civil Defense, Civil Defense Coordinators Meeting, PowerPoint presentation, held at the State Civil Defense Emergency Operation Center, Honolulu, Hawai'i, May 14 2007. Unpublished oral remarks.

Browning, W. (2007b). Federal Emergency Management Agency Regional Interagency Steering Committees Conference, PowerPoint presentation, held at the Waikiki Beach Marriott Hotel, Honolulu, Hawai'i, May 22 2007. Unpublished oral remarks.

Bryce, M. (2007). Federal Emergency Management Agency Regional Interagency Steering Committees Conference, 'ESF#8, 'Public Health and Medical Services', PowerPoint presentation, held at the Waikiki Beach Marriott Hotel, Honolulu, Hawai'i, May 22 2007. Unpublished oral remarks.

Dacosta, D. (2007). Federal Emergency Management Agency Regional Interagency Steering Committees Conference, 'ESF#13, 'Public Safety and Security', Power-Point presentation, held at the Waikiki Beach Marriott Hotel, Honolulu, Hawai'i, May 22 2007. Unpublished oral remarks.

Fenton, R. (2007). Federal Emergency Management Agency Regional Interagency Steering Committees Conference, 'ESF#5, 'Emergency Management', Power-Point presentation, held at the Waikiki Beach Marriott Hotel, Honolulu, Hawai'i, May 22 2007. Unpublished oral remarks.

Gilbert, K. (2007a). Department of Emergency Management. Interview. April 24, 2007.

Gilbert, K. (2007b). Department of Emergency Management. Interviews. May 15–16, 2007.

Hirai, P. (2007a). City and County Department of Emergency Management. 'Executive Briefing, Makani Pahili 2007 Hurricane Exercise'. PowerPoint presentation, held at the City and County Department of Emergency Management

Emergency Operation Center, Honolulu, Hawai'i, May 16 2007. Unpublished oral remarks.

Hirai, P. (2007b). O'ahu Civil Defense Agency. Interview. January 19, 2007.

Imamura, G (2007). American Red Cross. Shelter Simulation, held at the Mililani Uka Elementary School. Interview. May 19, 2007.

Latham, R. (2007). Federal Emergency Management Agency Regional Interagency Steering Committees Conference, held at the Waikiki Beach Marriott Hotel, Honolulu, Hawai'i, May 23 2007. Unpublished oral remarks.

Lum, A. (2007). Federal Emergency Management Agency Regional Interagency Steering Committees Conference, 'ESF#11, 'Agriculture and Natural Resources', PowerPoint presentation, held at the Waikiki Beach Marriott Hotel, Honolulu, Hawai'i, May 22 2007. Unpublished oral remarks.

Martin, G. (2007). Federal Emergency Management Agency Regional Interagency Steering Committees Conference, 'USCG/COMPACAREA support to FEMA', PowerPoint presentation, held at the Waikiki Beach Marriott Hotel, Honolulu, Hawai'i, May 22 2007. Unpublished oral remarks.

Nolan, J. (2007). Department of Planning and Permitting. Interview, April 14, 2007.

Richards, K. (2007a). Initial Planning Conference of the Makani Pahili Exercise, held at the Blaisdell Conference Room, University of Hawaii at Mānoa , Honolulu, Hawai'i, January 26, 2007. PowerPoint presentation.

Richards, K. (2007b). Mid Planning Conference of the Makani Pahili Exercise, held at the Blaisdell Conference Room, University of Hawaii at Mānoa , Honolulu, Hawai'i, March 30, 2007. PowerPoint presentation.

Richards, K. (2007c). Final Planning Conference of the Makani Pahili Exercise, held at the Blaisdell Conference Room, University of Hawaii at Mānoa , Honolulu, Hawai'i, May 4, 2007. PowerPoint presentation.

Richards, K. (2007d). Hawai'i State Civil Defense Multi-agency Exercise, held at the State Civil Defense, Honolulu, Hawai'i, May 4, 2007. Unpublished oral remarks.

Richards, K. (2007e). Hawai'i State Civil Defense. Civil Defense Coordinators Meeting, held at the State Civil Defense Emergency Operation Center, Honolulu, Hawai'i, May 14, 2007. Unpublished oral remarks.

Richards, K. (2007f). Seminars, held at the State Civil Defense, Honolulu, Hawai'i, May 17, 2007. Unpublished oral remarks.

Richards, K. (2007g). Federal Emergency Management Agency Regional Interagency Steering Committees Conference, held at the Waikiki Beach Marriott Hotel, Honolulu, Hawai'i. Informal conversation, May 22 2007. Unpublished oral remarks.

Richards, K. (2007h). Federal Emergency Management Agency Regional Interagency Steering Committees Conference, held at the Waikiki Beach Marriott Hotel, Honolulu, Hawai'i, May 23 2007. Unpublished oral remarks.

Richards, K. Tengan, D., (2007). Hawai'i State Civil Defense. Interview. February 5, 2007.

Romaine, P. (2007). Department of Transportation. Interview. February 2, 2007.

Rosegg, P. 2007a. Hawai'ian Electric Company. Interview. February 26, 2007.

Rosenberg, L. (2007a). Federal Emergency Management Agency Regional Inter-agency Steering Committees Conference, held at the Waikiki Beach Marriott Hotel, Honolulu, Hawai'i, May 23, 2007. Unpublished oral remarks.

Rosenberg, L. (2007b). Federal Emergency Management Agency. Interview, May 18, 2007.

Rosenberg, L. (2007c). Federal Emergency Management Agency Regional Inter-agency Steering Committees Conference, 'Federal Support CONOP for a Cata-strophic Hurricane impacting the State of Hawai'i', PowerPoint presentation, held at the Waikiki Beach Marriott Hotel, Honolulu, Hawai'i, May 22, 2007. Unpublished oral remarks.

Schroeder, T. (2005). Department of Meteorology, University of Hawai'i at Mānoa , presentation, 27 October 2005.

Schwarz, R. (2007). United States Coast Guard. ICS training. Informal talk, May 20, 2007. Unpublished oral remarks.

Shigetani, M. (2007). Federal Emergency Management Agency Regional Interagen-cy Steering Committees Conference, 'ESF#6, 'Mass Care, Housing and Human Services', PowerPoint presentation, held at the Waikiki Beach Marriott Hotel, Honolulu, Hawai'i, May 22 2007. Unpublished oral remarks.

Suizo, K. (2007). Army Corps of Engineers. Interview. February 21, 2007.

Tengan, D. (2007a). American Red Cross. Shelter Simulation, Mililani Uka Elemen-tary School. Interview. May 19, 2007.

Tengan, D. (2007b). Federal Emergency Management Agency Regional Interagency Steering Committees Conference, PowerPoint presentation, held at the Waikiki Beach Marriott Hotel, Honolulu, Hawai'i, May 22 2007. Unpublished oral re-marks.

Teixeira, E. (2007a). State Civil Defense, Diamond Head Chapter, presentation, October 2005. Unpublished oral remarks.

Teixeira, E. (2007b). Federal Emergency Management Agency Regional Interagency Steering Committees Conference, held at the Waikiki Beach Marriott Hotel, Honolulu, Hawai'i, May 23 2007. Unpublished oral remarks.

Weyman, J. (2007a). Makani Pahili Mid Planning Conference, State Civil Defense, PowerPoint presentation, held at the Waikiki Beach Marriott Hotel, Honolulu, Hawai'i, March 30 2007. Unpublished oral remarks.

Weyman, J. (2007b). State Civil Defense, Civil Defense Coordinators meeting, held at the State Civil Defense Emergency Operation Center, May 14, 2007. Unpub-lished oral remarks.

Witwer, R. (2007). Federal Emergency Management Agency Regional Interagency Steering Committees Conference, 'ESF#4, 'Firefighting', PowerPoint presenta-tion, held at the Waikiki Beach Marriott Hotel, Honolulu, Hawai'i, May 22 2007. Unpublished oral remarks.

Zingman, C. (2007). Federal Emergency Management Agency Regional Interagency Steering Committees Conference, 'ESF#12, 'Energy', PowerPoint presentation, held at the Waikiki Beach Marriott Hotel, Honolulu, Hawai'i, May 22 2007. Unpublished oral remarks.

Events and conferences

Department of Emergency Management, (2007). Emergency Operations Center, Observations, May 16 2007, O'ahu Civil Defense Agency EOC.
Breakout Session Infrastructure, (2007). Federal Emergency Management Agency Regional Interagency Steering Committees Conference, May 23 2007.

Grey literature

American Red Cross, (2005). *Shelter operations participant's workbook.* 3068–11. September 2005. p. 51–52.
Leonard, A. (2004). Coming Concepts: The Cybernetic Glossary for new management. Revised version.
Norcross-Nu'u, et al. (2007). Rising sea levels in Hawai'i: Impacts and Implications. Hand out. School of Ocean and Earth Science and Technology. University of Hawai'i, Honolulu.
Hawai'ian Electric Company, Maui Electric Company, Hawai'i Electric Light Company, (n.d.). Information. Handbook for Emergency Preparedness. Be Prepared – Be Informed.
Tengan, D. (2007c). PowerPoint Handout. State Civil Defense. February 5 2007.
State Civil Defense (2007). Exercise Plan Makani Pahili,. May 14–25 2007. Annual State of Hawai'i Hurricane Exercise. Distributed at Makani Pahili Final Planning Conference.
Hawai'i Civil Defense (n.d.). Hawai'i's costliest natural disasters. Table.
Hawai'i State Civil Defense (2007d). Makani Pahili Impacts 2007. Handout.
U.S. Army Corps of Engineers (2007). Graphs and maps generated for the Makani Pahili Exercise 2007. U.S. Army Corps of Engineers.

Newspaper Articles

Honolulu Advertiser (2005a). Military 'a resource we treasure' in a crisis. September 18, 2005.

Honolulu Advertiser (2005b). Shelters, sirens are state's weak links. September 18, 2005.

Honolulu Advertiser (2005c). Adequate shelter a key concern. September 18, 2005.

Honolulu Advertiser (2006a). Hawai'i rattles, then loses power statewide. October 16, 2006.

Honolulu Advertiser (2006b). No answers yet in Nanakuli. March 17, 2006.

Starbulletin (2002a). 'Iniki: Deadly power. A decade after the disaster. September 8, 2002

Starbulletin (2002b). Lingering fear. A decade after the disaster. September 8, 2002

Starbulletin (2002c). A decade after the disaster. September 8, 2002.

Starbulletin (2002d). First-hand view of catastrophe gives new outlook. A decade after the disaster. September 8, 2002.

Starbulletin (2002e). Resort's ruins remain. A decade after the disaster. September 8, 2002.

Starbulletin (2006a). Campbell offering 100 acres. Starbulletin. February 10, 2006.

Starbulletin (2006b). Officials admit to alarm deficiencies. October 29, 2006.

United Press International (1992). Hurricane 'Iniki hits Hawai'i. September 11, 1992.

E-mail contacts

Browning, W. (2007c). National Weather Service. Personal communication, email of October 5, 2007.

Browning, W. (2008a). National Weather Service. Personal communication, email of February 15, 2008.

Browning, W. (2008b). National Weather Service. Personal communication, email of February 25, 2008.

Emanuel, K. (2008). Professor of Atmospheric Science, MIT. Personal communication, email of February 25, 2008.

Leonard, A. (2006). Personal communication, email of March 13, 2006.

McCoy, M. (2008). Department of Homeland Security. FEMA. Personal communication, email of June 13, 2008.

Nolan, J. (2008). Department of Planning and Permitting. Personal communication, email of February 27, 2008.

Rosegg, P. (2007b). Hawai'i Electric Company. Personal communication, email of October 4, 2007.

Siemsen, T. (2008). U.S. Army Corps of Engineers. Personal communication, email of February 22, 2008.

Glossary

Glossary of Beer's cybernetic language

This glossary is not comprehensive but should serve to understand the main cybernetic concepts and the VSM application more easily.

Algedonic Signal	Preemptive message about dysfunction
Variety	Measure of the number of possible states of a system
Variety Engineering	Art of management
Black Box	Model of a system whose inner workings are not open to examination
Channel Capacity	Measure of the amount of information to be transmitted in time X
Cohesion	Balance of freedom and constraint within a system to provide a workable level of autonomy
Environment	Environment of a system consists of all of the factors which may separately or in combination change its state
Homeostasis	Process whereby critical variables are held within acceptable limits by self-regulatory processes
Identity	The mark of a whole; an indication of a distinction which may be consistently recognized or which persists over time
Metasystem	System which operates on a higher level of logic and which is capable of taking a larger view of system behavior
Metasystemic Calm	State of the Metasystem in which Algedonic Alarms can be fixed within the Relaxation Time
Recursion	Series of systems embedded in one another are called recursive structure; in such a structure, the same features are repeated invariantly from a system to its Metasystem to its Metasystem (like Russian Dolls). A Level of Recursion refers to one system.
Relaxation Time	Time it takes to return to equilibrium after a disturbance
Transduction	Information in one language or realm of reference is sent to another

For a more detailed Glossary see Leonard [2004].

Glossary of rules for the Viable System [Beer, 1979, pp. 565]

Aphorisms

The First Regulatory Aphorism: It is not necessary to enter the Black Box to understand the nature of the function it performs.

The Second Regulatory Aphorism: It is not necessary to enter the Black Box to calculate the Variety that it potentially may generate.

Principles

First Principle of Organization: Managerial, operational and environmental varieties, diffusing through an institutional system, tend to equate; they should be designed to do so with minimal damage to people and cost.

Second Principle of Organization: The four directional channels carrying information between the management unit, the operation and the Environment must each have a higher capacity to transmit a given amount of information relevant to Variety selection in a given time than the originating sub-system has to generate it in that time.

Third Principle of Organization: Wherever the information carried on a channel capable of distinguishing a given Variety crosses a boundary, it undergoes Transduction; the Variety of the transducer must be at least equivalent to the Variety of the channel.

Fourth Principle of Organization: The operations of the first three principles must be cyclically maintained through time without hiatus or lags.

Theorem

Recursive System Theorem: In a recursive organizational structure, any viable system contains, and is contained in, a viable system.

Axioms

The First Axiom of Management: The sum of horizontal Variety disposed by n operational elements equals the sum of vertical Variety disposed on the six vertical components of corporate cohesion.

The Second Axiom of Management: The Variety disposed by System 3 (operational control) resulting from the operation of the First Axiom equals the Variety disposed by System 4 (intelligence).

The Third Axiom of Management: The Variety disposed by System 5 (policy) equals the residual Variety generated by the operation of the Second Axiom.

Law

The Law of Cohesion for Multiple Recursions of the Viable System: The System 1 Variety accessible to System 3 (operational control) of Recursion x equals the Variety disposed by the sum of the Metasystem of Recursion y for every recursive pair.

Glossary of FEMA's acronyms

AC(P)	Area Command (Post)
ARC	American Red Cross
CONOP	Federal Support Concept of Operations for a catastrophic hurricane impacting the State of Hawaii
DEM	Department of Emergency Management
EOC	Emergency Operations Center:

The physical location at which the coordination of information and resources to support local or State incident management activities normally takes place.

EOP	Emergency Operations Plan
ESF	Emergency Support Function:

A grouping of government and certain private-sector capabilities into an organizational structure to provide the support, resources, program implementation, and services for disaster management activities.

FEMA	Federal Emergency Management Agency
HSEEP	Homeland Security Exercise and Evaluation Program
IC(S)	Incident Command (System)
JFO	Joint Field Office:

temporary Federal facility established to coordinate operational Federal assistance activities to the affected jurisdiction(s) during Incidents of National Significance.

NIMS	National Incident Management System
NRP	National Response Plan
RISC	Regional Interagency Steering Committees
SCD	State Civil Defense
UC(P)	Unified Command (Post)
USACE	US Army Corps of Engineers

Index